Personal Reminiscences of
EARLY DAYS IN CALIFORNIA

A Da Capo Press Reprint Series

THE AMERICAN SCENE
Comments and Commentators

GENERAL EDITOR: WALLACE D. FARNHAM
University of Illinois

Personal Reminiscences of
EARLY DAYS IN CALIFORNIA

BY STEPHEN J. FIELD

———————————•———————————

To which is added the story of his attempted
assassination by a former associate on the
supreme bench of the state

BY GEORGE C. GORHAM

Da Capo Press · New York · 1968

A Da Capo Press Reprint Edition

This Da Capo Press edition of *Personal Reminiscences of Early Days in California* is an unabridged republication of the first edition published in 1893.

Library of Congress Catalog Card Number 68-29601

Da Capo Press
A Division of Plenum Publishing Corporation
227 West 17th Street
New York, N.Y. 10011

Printed in the United States of America

PERSONAL REMINISCENCES

OF

EARLY DAYS IN CALIFORNIA,

WITH

OTHER SKETCHES.

BY

STEPHEN J. FIELD.

———

TO WHICH IS ADDED THE STORY OF HIS ATTEMPTED
ASSASSINATION BY A FORMER ASSOCIATE ON
THE SUPREME BENCH OF THE STATE.

BY

Hon. GEORGE C. GORHAM.

THE following sketches were taken down by a stenographer in the summer of 1877, at San Francisco, from the narrative of Judge Field. They are printed at the request of a few friends, to whom they have an interest which they could not excite in others.

INDEX.

WHY AND HOW I CAME TO CALIFORNIA.

SOME months previous to the Mexican War, my brother David Dudley Field, of New York City, wrote two articles for the Democratic Review upon the subject of the Northwestern Boundary between the territory of the United States and the British Possessions. One of these appeared in the June, and the other in the November number of the Review for 1845.* While writing these articles he had occasion to examine several works on Oregon and California, and, among others, that of Greenhow, then recently published, and thus became familiar with the geography and political history of the Pacific Coast. The next Spring, and soon after the war broke out, in the course of a conversation upon its probable results, he remarked, that if he were a young man, he would go to San Francisco; that he was satisfied peace would never be concluded without our acquiring the harbor upon which it was situated; that there was no other good harbor on the coast, and that, in his opinion, that town would, at no distant day, become a great city. He also remarked that if I would go he would furnish the means, not only for the journey, but also for the purchase of land at San Francisco and in its vicinity. This conversation was the first germ of my project of coming to California.

---

* The first article was entitled "The Oregon Question," and the second "The Edinburgh and Foreign Quarterly on the Oregon Question."

Some months afterwards, and while Col. Stevenson's regiment was preparing to start from New York for California, my brother again referred to the same subject and suggested the idea of my going out with the regiment. We had at that time a clerk in the office by the name of Sluyter, for whom I had great regard. With him I talked the matter over, it being my intention, if I should go at all, to induce him if possible to accompany me. But he wished to get married, and I wished to go to Europe. The result of our conference was, that the California project was deferred, with the understanding, however, that after my return from Europe we should give it further consideration. But the idea of going to California thus suggested, made a powerful impression upon my mind. It pleased me. There was a smack of adventure in it. The going to a country comparatively unknown and taking a part in fashioning its institutions, was an attractive subject of contemplation. I had always thought that the most desirable fame a man could acquire was that of being the founder of a State, or of exerting a powerful influence for good upon its destinies; and the more I thought of the new territory about to fall into our hands beyond the Sierra Nevada, the more I was fascinated with the idea of settling there and growing up with it.

But I was anxious first to visit, or rather to revisit, Europe. I was not able, however, to make the necessary arrangements to do so until the Summer of 1848. On the first of May of that year, I dissolved partnership with my brother, and in June started for Europe. In the following December, while at Galignani's News Room in Paris, I read in the New York Herald the message of President Polk, which confirmed previous reports, that gold had been discovered in California, then recently acquired. It is difficult to describe the effect which that message produced upon my mind. I read and re-read it, and the suggestion of my brother to go to that country recurred to me, and I felt some regret that I had not followed it. I remained in Europe, however, and carried out my original plan of seeing its most interesting cities, and returned to the United States in 1849, arriving at New York on the 1st of October of that year.

There was already at that early period a steamer leaving that city once or twice every month for Chagres. It went crowded every trip. The impulse which had been started in me by my brother in 1846, strengthened by the message of President Polk, had now become irresistible. I joined the throng, and on November 13th, 1849, took passage on the " Crescent City ;" and in about a week's time, in company with many others, I found myself at the little old Spanish-American town of Chagres, on the Isthmus of Panama. There we took small boats and were poled up the river by Indians to Cruces, at which place we mounted mules and rode over the mountain to Panama. There I found a crowd of persons in every degree of excitement, waiting for passage to California. There were thousands of them. Those who came on the " Crescent City " had engaged passage on the Pacific side also ; but such was the demand among the multitude at Panama for the means of transportation, that some of the steerage passengers sold their tickets from that place to San Francisco for $750 apiece and took their chances of getting on cheaper. These sales, notwithstanding they appeared at the time to be great bargains, proved, in most cases, to be very unfortunate transactions; for the poor fellows who thus sold their tickets, besides losing their time, exposed themselves to the malaria of an unhealthy coast. There was in fact a good deal of sickness already among those on the Isthmus, and many deaths afterwards occurred; and among those who survived there was much suffering before they could get away.

The vessel that conveyed us, and by "us" I mean the passengers of the "Crescent City," and as many others as could by any possibility procure passage from Panama to San Fransisco was the old steamer "California." She was about one thousand tons burden; but probably no ship of two thousand ever carried a greater number of passengers on a long voyage. When we came to get under way, there did not seem to be any spare space from stem to stern. There were over twelve hundred persons on board, as I was informed.* Unfortunately many of them carried with them the seeds of disease. The infection contracted under a tropical sun, being aggravated by hardships, insufficient food, and the crowded condition of the steamer, developed as the voyage proceeded. Panama fever in its worst form broke out; and it was not long before the main deck was literally covered with the sick. There was a physician attached to the ship; but unfortunately he was also prostrated. The condition of things was very sad and painful.

Among the passengers taken sick were two by the name of Gregory Yale and Stephen Smith; and I

* Note.— The number of passengers reported to the journals of San Francisco on the arrival of the steamer was much less than this, probably to avoid drawing attention to the violation of the statute which restricted the number.

turned myself into a nurse and took care of them. Mr. Yale, a gentleman of high attainments, and who afterwards occupied a prominent place at the bar of the State, was for a portion of the time dangerously ill, and I believe that but for my attentions he would have died. He himself was of this opinion, and afterwards expressed his appreciation of my attention in every way he could. In the many years I knew him he never failed to do me a kindness whenever an opportunity presented. Finally, on the evening of December 28, 1849, after a passage of twenty-two days from Panama, we reached San Francisco, and landed between eight and nine o'clock that night.

FIRST EXPERIENCES IN SAN FRANCISCO.

UPON landing from the steamer, my baggage consisted of two trunks, and I had only the sum of ten dollars in my pocket. I might, perhaps, have carried one trunk, but I could not manage two; so I was compelled to pay out seven of my ten dollars to have them taken to a room in an old adobe building on the west side of what is now known as Portsmouth Square. This room was about ten feet long by eight feet wide, and had a bed in it. For its occupation the sum of $35 a week was charged. Two of my fellow-passengers and myself engaged it. They took the bed, and I took the floor. I do not think they had much the advantage on the score of comfort.

The next morning I started out early with three dollars in my pocket. I hunted up a restaurant and ordered the cheapest breakfast I could get. It cost me two dollars. A solitary dollar was, therefore, all the money in the world I had left, but I was in no respect despondent over my financial condition. It was a beautiful day, much like an Indian Summer day in the East, but finer. There was something exhilarating and exciting in the atmosphere which made everybody cheerful and buoyant. As I walked along the streets, I met a great many persons I had known in New York, and they all seemed to be in the highest spirits. Every one in greeting me, said "It is a glorious country," or "Isn't it a glorious country?" or "Did you ever see a more glorious country?" or something to that effect. In every case the word "glorious" was sure to come out. There was something infectious in the use of the word, or rather in the feeling, which made its use natural. I had not been out many hours that morning before I caught the infection; and though I had but a single dollar in my pocket and no business whatever, and did not know where I was to get the next meal, I found myself saying to everybody I met, "It is a glorious country."

The city presented an appearance which, to me, who had witnessed some curious scenes in the course of my travels, was singularly strange and wild. The Bay then washed what is now the east side of Montgomery street, between Jackson and Sacramento streets; and the sides of the hills sloping back from the water were covered with buildings of various kinds, some just begun, a few completed,—all, however, of the rudest sort, the greater number being merely canvas sheds. The locality then called Happy Valley, where Mission and Howard streets now are, between Market and Folsom streets, was occupied in a similar way. The streets were filled with people, it seemed to me, from every nation under Heaven, all wearing their peculiar costumes. The majority of them were from the States; and each State had furnished specimens of every type within its borders. Every country of Europe had its representatives; and wanderers without a country were there in great numbers. There were also Chilians, Sonorians, Kanakas from the Sandwich Islands, and Chinese from Canton and Hong Kong. All seemed, in hurrying to and fro, to be busily occupied and in a state of pleasurable excitement. Everything needed for their wants; food, clothing, and lodging-quarters, and everything required for transportation and mining, were in urgent demand and obtained extravagant prices. Yet no one seemed to complain of the charges made. There was an apparent disdain of all attempts to cheapen articles and reduce prices. News from the East was eagerly sought from all new-comers. Newspapers from New York were sold at a dollar apiece. I had a bundle of them, and seeing the price paid for such papers, I gave them to a fellow-passenger, telling him he might have half he could get for them. There were sixty-four numbers, if I recollect aright, and the third day after our arrival, to my astonishment he handed me thirty-two dollars, stating that he had sold them all at a dollar apiece. Nearly everything else brought a similarly extravagant price. And this reminds me of an experience of my own with some chamois skins. Before I left New York, I purchased a lot of stationery and the usual accompaniments of a writing-table, as I intended to practise my profession in California. The stationer, learning from some remark made by my brother Cyrus, who was with me at the time, that I intended to go to California, said that I ought to buy some chamois skins in which to wrap the stationery, as they would be needed there to make bags for carrying gold-dust. Upon this suggestion, I bought a dozen skins for ten dollars. On unpacking my trunk, in Marysville, these chamois skins were of course exposed, and a gentleman calling at the tent, which I then occupied, asked me what I would take for them. I answered by inquiring what he would give for them. He replied at once, an ounce apiece. My astonishment nearly choked me, for an ounce was taken for sixteen dollars; at the mint, it often yielded eighteen or nineteen dollars in coin. I, of course, let the skins go, and blessed the hunter who brought the chamois down. The purchaser made bags of the skins, and the profit to him from their sale amounted to two ounces on each skin. From this transaction, the story arose that I had sold porte-monnaies in Marysville before practising law, which is reported in the interesting book of Messrs. Barry and Patten, entitled "Men and Memories of San Francisco in the Spring of 1850." The story has no other foundation.

But I am digressing from the narrative of my first experience in San Francisco. After taking my breakfast, as already stated, the first thing I noticed was a small building in the Plaza, near which a crowd was gathered. Upon inquiry, I was told it was the courthouse. I at once started for the building, and on entering it, found that Judge Almond, of the San Francisco District, was holding what was known as the Court of First Instance, and that a case was on trial. To my astonishment I saw two of my fellow-passengers, who had landed the night before, sitting on the jury. This seemed so strange that I waited till the case was over, and then inquired how it happened they were there. They said that they had been attracted to the building by the crowd, just as I had been, and that while looking on the proceedings of the court the sheriff had summoned them. They replied to the summons, that they had only just arrived in the country. But he said that fact made no difference; nobody had been in the country three months. They added that they had received eight dollars each for their services. At this piece of news I thought of my solitary dollar, and wondered if similar good fortune might not happen to me. So I lingered in the

court-room, placing myself near the sheriff in the hope
that on another jury he might summon me. But it
was not my good luck. So I left the temple of justice
and strolled around the busy city, enjoying myself
with the novelty of everything. Passing down Clay
street, and near Kearney street, my attention was attracted by a sign in large letters, "Jonathan D. Stevenson, Gold Dust Bought and Sold Here." As I saw
this inscription I exclaimed, "Hallo, here is good
luck," for I suddenly recollected that when I left New
York my brother Dudley had handed me a note
against Stevenson for $350 or $400; stating that he
understood the Colonel had become rich in California
and telling me, that if such was the case, to ask him
to pay the note. I had put the paper in my pocket-
book and thought no more of it until the sight of the
sign brought it to my recollection, and also reminded
me of my solitary dollar. Of course I immediately
entered the office to see the Colonel. He had known
me very well in New York, and was apparently delighted to see me, for he gave me a most cordial greeting. After some inquiries about friends in New York,
he commenced talking about the country. "Ah," he
continued, "it is a glorious country. I have made
two hundred thousand dollars." This was more than
I could stand. I had already given him a long shake
of the hand but I could not resist the impulse to
shake his hand again, thinking all the time of my
financial condition. So I seized his hand again and
shook it vigorously, assuring him that I was delighted
to hear of his good luck. We talked over the matter,
and in my enthusiasm I shook his hand a third time,
expressing my satisfaction at his good fortune. We
passed a long time together, he dilating all the while

upon the fine country it was in which to make money. At length I pulled out the note and presented it to him. I shall never forget the sudden change, from wreaths of smiles to an elongation of physiognomy, expressive of mingled surprise and disgust, which came over his features on seeing that note. He took it in his hands and examined it carefully; he turned it over and looked at its back, and then at its face again, and then, as it were, at both sides at once. At last he said in a sharp tone, "That's my signature," and began to calculate the interest; that ascertained, he paid me the full amount due. If I remember rightly he paid me $440 in Spanish doubloons, but some of it may have been in gold dust. If it had not been for this lucky incident, I should have been penniless before night.

The good fortune which the Colonel then enjoyed has not always attended him since. The greater part of his property he lost some years afterwards, but he has always retained, and now in his seventy-eighth year* still retains, great energy and vigor of mind, and a manly independence of character, which have made him warm friends. In all the changes of my life his name is pleasantly associated with the payment of the note, and the timely assistance which he thus gave me. His career as commander of the well-known regiment of New York volunteers which arrived in California in March, 1847, and subsequently in the State, are matters of public history.

As soon as I found myself in funds I hired a room as an office at the corner of Montgomery and Clay streets for one month for $300, payable in advance.

---

* Col. Stevenson was born at the commencement of the century, and is therefore now, 1893, in his ninety-fourth year.

It was a small room, about fifteen feet by twenty. I then put out my shingle as attorney and counsellor-at-law, and waited for clients; but none came. One day a fellow-passenger requested me to draw a deed, for which I charged him an ounce. He thought that too much, so I compromised and took half an ounce. For two weeks this was the only call I had upon my professional abilities. But I was in no way discouraged. To tell the truth I was hardly fit for business. I was too much excited by the stirring life around me. There was so much to hear and see that I spent half my time in the streets and saloons talking with people from the mines, in which I was greatly interested. I felt sure that there would soon be occasion in that quarter for my services.

Whilst I was excited over the news which was daily brought from the mines in the interior of the State, and particularly from the northern part, an incident occurred which determined my future career in California. I had brought from New York several letters of introduction to persons who had preceded me to the new country, and among them one to the mercantile firm of Simmons, Hutchinson & Co., of San Francisco, upon whom I called. They received me cordially, and inquired particularly of my intentions as to residence and business. They stated that there was a town at the head of river navigation, at the junction of Sacramento and Feather Rivers, which offered inducements to a young lawyer. They called it Vernon, and said they owned some lots in it which they would sell to me. I replied that I had no money. That made no difference, they said; they would let me have them on credit; they desired to build up the town and would let the lots go cheap to encourage its settlement. They added that they owned the steamer "McKim," going the next day to Sacramento, and they offered me a ticket in her for that place, which they represented to be not far from Vernon. Accordingly I took the ticket, and on January 12th, 1850, left for Sacramento, where I arrived the next morning. It was the time of the great flood of that year, and the entire upper country seemed to be under water. Upon reaching the landing place at Sacramento, we took a small boat and rowed to the hotel. There I found a great crowd of earnest and enthusiastic people, all talking about California, and in the highest spirits. In fact I did not meet with any one who did not speak in glowing terms of the country and anticipate a sudden acquisition of fortune. I had already caught the infection myself, and these new crowds and their enthusiasm increased my excitement. The exuberance of my spirits was marvelous. The next day I took the little steamer "Lawrence," for Vernon, which was so heavily laden as to be only eighteen inches out of water; and the passengers, who amounted to a large number, were requested not to move about the deck, but to keep as quiet as possible. In three or four hours after leaving Sacramento, the Captain suddenly cried out with great energy, "Stop her! stop her!"; and with some difficulty the boat escaped running into what seemed to be a solitary house standing in a vast lake of water. I asked what place that was, and was answered, "Vernon,"—the town where I had been advised to settle as affording a good opening for a young lawyer. I turned to the Captain and said, I believed I would not put out my shingle at Vernon just yet, but would go further on. The next place we stopped at was Nicolaus, and the following day we arrived at a place called Nye's Ranch, near the junction of Feather and Yuba Rivers.

No sooner had the vessel struck the landing at Nye's Ranch than all the passengers, some forty or fifty in number, as if moved by a common impulse, started for an old adobe building, which stood upon the bank of the river, and near which were numerous tents. Judging by the number of the tents, there must have been from five hundred to a thousand people there. When we reached the adobe and entered the principal room, we saw a map spread out upon the counter, containing the plan of a town, which was called " Yubaville," and a man standing behind it, crying out, " Gentlemen, put your names down ; put your names down, all you that want lots." He seemed to address himself to me, and I asked the price of the lots. He answered, "Two hundred and fifty dollars each for lots 80 by 160 feet." I replied, " But, suppose a man puts his name down and afterwards don't want the lots?" He rejoined, " Oh, you need not take them if you don't want them : put your names down, gentlemen, you that want lots." I took him at his word and wrote my name down for sixty-five lots, aggregating in all $16,250. This produced a great sensation. To the best of my recollection I had only about twenty dollars left of what Col. Stevenson had paid me ; but it was immediately noised about that a great capitalist had come up from San Francisco to invest in lots in the rising town. The consequence was that the proprietors of the place waited upon me and showed me great attention.

Two of the proprietors were French gentlemen, named Covillaud and Sicard. They were delighted when they found I could speak French and insisted on showing me the town site. It was a beautiful spot, covered with live-oak trees that reminded me of the oak parks in England, and the neighborhood was lovely. I saw at once that the place, from its position at the head of practical river navigation, was destined to become an important depot for the neighboring mines, and that its beauty and salubrity would render it a pleasant place for residence. In return for the civilities shown me by Mr. Covillaud, and learning that he read English, I handed him some New York papers I had with me, and among them a copy of the New York "Evening Post" of November 13th, 1849, which happened to contain a notice of my departure for California with an expression of good wishes for my success.* The next day Mr. Covillaud came to me and in an excited manner said: "Ah, Monsieur, are you the Monsieur Field, the lawyer from New York, mentioned in this paper?" I took the paper and looked at the notice with apparent surprise that it was marked, though I had myself drawn a pencil line around it, and replied, meekly and modestly, that I believed I was. "Well, then," he said, "we must have a deed drawn for our land." Upon making inquiries I found that the proprietors had purchased the tract upon which the town was laid out, and several leagues of land adjoining, of General—then Captain—John A. Sutter, but had not yet received a conveyance of the property. I answered that I would draw the necessary deed; and they immediately dispatched a couple of vaqueros for Captain Sutter, who lived at Hock Farm, six miles below, on Feather River. When he arrived the deed was ready for signature. It was for some leagues of land; a

---

* See Exhibit A, in Appendix.

considerably larger tract than I had ever before put
into a conveyance. But when it was signed there was
no officer to take the acknowledgment of the grantor,
nor an office in which it could be recorded, nearer
than Sacramento.

I suggested to those present on the occasion, that
in a place of such fine prospects, and where there was
likely in a short time to be much business and many
transactions in real property, there ought to be an
officer to take acknowledgments and record deeds,
and a magistrate for the preservation of order and the
settlement of disputes. It happened that a new house,
the frame of which was brought in the steamer, was
put up that day; and it was suggested by Mr. Covillaud that we should meet there that evening and
celebrate the execution of the deed, and take into
consideration the subject of organizing a town by the
election of magistrates. When evening came the
house was filled. It is true it had no floor, but the
sides were boarded up and a roof was overhead, and
we improvised seats out of spare planks. The proprietors sent around to the tents for something to
give cheer to the meeting, and, strange as it may seem,
they found two baskets of champagne. These they
secured, and their contents were joyously disposed of.
When the wine passed around, I was called upon and
made a speech. I started out by predicting in glowing colors the prosperity of the new town, and spoke
of its advantageous situation on the Feather and Yuba
Rivers; how it was the most accessible point for vessels coming up from the cities of San Francisco and
Sacramento, and must in time become the depot for
all the trade with the northern mines. I pronounced
the auriferous region lying east of the Feather River

and north of the Yuba the finest and richest in the
country ; and I felt certain that its commerce must
concentrate at the junction of those rivers. But, said
I, to avail ourselves of all these advantages we must
organize and establish a government, and the first
thing to be done is to call an election and choose
magistrates and a town council. These remarks met
with general favor, and it was resolved that a public
meeting should be held in front of the Adobe house
the next morning, and if it approved of the project,
that an election should be held at once.

Accordingly, on the following morning, which was the
18th of January, 1850, a public meeting of citizens was
there held, and it was resolved that a town government
should be established and that there should be elected
an Ayuntamiento or town council, a first and second
Alcalde, (the latter to act in the absence or sickness
of the former,) and a Marshal. The Alcalde was a
judicial officer under the Spanish and Mexican laws,
having a jurisdiction something like that of a Justice
of the Peace; but in the anomalous condition of
affairs in California at that time, he, as a matter of
necessity, assumed and exercised very great powers.
The election ordered took place in the afternoon of
the same day. I had modestly whispered to different
persons at the meeting in the new house the night
before, that my name was mentioned by my friends
for the office of Alcalde; and my nomination followed.
But I was not to have the office without a struggle ;
an opposition candidate appeared, and an exciting
election ensued. The main objection urged against
me was that I was a new-comer. I had been there
only three days; my opponent had been there six.
I beat him, however, by nine votes.*

---

* See Exhibit B, in Appendix.

On the evening of the election, there was a general gathering of people at the Adobe house, the principal building of the place, to hear the official announcement of the result of the election. When this was made, some one proposed that a name should be adopted for the new town. One man suggested " Yubafield," because of its situation on the Yuba River; and another, " Yubaville," for the same reason. A third, urged the name " Circumdoro," (surrounded with gold, as he translated the word,) because there were mines in every direction round about. But there was a fourth, a solid and substantial old man, evidently of kindly domestic affections, who had come out to California to better his fortunes. He now rose and remarked that there was an American lady in the place, the wife of one of the proprietors; that her name was Mary; and that, in his opinion, her name ought to be given to the town, and it should be called, in her honor, " Marysville." No sooner had he made the suggestion, than the meeting broke out into loud hurrahs; every hat made a circle around its owner's head, and we christened the new town " Marysville," without a dissenting voice. For a few days afterwards, the town was called both Yubaville and Marysville, but the latter name was soon generally adopted, and the place is so called to this day. The lady in whose honor it was named was Mrs. Covillaud. She was one of the survivors of the Donner party, which suffered so frightfully while crossing the Sierra Nevadas in the winter of 1846–7, and had been living in the country ever since that terrible time.

With my notions of law, I did not attach much importance to the election, but I had a certificate of election made out and signed by the Inspectors, stating that at a meeting of the residents of the District of Yubaville, on the day named, an election for officers had been held, and designating the Inspectors who were appointed, the number of votes that had been cast for the office of Alcalde, and the number received by myself, and the number received by my opponent, and that as I had received a majority of all the votes cast, I was elected to that office. It was made out with all possible formality, and when completed, was sent to the Prefect of the District. This officer, a Mr. E. O. Crosby, afterwards Minister to one of the South American Republics, wrote back approving my election, and advising me to act. His advice, under the circumstances, was a matter of some moment. The new Constitution of the State had gone into effect, though it was still uncertain whether it would be recognized by Congress. Mr. Crosby, therefore, thought it best for me to procure, in addition to my commission as Alcalde, an appointment as Justice of the Peace; and through his kind offices, I obtained from Governor Burnett the proper document bearing his official seal. After my election, I went to Sacramento, and on the 22d of January, 1850, was sworn into office as first Alcalde of Yubaville, by the Judge of the Court of First Instance, as that was the name of the district in the certificate of election; but I was always designated, after the name of the town had been adopted, as First Alcalde of Marysville.*

Captain Sutter, whose deed I had drawn, was a remarkable character. He was about five feet nine inches in height, and was thick-set. He had a large head and an open, manly face, somewhat hardened and bronzed by his life in the open air. His hair was

---

* See Exhibit C, in Appendix.

thin and light, and he wore a mustache. He had the appearance of an old officer of the French army, with a dignified and military bearing. I subsequently became well acquainted with him, and learned both to respect and to pity him. I respected him for his intrepid courage, his gentle manners, his large heart, and his unbounded benevolence. I pitied him for his simplicity, which, while suspecting nothing wrong in others, led him to trust all who had a kind word on their lips, and made him the victim of every sharper in the country. He was a native of Switzerland and was an officer in the Swiss Guards, in the service of the King of France, in 1823, and for some years afterwards. In 1834, he emigrated to America, and had varied and strange adventures among the Indians at the West; in the Sandwich Islands, at Fort Vancouver, in Alaska, and along the Pacific Coast. In July, 1839, the vessel which he was aboard of, was stranded in the harbor of San Francisco. He then penetrated into the interior of California and founded the first white settlement in the valley of the Sacramento, on the river of that name, at the mouth of the American River, which settlement he named Helvetia. He built a fort there and gathered around it a large number of native Indians and some white settlers. In 1841, the Mexican government granted to him a tract of land eleven square leagues in extent; and, subsequently, a still larger concession was made to him by the Governor of the Department. But the Governor being afterwards expelled from the country, the concession was held to be invalid. The emigrants arriving in the country after the discovery of gold proved the ruin of his fortunes. They squatted upon his land, denied the validity of his title, cut down his

timber, and drove away his cattle. Sharpers robbed
him of what the squatters did not take, until at last
he was stripped of everything; and, finally, he left
the State, and for some years has been living with
relatives in Pennsylvania. Even the stipend of $2,500,
which the State of California for some years allowed
him, has been withdrawn, and now in his advanced
years, he is almost destitute. Yet, in his days of
prosperity, he was always ready to assist others.
His fort was always open to the stranger, and food,
to the value of many thousand dollars, was, every
year, so long as he had the means, sent out by him
for the relief of emigrants crossing the plains. It is
a reproach to California that she leaves the pioneer
and hero destitute in his old age.

UNDER the Mexican law, Alcaldes had, as already stated, a very limited jurisdiction. But in the anomalous condition of affairs under the American occupation, they exercised almost unlimited powers. They were, in fact, regarded as magistrates elected by the people for the sake of preserving public order and settling disputes of all kinds. In my own case, and with the approval of the community, I took jurisdiction of every case brought before me. I knew nothing of Mexican laws; did not pretend to know anything of them; but I knew that the people had elected me to act as a magistrate and looked to me for the preservation of order and the settlement of disputes; and I did my best that they should not be disappointed. I let it be known that my election had been approved by the highest authority.

The first case I tried was in the street. Two men came up to me, one of them leading a horse. He said, "Mr. Alcalde, we both claim this horse, and we want you to decide which of us is entitled to it." I turned to the man who had the horse, administered an oath to him, and then examined him as to where he got the horse, of whom and when, whether he had a bill of sale, whether there was any mark or brand on the animal, and, in short, put all those questions which would naturally be asked in such a case to elicit the truth. I then administered an oath to the other man and put him through a similar examination, paying careful attention to what each said. When the examination was completed I at once decided the case. "It is very plain, gentlemen," I said, "that the horse belongs to this man (pointing to one of them) and the other must give him up." "But," said the man who had lost and who held the horse, "the bridle certainly belongs to me, he does not take the bridle, does he?" I said, "Oh no, the bridle is another matter." As soon as I said this the owner of the bridle turned to his adversary and said, "What will you take for the horse?" "Two hundred and fifty dollars," was the instant reply. "Agreed," retorted the first, and then turning to me, he continued: "And now, Mr. Alcalde, I want you to draw me up a bill of sale for this horse which will stick." I, of course, did as he desired. I charged an ounce for trying the case and an ounce for the bill of sale; charges which were promptly paid. Both parties went off perfectly satisfied. I was also well pleased with my first judicial experience.

Soon after my election I went to San Francisco to get my effects; and while there I purchased, on credit a frame house and several zinc houses, which were at once shipped to Marysville. As soon as the frame house was put up I opened my office in it, and exercised not only the functions of a magistrate and justice, but also of a supervisor of the town. I opened books for the record of deeds and kept a registry of conveyances in the district. I had the banks of the river graded so as to facilitate the landing from vessels. The marshal of my court, elected at the same time with myself, having refused to act, I appointed an active and courageous person in his place, R. B. Buchanan by name, and directed him to see that peace was preserved, and for that purpose to appoint as many deputies as might be necessary. He did so, and order and peace were preserved throughout the district, not only in Marysville, but for miles around.

As a judicial officer, I tried many cases, both civil and criminal, and I dictated the form of process suited to the exigency. Thus, when a complaint was made to me by the owner of a river boat, that the steamer, which plied between Marysville and Sacramento, had run down his boat, by which a part of its cargo was lost, I at once dictated process to the marshal, in which the alleged injury was recited, and he was directed to seize the steamer, and hold it until further orders, unless the captain or owner gave security to appear in the action commenced by the owner of the boat, and pay any judgment that might be recovered therein. Upon service of the process the captain appeared, gave the required security, and the case was immediately tried. Judgment was rendered and paid within five hours after the commission of the injury.

In civil cases, I always called a jury, if the parties desired one; and in criminal cases, when the offence was of a high grade, I went through the form of calling a grand jury, and having an indictment found; and in all cases I appointed an attorney to represent the people, and also the accused, when necessary. The Americans in the country had a general notion of what was required for the preservation of order and the due administration of justice; and as I endeavored to administer justice promptly, but upon a due consideration of the rights of every one, and not rashly, I was sustained with great unanimity by the community.

I have reported a civil case tried before me as Alcalde. I will now give a few criminal prosecutions and their circumstances. One morning, about five o'clock, a man tapped at my window, and cried, "Alcalde, Alcalde, there has been a robbery, and you are wanted." I got up at once, and while I was dressing he told his story. Nearly every one in those days lived in a tent and had his gold dust with him. The man, who proved to be Gildersleeve, the famous runner, upon going to bed the previous evening had placed several pounds of gold dust in his trunk, which was not locked. In the night some one had cut through his tent and taken the gold dust. I asked him if he suspected anybody; and he named two men, and gave such reasons for his suspicion that I immediately dictated a warrant for their arrest; and in a short time the two men were arrested and brought before me. The gold dust was found on one of them. I immediately called a grand jury, by whom he was indicted. I then called a petit jury, and assigned counsel for the prisoner. He was immediately placed upon his trial, and was convicted. The whole proceeding occupied only a part of the day. There was a great crowd and much excitement, and some talk of lynching. Curiously enough, my real trouble did not commence until after the conviction. What was to be done with the prisoner? How was he to be punished? Imposing a fine would not answer; and, if he had been discharged, the crowd would have immediately hung him. When at San Francisco, Mayor Geary, of that place, told me if I would send my convicts to him, with money enough to pay for a ball and chain for each one, he would put them in the chain-gang. But at that time the price of passage by steamer from Marysville to San Francisco was fifty dollars, which, with the expense of an officer to accompany the prisoner, and the price of a ball and chain, would have amounted to a much larger sum than the prosecution could afford; so it was clearly impracticable to think of sending him to San Francisco. Nor is it at all likely that the people would have consented to his removal. Under these circumstances there was but one course to pursue, and, however repugnant it was to my feelings to adopt it, I believe it was the only thing that saved the man's life. I ordered him to be publicly whipped with fifty lashes, and added that if he were found, within the next two years, in the vicinity of Marysville, he should be again whipped. I, however, privately ordered a physician to be present so as to see that no unnecessary severity was practiced. In accordance with this sentence, the fellow was immediately taken out and flogged; and that was the last seen of him in that region. He went off and never came back. The latter part of the sentence, however, was supererogatory; for there was something so degrading in a public whipping, that I have never known a man thus whipped who would stay longer than he could help, or ever desire to return. However this may have been, the sense of justice of the community was satisfied. No blood had been shed; there had been no hanging; yet a severe public example had been given.

On another occasion a complaint was made that a man had stolen fifteen hundred dollars from a woman. He was arrested, brought before me, indicted, tried, and convicted. I had the same compunctions about punishment as before, but, as there was no other course, I ordered him to receive fifty lashes on his back on two successive days, unless he gave up the money, in which case he was to receive only fifty lashes. As soon as the sentence was written down the marshal marched the prisoner out to a tree, made him hug the tree, and in the presence of the crowd that followed, began inflicting the lashes. The man stood it for awhile without flinching, but when he had received the twenty second lash he cried out, " Stop, for God's sake, and I will tell you where the money is." The marshal stopped and, accompanied by the crowd, took the man to the place indicated, where the money was recovered ; and the thief was then made to carry it back to the woman and apologize for stealing it. The marshal then consulted the sentence, and, finding that it prescribed fifty lashes at any rate, he marched the wretch back to the tree and gave him the balance, which was his due.

But the case which made the greatest impression upon the people, and did more to confirm my authority than anything else, was the following : There was a military encampment of United States soldiers on Bear River, about fifteen miles from Marysville, known as " Camp Far West." One day an application was made to me to issue a warrant for the arrest of one of the soldiers for a larceny he had committed. It was stated that a complaint had been laid before the local Alcalde near the camp ; but that the officer in charge had refused to give up the soldier unless a warrant for that purpose were issued by me, it being the general impression that I was the only duly commissioned Alcalde in the district above Sacramento. On this showing I issued my warrant, and a lieutenant of the army brought the soldier over. The soldier was indicted, tried, convicted, and sentenced to be publicly whipped with the usual number of lashes, and the officer stood by and saw the punishment inflicted. He then took the soldier back to camp, where it was afterwards reported that he received an additional punishment. But before the lieutenant left me that day, and while we were dining together, he took occasion to say that, if at any time I had any trouble in enforcing the law, I had but to send him word and he would order out a company of troops to support me. This offer I permitted to become known through the town; and people said—and with what effect may be imagined—"Why here is an Alcalde that has the troops of the United States at his back."

I have already stated that I had the banks of the Yuba River graded so as to facilitate the landing from vessels. I will now mention another instance of my administration as general supervisor of the town. There were several squatters on the landing at the river, which, according to the plan of the town, was several hundred feet wide. The lots fronting on this landing being the best for business, commanded the highest prices. But on account of the squatters the owners were deprived of the benefit of the open ground of the landing in front of their property, and they complained to me. I called upon the squatters and told them that they must leave, and that if they were not gone by a certain time, I should be compelled to remove them by force, and, if necessary, to call to my aid the troops of the United States. This was enough; the squatters left, the landing was cleared, and business went on smoothly.

In addition to my ordinary duties as a judicial officer and as general supervisor of the town, I acted as arbitrator in a great number of controversies which

arose between the citizens. In such cases the parties
generally came to my office together and stated that
they had agreed to leave the matter in dispute between them to my decision. I immediately heard
their respective statements—sometimes under oath,
and sometimes without oath—and decided the matter
at once. The whole matter was disposed of without
any written proceedings, except in some instances I
gave to parties a memorandum of my decision. Thus
on one occasion a dispute arose as to the rate of wages,
between several workmen and their employer; the
workmen insisting upon twelve dollars a day and the
employer refusing to give more than ten. To settle
the dispute they agreed to leave the matter to me.
I heard their respective statements, and after stating that both of them ought to suffer a little for
not having made a specific contract at the outset, decided that the workingmen should receive eleven
dollars a day, with which both appeared to be well
satisfied. On another occasion parties disputed as
to whether freight on a box of crockery should be
charged by measurement or by weight, a specific
contract having been made that all articles shipped
by the owner should be carried at a fixed price per
hundred pounds. They agreed to leave the matter
to my determination, and I settled it in five minutes.
Again, on one occasion a woman, apparently about
fifty-six, rushed into my office under great excitement, exclaiming that she wanted a divorce from
her husband, who had treated her shamefully. A
few moments afterwards the husband followed, and
he also wanted relief from the bonds of matrimony.
I heard their respective complaints, and finding that
they had children, I persuaded them to make peace,

kiss, and forgive; and so they left my office arm-in-arm, each having promised the other never to do so again, amid the applause of the spectators. In this way I carried out my conception of the good Cadi of the village, from which term (Al Cadi) my own official designation, Alcalde, was derived.

To make a long story short, until I was superseded by officers under the State government, I superintended municipal affairs and administered justice in Marysville with success. Whilst there was a large number of residents there of high character and culture, who would have done honor to any city, there were also unfortunately many desperate persons, gamblers, blacklegs, thieves, and cut-throats; yet the place was as orderly as a New England village. There were no disturbances at night, no riots, and no lynching. It was the model town of the whole country for peacefulness and respect for law.

And now a word about my speculations. In a short time after going to Marysville and writing my name down for sixty-five town lots, property increased tenfold in value. Within ninety days I sold over $25,000 worth, and still had most of my lots left. My frame and zinc houses brought me a rental of over $1,000 a month. The emoluments of my office of Alcalde were also large. In criminal cases I received nothing for my services as judge, and in civil cases the fees were small; but as an officer to take acknowledgments and affidavits and record deeds, the fees I received amounted to a large sum. At one time I had $14,000 in gold dust in my safe, besides the rentals and other property.

One day whilst I was Alcalde, a bright-looking lad, with red cheeks and apparently about seventeen years

of age, came into the office and asked if I did not
want a clerk. I said I did, and would willingly give
$200 a month for a good one; but that I had written
to Sacramento and was expecting one from there.
The young man suggested that perhaps the one from
Sacramento would not come or might be delayed,
and he would like to take the place in the meanwhile.
I replied, very well, if he was willing to act until the
other arrived, he might do so. And thereupon he
took hold and commenced work. Three days afterwards the man from Sacramento arrived; but in the
meanwhile I had become so much pleased with the
brightness and quickness of my young clerk that I
would not part with him. That young clerk was
George C. Gorham, the present Secretary of the
United States Senate. I remember him distinctly as
he first appeared to me, with red and rosy cheeks.
His quickness of comprehension was really wonderful.
Give him half an idea of what was wanted, and he
would complete it as it were by intuition. I remember on one occasion he wanted to know what was
necessary for a marriage settlement. I asked him
why. He replied that he had been employed by a
French lady to prepare such a settlement, and was
to receive twenty-five dollars for the instrument. I
gave him some suggestions, but added that he had
better let me see the document after he had written
it. In a short time afterwards he brought it to me,
and I was astonished to find it so nearly perfect.
There was only one correction to make. And thus
ready I always found him. With the most general
directions he would execute everything committed to
his charge, and usually with perfect correctness. He
remained with me several months, and acted as clerk

of my Alcalde court, and years afterwards, at different times, was a clerk in my office. When I went upon the bench of the Supreme Court, I appointed him clerk of the Circuit Court of the United States for the District of California, and, with the exception of the period during which he acted as secretary of Gov. Low, he remained as such clerk until he was nominated for the office of governor of the State, when he resigned. Through the twenty-seven years of our acquaintance, from 1850 to the present time, July, 1877, his friendship and esteem have been sincere and cordial, which no personal abuse of me could change and no political differences between us could alienate. His worldly possessions would have been more abundant had he pursued the profession of the law, which I urged him to do; and his success as a public man would have been greater, had he been more conciliatory to those who differed from him in opinion.

THE TURNER CONTROVERSY.

Towards the end of May, 1850, William R. Turner, who had been appointed Judge of the Eighth Judicial District of the State by the first Legislature which convened under the Constitution, made his appearance and announced that he intended to open the District Court at Marysville on the first Monday of the next month. We were all pleased with the prospect of having a regular court and endeavored, as far as lay in our power, to make the stay of the Judge with us agreeable. I had been in the habit of receiving a package of New York newspapers by every steamer, and among them came copies of the New York " Evening Post," which was at that time the organ of the so-called Free-soil party. When Judge Turner arrived, I waited on him to pay my respects, and sent him the various newspapers I had received. He had lived for years in Texas, and, as it proved, was a man of narrow mind and bitter prejudices. He seems to have had a special prejudice against New Yorkers and regarded a Free-soiler as an abomination. I have been told, and I believe such to be the fact, that my sending him these newspapers, and particularly the " Evening Post," led him to believe that I was an " Abolitionist "—a person held in special abhorrence in those days by gentlemen from the South. At any rate he conceived a violent dislike of me, which was destined in a short time to show itself and cause me great annoyance. What was intended on my part as an act of courtesy, turned out to be the beginning of a long, bitter, and on his part, ferocious quarrel. At that time my affairs were in a very prosperous condition, as I have already stated. I had $14,000 in gold dust, a rental of over a thousand dollars a month, and a large amount of city property constantly increasing in value. Such being the case, I thought I would go East on a visit, and accordingly began making arrangements to leave. But shortly before the opening of the June term of the District Court, Captain Sutter came to me and told me he had been sued by a man named Cameron, and wished me to appear as his counsel. I answered that I was making arrangements to go East and he had better retain some one else. He replied that I ought to remain long enough to appear for him and assist his attorney, and begged of me as an act of friendship to do so. I finally consented, and deferred my departure.

Soon after the opening of the court, some time during the first week, the case of Captain Sutter was called. A preliminary motion, made by his attorney, was decided against him. Mr. Jesse O. Goodwin, a member of the bar, sitting near, said to me that the practice act, passed at the recent session of the Legislature, contained a section bearing upon the question ; and at the same time handed me the act. I immediately rose, and addressing the court, remarked that I was informed there was a statutory provision applicable to the point, and begged permission to read it ; and commenced turning over the pages of the act in search of it, when Judge Turner, addressing me and apparently irritated, said in a petulant manner:—"The court knows the law—the mind of the court is made up—take your seat, sir." I was amazed at hearing such language ; but in a respectful and quiet manner stated that I excepted to the decision, and appealed, or would appeal from the order. The Judge instantly replied, in a loud and boisterous manner, " Fine that gentleman two hundred dollars." I replied quietly, " Very well," or " Well, sir." He immediately added, in an angry tone, " I fine him three hundred dollars, and commit him to the custody of the sheriff eight hours." I again replied, " Very well." He instantly exclaimed, in the same violent manner, " I fine him four hundred dollars and commit him twelve hours." I then said that it was my right by statute to appeal from any order of his honor, and that it was no contempt of court to give notice of an exception or an appeal, and asked the members of the bar present if it could be so regarded. But the Judge, being very ignorant of the practice of the law, regarded an exception to his decision as an impeachment of his judgment, and, therefore, something like a personal affront. And so, upon my statement, he flew into a perfect rage, and in a loud and boisterous tone cried out, " I fine him five hundred dollars and commit him twenty-four hours—forty-eight hours—turn him out of court— subpœna a posse—subpœna me." I then left the court-room. The attorney in the case accompanied me, and we were followed by the deputy sheriff. After going a few steps we met the coroner, to whom the deputy sheriff transferred me ; and the coroner accompanied me to my office, and after remaining there a few moments left me to myself. On the way an incident occurred, which probably inflamed Judge Turner against me more than anything else that could have happened. The attorney, who was much exasperated at the conduct of the Judge, said to me as we met the coroner, " Never mind what the Judge does ; he is an old fool." I replied, " Yes, he is an old jackass." This was said in an ordinary conversational tone; but a man by the name of Captain Powers, with whom Turner boarded, happened to overhear it, and running to the court-house, and opening the door, he hallooed out, " Judge Turner! oh, Judge Turner! Judge Field says you are an old jackass." A shout followed, and the Judge seemed puzzled whether or not he should send an officer after me, or punish his excitable friend for repeating my language.

I remained in my office the remainder of the day, and many people who were present in court, or heard of what had occurred, called to see me. I immediately wrote out a full statement of everything that happened in the court-room, and had it verified by a number of persons who were eye and ear witnesses of the affair. Towards evening the deputy sheriff met the Judge, who asked him what he had done with me. The deputy answered that I had gone to my office and was still there. The Judge said, " Go and put him under lock and key, and, if necessary, put him in irons." The deputy came to me and said, " The Judge has sent me to put you under lock and key; let me turn the key upon you in your own office." At this I became indignant, and asked for his warrant or commitment to hold me. He replied that he had none, that only a verbal order was given to him by the Judge in the street. I then told him he must go away from me and leave me alone. He replied that, "as he was acting by the orders of the sheriff, whose deputy he was, in obeying the Judge, he must do as he had been directed." He added, "I will lock the door anyway," and doing so he went off. I immediately sued out a writ of habeas corpus returnable before Henry P.

Haun, the County Judge. The writ was executed forthwith, and the same evening I was taken before the Judge. There was a great crowd present. I called the sheriff to the stand and asked him if he had any writ, process, commitment, or order by which he held me in custody. He replied that he had none. I then put on the stand Samuel B. Mulford and Jesse O. Goodwin and several others, who were present in the District Court where the scenes narrated had occurred, and they testified that there was nothing disrespectful in my language or manner ; that I had not used an expression at which anybody could justly take offence ; and that they had been utterly surprised at the conduct of the Judge, which was violent and tyrannical; and that they saw no possible excuse for it. This testimony was of course of no consequence on the question presented by the habeas corpus ; because, as there was no order or warrant for my arrest in the possession of the officer, I could not, under any circumstances, be held; but I wished to show my friends, who had not been present in the court-room, the facts of the case.

I was of course at once discharged. But the matter did not end there. An excited crowd was present, and as I left the court-room they cheered enthusiastically. I thereupon invited them to the Covillaud House, a public house in the town, and directed the keeper to dispense to them the good things of his bar. The champagne was accordingly uncorked without stint, and the best Havana boxes were soon emptied of their most fragrant cigars. A bill of $290 paid the next day settled the account. Whilst the boys were thus enjoying themselves, Judge Turner, who was not far off, entered the Covillaud

House, perfectly furious, and applied obscene and vile epithets to the County Judge, declaring with an oath that he would teach "that fellow" that he was an inferior judge, and that the witnesses before him were a set of "perjured scoundrels" who should be expelled from the bar. Similar threats were made by him in different saloons in the town, to the disgust of every one. That evening he was burned in effigy in the public plaza. I had nothing to do with that act, and did not approve of it. I did not know then, and do not know to this day who were engaged in it. He attributed it to me, however, and his exasperation towards me in consequence became a malignant fury.

On the Monday following, June 10th, which was the first day on which the court was held after the scenes narrated, Judge Turner, on the opening of the court, before the minutes of the previous session were read, and without notice to the parties, or any hearing of them, although they were present at the time, ordered that Judge Haun be fined fifty dollars and be imprisoned forty-eight hours for his judicial act in discharging me from arrest, under some pretence that the order of the court had been thus obstructed by him. At the same time he ordered that I should be reimprisoned, and that Mr. Mulford, Mr. Goodwin, and myself should be expelled from the bar; myself for suing out the writ, and those two gentlemen for being witnesses on its return, under the pretence that we had "vilified the court and denounced its proceedings." Judge Haun paid his fine and left the court-room, and I was again taken into custody by the sheriff.*

---

* See Exhibit D, in Appendix.

It happened to be the day appointed by law for the opening of the Court of Sessions of the county, over which the County Judge presided. Judge Haun proceeded from the District Court to the room engaged for the Court of Sessions, and there, in connection with an associate justice, opened that court. Immediately afterwards I sued out another writ of *habeas corpus*, returnable forthwith, and whilst before the court arguing for my discharge under the writ, the sheriff entered and declared his intention of taking me out of the room, and of taking Judge Haun from the bench and putting us in confinement, pursuant to the order of Judge Turner. Judge Haun told the sheriff that the Court of Sessions was holding its regular term; that he was violating the law, and that the court must not be disturbed in its proceedings. Judge Turner was then informed that the Court of Sessions was sitting; that Judge Haun was on the bench, and that I was arguing before the court on a writ of habeas corpus. Judge Turner immediately ordered a posse to be summoned and appealed to gentlemen in the court-room to serve on it, and directed the sheriff to take Judge Haun and myself into custody by force, notwithstanding Judge Haun was on the bench, and I was arguing my case; and if necessary to put Judge Haun in irons—to handcuff him. Soon afterwards the sheriff, with a posse, entered the room of the Court of Sessions, and forced me out of it, and was proceeding to seize Judge Haun on the bench, when the Judge stepped to a closet and drew from it a navy revolver, cocked it, and, pointing it towards the sheriff, informed him in a stern manner that he was violating the law; that whilst on the bench he, the Judge, could not be arrested, and that if the sheriff attempted to do so he would kill him. At the same time he fined the sheriff for contempt of court $200, and appointed a temporary bailiff to act, and directed him to clear the court-room of the disturbers. The new bailiff summoned all the bystanders, who instantly responded, and the court-room was immediately cleared. Judge Haun then laid his revolver on a drawer before him, and inquired if there was any business ready; for if so the court would hear it. There being none, the court adjourned.

I regret to be compelled to add, that notwithstanding the manly and courageous conduct which Judge Haun had thus shown, no sooner was the court adjourned than he was persuaded to make a qualified apology to the District Court for discharging me, by sending a communication to it, stating "that if he was guilty of obstructing the order of the court in releasing Field, he did it ignorantly, not intending any contempt by so doing;" and thereupon the District Court ordered that he be released from confinement, and that his fine be remitted.*

Of course there was great excitement through the town as soon as these proceedings became known. That night nearly all Marysville came to my office. I made a speech to the people. Afterwards some of them passed in front of Turner's house, and gave him three groans. They then dispersed, and in returning home some of them fired off their pistols as a sort of finale to the proceedings of the evening. The firing was not within three hundred yards of Turner's house; but he seized hold of the fact of firing, and stated that he had been attacked in his house by an armed mob. He also charged that I had instigated the crowd to

---

* See Exhibit E, in Appendix.

attack him, but the facts are as I have stated them. There was a great deal of feeling on the part of the people, who generally sided with me; but I did nothing to induce them to violate the law or disturb the peace. Even if I wished to do so, prudence and policy counselled otherwise.

When Turner caused the names of Mulford, Goodwin, and myself, to be stricken from the roll of attorneys, we, of course, could no longer appear as counsel in his court. I at once prepared the necessary papers, and applied to the Supreme Court of the State for a mandamus to compel him to vacate the order and re-instate us. I took the ground that an attorney and counsellor, by his admission to the bar, acquired rights of which he could not be arbitrarily deprived; that he could not, under any circumstances, be expelled from the bar without charges being preferred against him and an opportunity afforded to be heard in his defence; that the proceedings of Judge Turner being ex-parte, without charges preferred, and without notice, were void; and that a mandate, directing him to vacate the order of expulsion and restore us to the bar, ought to be issued immediately.

In addition to this application, I also moved for a mandamus to him to vacate the order imposing a fine and imprisonment upon me for the alleged contempt of his court, or for such other order in the premises as might be just. I took the ground, that as the order did not show any act committed which could constitute a contempt of court, it was void on its face, and should be so declared. My old friend, Gregory Yale, assisted me in the presentation of these motions. In deciding them, the court delivered two opinions, in which these positions were sustained. They are reported under the titles of People, ex rel. Mulford et al., vs. Turner, 1 Cal., 143 ; and People, ex rel. Field vs. Turner, 1 Cal., 152. In the first case, a peremptory writ of mandamus was issued, directed to Judge Turner, ordering him to reinstate us as attorneys ; in the second, a writ of certiorari was issued to bring up the order imposing a fine, which was subsequently reversed and vacated, as shown in Ex-parte Field, 1 Cal., 187. The opinions referred to were delivered by Judge Bennett, and are models of their kind. Many years afterwards, when a somewhat similar question came before the Supreme Court of the United States, I was called upon to announce its judgment ; and in doing so, I followed these opinions, as may be seen by reference to the case of Ex-parte Robinson, 19 Wallace, 510. I there repeated substantially the doctrine of Judge Bennett, which is the only doctrine that will protect an attorney and counsellor from the tyranny of an arbitrary and capricious officer, and preserve to him his self-respect and independence.

When the order for our restoration came down from the Supreme Court, Turner refused to obey it ; and wrote a scurrilous "Address to the Public" about us, which he published in one of the newspapers. We replied in a sharp and bitter article, signed by ourselves and five other gentlemen ; and at the same time we published a petition to the Governor, signed by all the prominent citizens of Marysville, asking for Judge Turner's removal. There was a general impression in those days that Judges appointed before the admission of the State into the Union held their offices subject to removal by the Governor. I hardly know how this impression originated, but probably in some vague notions about the powers of Mexican Governors. However this may be, such was the general notion, and in accordance with it, a petition for Turner's removal was started, and, as I have said, was very generally signed.* The matter had by this time assumed such a serious character, and the Judge's conduct was so atrocious, that the people became alarmed and with great unanimity demanded his deposition from office.

In the article referred to as published by us, we said, after setting forth the facts, that "Judge Turner is a man of depraved tastes, of vulgar habits, of an ungovernable temper, reckless of truth when his passions are excited, and grossly incompetent to discharge the duties of his office." Unfortunately the statement was perfectly true. He refused to obey the mandate of the Supreme Court, even talked of setting that court at defiance, and went around saying that every one who had signed an affidavit against him was a "perjured villain," and that as to Goodwin, Mulford, and Field, he would "cut their ears off." He frequented the gambling saloons, associated with disreputable characters, and was addicted to habits of the most disgusting intoxication. Besides being abusive in his language, he threatened violence, and gave out that he intended to insult me publicly the first time we met, and that, if I resented his conduct, he would shoot me down on the spot. This being reported to me by various persons, I went to San Francisco and consulted Judge Bennett as to what course I ought to pursue. Judge Bennett asked if I were certain that he had made such a threat. I replied I was. "Well," said the Judge, "I will not give you any advice; but if it were my case, I think I should get a

---

* See Exhibit F, in Appendix.

shot-gun and stand on the street, and see that I had the first shot." I replied that "I could not do that; that I would act only in self-defence." He replied, "That would be acting in self defence." When I came to California, I came with all those notions, in respect to acts of violence, which are instilled into New England youth; if a man were rude, I would turn away from him. But I soon found that men in California were likely to take very great liberties with a person who acted in such a manner, and that the only way to get along was to hold every man responsible, and resent every trespass upon one's rights. Though I was not prepared to follow Judge Bennett's suggestion, I did purchase a pair of revolvers and had a sack-coat made with pockets in which the barrels could lie, and be discharged; and I began to practice firing the pistols from the pockets. In time I acquired considerable skill, and was able to hit a small object across the street. An object so large as a man I could have hit without difficulty. I had come to the conclusion that if I had to give up my independence; if I had to avoid a man because I was afraid he would attack me; if I had to cross the street every time I saw him coming, life itself was not worth having.

Having determined neither to seek him nor to shun him, I asked a friend to carry a message to him, and to make sure that it would reach him, I told different parties what I had sent, and I was confident that they would repeat it to him. "Tell him from me," I said, "that I do not want any collision with him; that I desire to avoid all personal difficulties; but that I shall not attempt to avoid him; that I shall not cross the street on his account, nor go a step out of my way for him; that I have heard of his threats, and that if

he attacks me or comes at me in a threatening manner
I will kill him."* I acted on my plan. I often met
him in the streets and in saloons, and whenever I drew
near him I dropped my hand into my pocket and
cocked my pistols to be ready for any emergency.
People warned me to look out for him ; to beware of
being taken at a disadvantage; and I was constantly
on my guard. I felt that I was in great danger; but
after awhile this sense of danger had a sort of fasci-
nation, and I often went to places where he was, to
which I would not otherwise have gone. Whenever
I met him I kept my eye on him, and whenever I
passed him on the street I turned around and narrowly. watched him until he had gone some distance.
I am persuaded if I had taken any other course, I
should have been killed. I do not say Turner would
have deliberately shot me down, or that he would have
attempted anything against me in his sober moments ;
but when excited with drink, and particularly when in
the presence of the lawless crowds who heard his
threats, it would have taken but little to urge him on.
As it turned out, however, he never interfered with
me, perhaps because he knew I was armed and believed
that, if I were attacked, somebody, and perhaps more
than one, would be badly hurt. I have been often
assured by citizens of Marysville that it was only the
seeming recklessness of my conduct, and the determination I showed not to avoid him or go out of his
way, that saved me. But at the same time my business was ruined. Not only was I prevented, by his
refusal to obey the mandate of the Supreme Court,
from appearing as an advocate, but I could not, on
account of the relation I occupied towards him, prac-

---

* See Exhibit G, in Appendix.

tice at all; nor could I, under the circumstances, leave Marysville and make my intended visit East. Having nothing else to do, I went into speculations which failed, and in a short time—a much shorter time than it took to make my money—I lost nearly all I had acquired and became involved in debt.

ONE morning about this time I unexpectedly found myself in the newspapers, nominated by my friends as a candidate for the lower house of the Legislature. Who the friends were that named me I did not know; but the nomination opened a new field and suggested new ideas. I immediately accepted the candidacy. Judge Turner had threatened, among other things, to drive me into the Yuba River. I now turned upon him, and gave out that my object in wishing to go to the Legislature was to reform the judiciary, and, among other things, to remove him from the district. I canvassed the county thoroughly and was not backward in portraying him in his true colors. He and his associates spared no efforts to defeat me. Their great reliance consisted in creating the belief that I was an abolitionist. If that character could have been fastened upon me it would have been fatal to my hopes, for it was a term of great reproach. Yuba County then comprised the present county of that name, and also what are now Nevada and Sierra Counties. It was over a hundred miles in length and about fifty in width, and had a population of twenty-five thousand people, being the most populous mining region in the State. I visited nearly every precinct and spoke whenever I could get an audience. An incident of the canvass may not be uninteresting. I went to the town of Nevada a little more than a week before the election. As I was riding through its main street a gentleman whom I had long known, General John Anderson, hailed me, and, after passing a few words, said, " Field, you won't get fifty votes here." I asked, " Why not ? " He replied, " Because everybody is for McCarty, your opponent." I said, somewhat sharply, " Anderson, I have come here to fight my own battle and I intend to carry Nevada." He laughed and I rode on. The first man I met after reaching the hotel was Captain Morgan, who afterwards commanded a steamer on the Bay of San Francisco. After talking for some time on general topics, he asked me about a story in circulation that I was an abolitionist. I saw at once the work of enemies, and I now understood the meaning of General Anderson's remark. I assured Morgan that the story was entirely false, and added : " To-morrow will be Sunday ; everybody will be in town ; I will then make a speech and show the people what kind of a man I am, and what my sentiments are on this and other subjects." Accordingly, the next day, in the afternoon, when the miners from the country were in town and had nothing else to do than to be amused, I mounted a platform erected for the purpose in the main street, and commenced speaking. I soon had a crowd of listeners. I began about my candidacy, and stated what I expected to do if elected. I referred to the necessity of giving greater jurisdiction to the local magistrates, in order that contests of miners respecting their claims might be tried in their vicinity. As things then existed the right to a mule could not be litigated without going to the county seat, at a cost greater than the value of the animal. I was in favor of legislation which would protect miners in their claims, and exempt their tents, rockers, and utensils used in mining from forced sale.

I was in favor of dividing the county, and making
Nevada the seat of the new county. I had heard of
numerous measures they wanted, and I told them how
many of these measures I advocated. Having got
their attention and excited their interest, I referred to
the charge made against me of being an abolitionist,
and denounced it as a base calumny. In proof of the
charge I was told that I had a brother in New York
who was a free-soiler. So I had, I replied, and a noble
fellow he is—God bless him wherever he may be.
But I added, I have another brother who is a slave-
holder in Tennessee, and with which one, I asked, in
the name of all that is good, were they going to place
me. I wondered if these "honorable" men, who
sought by such littleness to defeat me, did not find
out whether I did not have some other relatives,—
women, perhaps, who believed in things unearthly
and spiritual,—whose opinions they could quote to
defeat me. Shame on such tactics, I said, and the
crowd answered by loud cheering. I then went on
to give my views of our government, of the relation
between the general government of the Union and
the government of the States, to show that the former
was created for national purposes which the States
could not well accomplish—that we might have uni-
formity of commercial regulations, one army and one
navy, a common currency, and the same postal system,
and present ourselves as one nation to foreign countries—but that all matters of domestic concern were
under the control and management of the States, with
which outsiders could not interfere ; that slavery was
a domestic institution which each State must regulate
for itself, without question or interference from others.
In other words, I made a speech in favor of State

Rights, which went home to my hearers, who were in great numbers from the South. I closed with a picture of the future of California, and of the glories of a country bounded by two oceans. When I left the platform the cheers which followed showed that I had carried the people with me. McCarty, my opponent, followed, but his speech fell flat. Half his audience left before he had concluded.

The election took place a week from the following Monday. I remained in Nevada until it was over. At the precinct in town where I had spoken, I had between three and four hundred majority, and in another precinct in the outskirts I had a majority of two to one. In the county generally I ran well, and was elected, notwithstanding the fact that I was not the nominee of any convention or the candidate of any party. The morning following the election, as I was leaving Nevada, I rode by the store of General Anderson, and hailing him, inquired what he thought now of my getting fifty votes in the town. "Well," he replied, "it was that Sunday speech of yours which did the business. McCarty could not answer it."

There was one thing in the election which I regretted, and that was that I did not carry Marysville; a majority of the votes of its citizens was cast for my opponent. It is true that there the greater number of gamblers and low characters of the county were gathered, but the better class predominated in numbers, and I looked with confidence to its support. My regret, however, was sensibly diminished when I learned the cause of the failure of a portion of the people to give me their votes. Some few weeks previous to the day of election a man was killed in the street by a person by the name of Keiger, who was immediately arrested. The person killed was about leaving the State, and owed a small debt to Keiger, which he refused either to pay or to give security for its payment. Exasperated by his refusal, Keiger drew a pistol and shot him. I was sent for by an acquaintance of Keiger to attend his examination before the local magistrate, by whom he was held for the action of the grand jury. In the afternoon of the same day a large crowd assembled in the streets, with the purpose of proceeding to the summary execution of Keiger. Whilst the people were in a great state of excitement I made a speech to them begging them not to resort to violence and thus cast reproach upon the good name of Marysville, but to let the law take its course, assuring them that justice would certainly be administered by the courts. My remarks were received with evident displeasure, and I am inclined to think that violence would have been resorted to had not the prisoner been secretly removed from the city and taken to Sacramento. The exasperation of a large number, at this escape of their intended victim, vented itself on me, and cost me at least a hundred votes in the city. I would not have acted otherwise had I known beforehand that such would be the result of my conduct. When the civil tribunals are open and in the undisturbed exercise of their jurisdiction, a resort to violence can never be approved or excused.

I witnessed some strange scenes during the campaign, which well illustrated the anomalous condition of society in the county. I will mention one of them. As I approached Grass Valley, then a beautiful spot among the hills, occupied principally by Mr. Walsh, a name since become familiar to Californians, I came

to a building by the wayside, a small lodging-house
and drinking-saloon, opposite to which a Lynch jury
were sitting, trying a man upon a charge of stealing gold
dust. I stopped and watched for awhile the progress
of the trial. On an occasion of some little delay in
the proceedings, I mentioned to those present, the
jury included, that I was a candidate for the Legislature, and that I would be glad if they would join me
in a glass in the saloon, an invitation which was seldom declined in those days. It was at once accepted,
and leaving the accused in the hands of an improvised
constable, the jury entered the house and partook of
the drinks which its bar afforded. I had discovered,
or imagined from the appearance of the prisoner, that
he had been familiar in other days with a very different life from that of California, and my sympathies
were moved towards him. So, after the jurors had
taken their drinks and were talking pleasantly together, I slipped out of the building and approaching
the man, said to him, " What is the case against you?
Can I help you? " The poor fellow looked up to me
and his eyes filled with great globules of tears as he
replied, " I am innocent of all I am charged with. I
have never stolen anything nor cheated any one ; but
I have no one here to befriend me." That was enough
for me. Those eyes, filled as they were, touched my
heart. I hurried back to the saloon ; and as the
jurors were standing about chatting with each other
I exclaimed, " How is this ? you have not had your
cigars ? Mr. bar-keeper, please give the gentlemen
the best you have ; and, besides, I added, let us have
another ' smile '—it is not often you have a candidate
for the Legislature among you." A laugh followed,
and a ready acceptance was given to the invitation.

In the meantime my eyes rested upon a benevolent-looking man among the jury, and I singled him out for conversation. I managed to draw him aside and inquired what State he came from. He replied, from Connecticut. I then asked if his parents lived there. He answered, with a faltering voice, "My father is dead ; my mother and sister are there." I then said, "Your thoughts, I dare say, go out constantly to them ; and you often write to them, of course." His eyes glistened, and I saw pearl like dew-drops gathering in them ; his thoughts were carried over the mountains to his old home. "Ah, my good friend," I added, "how their hearts must rejoice to hear from you." Then, after a short pause, I remarked, "What is the case against your prisoner? He, too, perhaps, may have a mother and sister in the East, thinking of him as your mother and sister do of you, and wondering when he will come back. For God's sake remember this." The heart of the good man responded in a voice which, even to this day—now nearly twenty-seven years past—sounds like a delicious melody in my ears : "I will do so." Passing from him I went to the other jurors, and, finding they were about to go back to the trial, I exclaimed, "Don't be in a hurry, gentlemen, let us take another glass." They again acceded to my request, and seeing that they were a little mellowed by their indulgence, I ventured to speak about the trial. I told them that the courts of the State were organized, and there was no necessity or justification now for Lynch juries ; that the prisoner appeared to be without friends, and I appealed to them, as men of large hearts, to think how they would feel if they were accused of crime where they had no counsel and no friends. "Better send him, gentle-

men, to Marysville for trial, and keep your own hands
free from stain." A pause ensued ; their hearts were
softened ; and, fortunately, a man going to Marysville
with a wagon coming up at this moment, I prevailed
upon them to put the prisoner in his charge to be
taken there. The owner of the wagon consenting,
they swore him to take the prisoner to that place and
deliver him over to the sheriff; and to make sure that
he would keep the oath, I handed him a " slug," a
local coin of octagonal form of the value of fifty
dollars, issued at that time by assayers in San Francisco. We soon afterwards separated. As I moved
away on my horse my head swam a little, but my
heart was joyous. Of all things which I can recall of
the past, this is one of the most pleasant. I believe
I saved the prisoner's life ; for in those days there was
seldom any escape for a person tried by a Lynch jury.

The expenses of the election were very great. It
was difficult to interest the miners in it ; most of them
had come to the country in the hope of improving
their fortunes in one or two years, and then returning
to " the States." It was, therefore, a matter of little
moment to them who were chosen members of the coming Legislature. Party lines were not regarded among
them, and party questions could not draw many of
them from their labors. As I was an independent
candidate, not supported by any party, I had to bear
the whole expenses of the campaign. How great
those expenses were may be imagined from the following bill, one of a large number sent to me after the
election. I had told the saloon-keepers in the vicinity
of the polling places in the different precincts to be
liberally disposed towards my friends on the day of
election. They took me literally at my word, as this

bill from the keeper of a saloon where the polls were opened in Downieville precinct will show :

Mr. S. J. FIELD,

To ORLEANS HOUSE.

To 460 drinks..............................	$230	00
275 cigars...........	68	75
	$298	75

DOWNIEVILLE, *October 9th*, 1850.

[Endorsed :]

" We hereby certify that the within account is correct.
" P. L. MOORE.
" WM. S. SPEAR."

" Received payment of the within bill in full from Stephen J. Field.
" J. STRATMAN.

" *October* 14*th*, 1850."

It was not until after my election that Judge Turner paid any attention to the mandate of the Supreme Court commanding him to vacate his order of expulsion against myself and Messrs. Goodwin and Mulford, and to restore us to the bar. The mandate was issued on the fourth of July, and was served on the Judge on the sixteenth. He immediately and publicly declared that he would not obey it, but would stand an impeachment first. Whilst attending the Supreme Court on the application for the writ, Mr. Goodwin, Mr. Mulford and myself, were admitted as attorneys and counsellors of that court, and that admission under its rules entitled us to practice in all the courts of the State. The effect of this, which reinstated us in the District Court, he determined to defeat. He accordingly directed the sheriff of the county to notify us to show cause before the court in Sutter County, why we should not be again expelled from the bar for the publication of the article in the Placer Times, to which I have referred, written in reply to his attack on us in his "Address to the Public." The order was dated on the fourth of October, and was served on the eighth, and required us to appear on the first Thursday of the month, which was the third. As the time for appearance was previous to the day of service and to the date of the order, no attention was paid to it. The Judge, however, proceeded, and on the eleventh of the month made another order of expulsion. After the adjournment of the court, he discovered his blunder, and at once issued another direction to the sheriff to notify us that the last order of expulsion was suspended until the twenty eighth of October, and to show cause on that day why we should not be again expelled. In the meantime, the Judge made no concealment of his purposes, but publicly declared in the saloons of the town that if we did not appear upon this second notice, he would make an order for our expulsion, and if we did appear, he would expel us for contempt in publishing the reply to his article, which he termed a false and slanderous communication. We knew, of course, that it would be useless to appear and attempt to resist his threatened action; still we concluded to appear and put in an answer. Accordingly, on the day designated, we presented ourselves before the court in Sutter County. I was the first one called upon to show cause why I should not be again expelled. I stated that I was ready, and first read an affidavit of one of the Associate Justices of the Court of Sessions, to show that the Judge had declared his purpose to expel myself and the other gentlemen in any event, and that it was an idle ceremony to call upon us to show cause against such threatened action. As soon as it was read, the Judge declared that it was not respectful and could not be received. I then began to read my answer to the order to show cause, but was stopped when I had read about one half of it, and was told that it was not respectful and could not be received. I then requested permission to file it, but my request was refused. Mr. Mulford being called upon to show cause why he should not be expelled, began to read an answer, but was stopped after reading a few lines. His answer was respectful, and was substantially to the effect that he had been admitted as attorney and counsellor in the Supreme Court on the previous July, and was thus entitled to practice in all the courts of the State; that the communication in the Placer Times was written in reply to an article of the Judge, and that he was ready at the proper time and place to substantiate its truth; and he protested against the Judge's interfering in the matter in the manner indicated in the notice. Mr. Goodwin being called upon, took in his answer substantially the same grounds as Mr. Mulford. Immediately after Mr. Goodwin took his seat, without a moment's hesitation, the Judge made an order that his previous order of the eleventh of October, expelling us, should be confirmed, and that the order should be published in the Sacramento Times and the San Francisco Herald. I immediately took the proper steps to obtain another mandate from the Supreme Court to vacate this second expulsion; and also to attach the Judge for non-compliance with the original mandate, the first order of expulsion still being unvacated on the records of the court. At the January term, 1851, the applications to the court in both cases were decided, and they are reported in the 1st California Reports, at pages 189 and 190. In the attachment case, the court denied the application on the ground that no motion had been made by us or any one on our behalf to cause the original order of expulsion to be vacated, and that the Judge had, in the proceedings to expel us, substantially recognized us as re-instated. In the other case, the court decided that the proceedings to re-expel us were irregular, and directed an alternative writ to issue, commanding the Judge to vacate the order and to permit us to practice in all the courts of the district, or to show cause to the contrary, at the next term. No cause was ever shown; and thus ended the attempts of an ignorant, malicious, and brutal judge to keep us out of the profession of our choice. Mr. Goodwin has since held many positions of honor and trust in the State. He was elected District Attorney at the same time that I was elected to the Legislature, and afterwards was Judge of Yuba County, and is now (1877) a member of the State Senate. Mr. Mulford was afterwards and until his death a successful practitioner at the bar of Marysville, and was in all the affairs of life respected as a high-spirited and honorable man.

But with Judge Turner I have not yet done. I have a long story still to relate with respect to him. After my election to the Legislature was ascertained, he became exceedingly solicitous to prevent in advance my exerting any influence in it. He expected that I would attack him, and endeavor to secure his impeachment, and he wanted to break me down if possible. He accordingly published a pamphlet purporting to be a statement of the charges that I preferred against him, which was, however, little else than a tirade of low abuse of myself and the editor of the Marysville Herald, in the columns of which the conduct of the Judge had been the subject of just criticism and censure. There was nothing in the miserable swaggering billingsgate of the publication which merited a moment's notice, but as in one passage he stated that he had attempted to chastise me with a whip, and that I had fled to avoid him, I published in the Marysville Herald the following card:

A CARD.

Judge William R. Turner, in a "statement" published over his signature on the 12th instant, asserts that he attempted to chastise me with a switch, and that I fled to avoid him. This assertion is a *shameless lie*. I never, to my recollection, saw Judge Turner with a switch or a whip in his hand. He has made, as I am informed, many threats of taking personal vengeance on myself, but he has never attempted to put any of them into execution. I have never avoided him, but on the contrary have passed him in the street almost every day for the last four months. When he attempts to carry any of his threats into execution, I trust that I shall not forget, at the time, what is due to myself.

Judge Turner says he holds himself personally responsible in and under all circumstances. This he says *in print ;* but it is well understood in this place that he has stated he should feel bound by his oath of office to endeavor to obtain an indictment against any gentleman who should attempt to call him to account. Shielded behind his oath of office he has displayed his character by childish boasts of personal courage and idle threats of vengeance.

STEPHEN J. FIELD.

MARYSVILLE, *Dec.* 21*st*, 1850.

There were also annexed to the publication of Turner, letters from different persons expressive of their opinion of his general bearing on the bench and courtesy to them. Among these was one from John T. McCarty, the candidate against me at the recent election, in which he spoke in high terms of the Judge's conduct on the bench, and assailed me as his calumniator, applying to me sundry coarse epithets. In answer to this letter I published in the Herald the following card :

JOHN T. McCARTY.

John T. McCarty, in a letter to Judge William R. Turner, dated the 22d of November, takes occasion to apply several vile epithets to myself, and uses the following language to Judge Turner : " Having been present at the first term of your court ever held in this district, and most of your courts since that time, and being familiar with almost every decision and your entire conduct upon the bench, I take pleasure in saying that I never have practiced before any court where there was so great a dispatch of business, so much order and general satisfaction rendered by the rules and decisions of the court, and that, notwithstanding the base denunciations of your enemies, a large majority of the people who have attended your courts approve and sustain your positions and decisions."

During the session of the District Court, at its first term, this same John T. McCarty was called before the County Judge to give his testimony on the return of a writ of *habeas corpus*, and then he testified " *that the conduct of Judge Turner on the bench was the most outrageous he had ever witnessed in any court in which he had practiced ;* " *and the tenor and effect of his whole testimony was in the highest degree condemnatory of the conduct of Judge Turner.*

One of two things follows : If the statement in the letter be true, then John T. McCarty was guilty of perjury before the County Judge ; but if he testified to the truth, then his statement in the letter is false. In the one case he is a liar and in the other a perjured scoundrel. Thus convicted out of his own mouth, his vile epithets respecting myself are not worth a moment's consideration.

STEPHEN J. FIELD.

MARYSVILLE, *Dec.* 21*st*, 1850.

On my return from the Legislature, and afterwards, this same McCarty was in my presence the most abject and humble wretch I knew in Marysville. He almost piteously begged recognition by me, and was ready to go down on his knees for it. He was a blustering miscreant, full of courage where no force was required, and ready to run at the first appearance of a fight. He was one of a class, all of whom are alike, in whom bluster, toadyism, and pusillanimity go in concert, and are about equally developed in degree.

LIFE IN THE LEGISLATURE.

IMMEDIATELY after the election I commenced the preparation of a bill relating to the courts and judicial officers of the State, intending to present it early in the session. The Legislature met at San José on the first Monday of January, 1851, and I was placed on the Judiciary Committee of the House. My first business was to call the attention of the Committee to the bill I had drawn. It met their approval, was reported with a favorable recommendation, and after a full discussion was passed. Its principal provisions remained in force for many years, and most of them are retained in the Code, which went into effect in January, 1873. It created eleven judicial districts and defined the jurisdiction and powers of every judicial officer in the State, from a Supreme Judge to a Justice of the Peace. It provided that the then incumbent District Judges should continue to be the Judges of the new Districts according to their respective numbers. At the same time I introduced a bill dividing the county of Trinity, and creating that of Klamath ; and also a bill dividing the county of Yuba, and creating that of Nevada ; and I so arranged it that out of Trinity and Klamath a new Eighth Judicial District was created, and out of Yuba, Nevada, and Sutter a Tenth Judicial District. Thus Turner, being Judge of the Eighth District, was sent to the then comparative wilderness of Trinity and Klamath ; and the Tenth District was to have a new judge. After this bill was passed I presented petitions from the citizens of Yuba County, and of that part which now constitutes Nevada County, praying for the impeachment of Turner, and his removal from office, charging as grounds for it his incompetency from ignorance to discharge its duties, his arbitrary and tyrannical conduct towards the County Judge and members of the Marysville bar, the particulars of which I have related, his contemptuous treatment of the writ of *habeas corpus*, and his general immoral conduct.

A committee was thereupon appointed to which the petitions were referred, with power to send for persons and papers. The testimony taken by them fully established the charges preferred. Indeed, there was no serious attempt made to refute them. The only evidence offered in behalf of the Judge was that of a few persons who testified that they had been treated by him with courtesy in some instances and that good order had been maintained in court when they were present. There is no doubt that the impeachment would have been ordered but for a strong desire of the members to bring the session to a close, and a report which had obtained credence, that after the passage of the court bill, by which Turner was sent out of the eighth district, I was content to let the question of impeachment be indefinitely postponed. The testimony taken was reported by the Committee on the 15th of April. His impeachment would have required a trial by the Senate, which would have prolonged the session at least a month, and to this members were much averse. Parties came to me and said, " Judge, what's the use of pressing this matter ? You have sent Turner where there are only grizzly bears and Indians ; why not let him remain there ? He can do no harm there." I replied that he was not fit to be a

judge anywhere, and I refused assent to a postponement of the matter. Afterwards, when the vote was
about to be taken, a Senator and a personal friend of
Turner, misinterpreting some expressions of mine that
I desired to bring the matter to a speedy close, privately stated to members of the House that I had declared myself satisfied by the passage of the court bill
and was willing to let the impeachment be dropped,
it being understood that this course would not be
taken as a sanction of the Judge's conduct. To my
astonishment, members who had said only half an
hour before that they should vote for the impeachment now voted for an indefinite postponement, which
was carried by three votes—fifteen to twelve. I did
not vote, and three members who strongly favored the
impeachment were absent at the time. Seven of the
members who voted for the indefinite postponement
afterwards informed me that they had done so under
the impression that such a disposition of the matter
would be satisfactory to me, and that if a direct vote
had been taken on the charges they should have voted
for the impeachment. Here the matter ended ; I did
not pursue it. Turner did not go back to Marysville
and I had no further trouble with him.*

To understand fully the legislation with which I
was connected, and its effect upon the State, one must
be familiar with the history of the country and the
condition of its people. In addition to the act concerning the courts and judicial officers referred to, I
took up the Code of Civil Procedure, as reported by
the Commissioners in New York, remodelled it so as
to adapt it to the different condition of things and
the different organization of the courts in California,

* See Exhibit H, in Appendix.

and secured its passage. It became what was known as the California Civil Practice Act, and was afterwards adopted in Nevada and in the Territories west of the Rocky Mountains.

I also took up the Code of Criminal Procedure, as reported by the same Commissioners, and remodelled that in the same way and secured its passage. It constituted what was afterwards known as the California Criminal Practice Act, and was also adopted in the State and Territories mentioned. The amount of labor bestowed upon these acts will be appreciated when I state that I recast, in the two, over three hundred sections, and added over one hundred new ones. I devoted so much attention and earnestness to the work, that in a short time the Legislature placed implicit confidence in everything relating to the judiciary which I recommended. The Criminal Practice Act, for instance, remodelled as stated, consisting of over six hundred sections, was never read before the Legislature at all. The rules were suspended and the bill read by its title and passed. When it came before the Governor, on the last day of the session, he said he could not sign it without reading it, and it was too late for him to do that. I represented to him that its passage was essential to secure the harmonious working of laws already passed. Turning to me he said, " You say it is all right?" I replied, " Yes ;" and thereupon he signed it.

I have already stated that I moved Turner's impeachment. After the testimony was taken I addressed the House upon the subject. In reply to my remarks a member, by the name of B. F. Moore, from Tuolumne County, took occasion to make an abusive attack on me. It was the common practice in those days to go armed. Of the thirty-six members of which the Assembly then consisted, over two-thirds never made their appearance without having knives or pistols upon their persons, and frequently both. It was a thing of every-day occurrence for a member, when he entered the House, before taking his seat, to take off his pistols and lay them in the drawer of his desk. He did it with as little concern and as much a matter of course, as he took off his hat and hung it up. Nor did such a thing excite surprise or comment. But when Mr. Moore rose to reply to me, he first ostentatiously opened his drawer, took out his revolvers, cocked them, and laid them in the open drawer before him. He then launched out into a speech of the most opprobrious language, applying to me offensive epithets, and frequently interspersing his remarks with the declaration that he was responsible for what he said, both there and elsewhere. It is difficult for me to describe the indignation I felt at this outrageous assault and the manner in which it was made. Its very fierceness made me calm, as it is said that a tempest at sea is sometimes so violent as to still the waves. So when I came to make my rejoinder, I answered only such portions of his speech as attempted argument, and made no allusion to the personal language he had used towards me. But as soon as the vote was had on the question of postponing the impeachment, I took measures to call him to account. For this purpose I applied to Mr. Samuel A. Merritt, a member from Mariposa County, to carry a note from me to him, calling upon him to apologize for his offensive conduct or give me the satisfaction which it was understood one gentleman had the right to demand from another.

At that time it was generally supposed that the constitutional provision in regard to duelling was self-operative, and that any person who either sent or accepted a challenge, or acted as a second to one who thus offended, would *ipso facto* be disqualified from afterwards holding any public office. Upon this understanding of the law, Mr. Merritt, with many expressions of regard for me and regret at the law, declined to carry the note. I then applied to Mr. Richardson, also a member, but he declined for the same reason. I was afraid, as matters stood, that I could not get anybody to act for me, and I did not know to whom to apply or what to do. Whilst thinking the matter over, I happened, about nine o'clock in the evening, to walk into the Senate Chamber, and there found Mr. David C. Broderick, afterwards United States Senator, sitting at his desk writing. He was at that time President *pro tem.* of the Senate. I had known him for some time, but not intimately; we were merely bowing acquaintances. As I entered he looked up and said, "Why, Judge, you don't look well, what is the matter?" I answered that I did not feel well, for I had not a friend in the world. He replied, "What is it that worries you?" I then related to him everything that had happened, giving the particulars of the gross and violent assault upon my character, and stated that I was determined, at all hazards, to call Moore to account. Mr. Broderick, without hesitation, said, "My dear Field, I will be your friend in this matter; go and write at once a note to Moore, and I will deliver it myself." I accordingly sat down at an adjoining desk and wrote him a note, the purport of which was that I required him either to make a public retraction of his insulting language in the

Legislature, or to give me the satisfaction I had a right to demand. Broderick approved of its terms and at once proceeded to deliver it.

When he called on Moore and presented it, the latter said he expected to be a candidate for Congress before the coming convention, and he could not accept a challenge because it would disqualify him under the constitution from holding the office. But at the same time he observed that he was willing to meet me at any time and place; in other words, that he had no objection to a street fight. Broderick replied that a street fight was not exactly the thing among gentlemen; but that if Moore would do no better, a street fight there should be; and thereupon named a time and place when and where I would be found the next morning. Within an hour afterwards Moore changed his mind, and informed Mr. Broderick that Drury Baldwin, another member of the House, would act as his friend, and give a reply to my note the next ·morning.

In anticipation of a possible collision, Mr. Broderick took me out early the following morning to try my skill in the use of a pistol. I tried a navy revolver and succeeded in hitting a knot on a tree, at a distance of thirty yards, three times out of five. Broderick declared himself satisfied, and I then urged upon him the necessity of bringing the matter to a speedy issue. In all this he concurred, and before the meeting of the House, called upon Baldwin for an answer to my note. Baldwin replied that his principal had made up his mind to do nothing further in the matter. "Then," said Broderick, "as soon as the House meets, Judge Field will arise in his seat and refer to the attack on him and to the language of

Moore, that he held himself responsible for what he said, and state that respect for the dignity of the House had prevented him from replying to the attack at the time in the terms it deserved; that he had since demanded satisfaction of Moore for his language, and that Moore had refused to respond, and will thereupon pronounce him a liar and a coward." " Then," said Baldwin, " Judge Field will get shot in his seat." "In that case," rejoined Broderick, "there will be others shot too." Mr. Broderick soon afterwards informed me of his conversation with Baldwin, and asked me if I would act as he had stated I would. " Most certainly," I replied; "never fear for me; I will meet the case as it should be met." Accordingly, when the House opened, I took my seat at my desk as usual. Looking around I saw that Broderick was seated near me, and behind him were eight or nine of his personal friends, all armed to the teeth and ready for any emergency. In the meantime, and just before the House met, General John E. Addison, who had found out what was going on and knew the seriousness of the affair, called on Moore, who was his friend, and urged him to retract what he had said and make a suitable apology, and for that purpose drew up a document for him to read to the House, but of this I was not at the time informed. As soon as the journal was read I rose in my seat and said, "Mr. Speaker." At the same moment Moore rose in his seat and said, " Mr. Speaker." The Speaker recognized Moore first; and Moore thereupon proceeded to read the written apology prepared by Addison for his conduct and language to me. It was full, ample, and satisfactory; and of course with that the matter ended. From that time forward to the end of the session I had no further trouble with any one.

THE narrative which I have given of my difficulty with Moore explains how Broderick befriended me at a very trying time. But that was not the only occasion on which he befriended me. When I came to San Francisco after the adjournment of the Legislature, in May, 1851, I went several times to see him at the hotel where he stopped. On one occasion, in the evening, while we were in the saloon of the hotel, he asked me to take a glass of wine with him. We stepped up to the bar and were about drinking, when he suddenly threw himself before me and with great violence pushed me out of the room. The proceeding was so sudden and unexpected that I was astonished and for a moment indignant. I demanded an explanation, saying "What does this mean, Mr. Broderick?" He then told me that while we were standing at the bar he had noticed Vi.—or to give his full name, Vicesimus—Turner, a brother of the Judge, a man of desperate character, come into the bar-room, throw back his Spanish cloak, draw forth a navy revolver, and level it at me. Seeing the movement, he had thrown himself between me and the desperado and carried me off. These good offices on the part of Mr. Broderick filled me with a profound sense of gratitude. For years afterwards I thought and felt as if there was nothing I could do that would be a sufficient return for his kindness. On his account I took much greater interest in political matters than I otherwise should. In order to aid him in his aspira-

tions for election to the United States Senate, upon
which he had set his heart, I attended conventions
and gave liberally, often to my great inconvenience,
to assist the side to which he belonged. To many
persons it was a matter of surprise that I should take
such an interest in his success and through good and
evil report remain so constant and determined in my
support of him; but the explanation lies in the circumstances I have narrated and the brave manner in
which he had stood by me in a most critical moment
of my life.

I regret to state that this friendship was ever
broken. It was not by me; but broken it was.
Shortly after Mr. Broderick was elected to the Senate, he quarrelled with Mr. Buchanan over appoint-
ments to office in California; and when he returned
to the State, he expressed a good deal of hostility to
the Administration. In that hostility I did not participate, and he complained of me for that reason. I
was then spoken of throughout the State as a probable candidate for the bench, and he announced his
opposition to my nomination. I made no complaints
of his conduct, but was much hurt by it. My nomination and election soon afterwards removed me from
the sphere of politics. I seldom met him after my
election, and never had any conversation with him.
Though he was offended at my failure to take sides
with him in his controversy with the President, and
our intimacy ceased, I could never forget his generous
conduct to me; and for his sad death there was no
more sincere mourner in the State.

My legislative career was not without good results.
I drew, as already stated, and carried through the
Legislature a bill defining the powers and jurisdiction
of the courts and judicial officers of the State; and
whilst thus doing good, I also got rid of the ignorant
and brutal judge of our district who had outraged my
rights, assaulted my character, and threatened my
life. I also, as I have mentioned, introduced bills
regulating the procedure in civil and criminal cases,
remodelled with many changes from the Codes of
Civil and Criminal Procedure reported by the Commissioners of New York; and secured their passage.

In the Civil Practice Act I incorporated provisions
making the most liberal exemptions from forced sale
of the personal property of a debtor, including not
merely a limited amount of household furniture, and
provisions sufficient for individual or family use for
one month, but also the instruments or tools by which
he earned his livelihood. The exemptions embraced
necessary household and kitchen furniture, wearing
apparel, beds and bedding of the debtor, whatever
his calling; and also the farming utensils and implements of husbandry of the farmer, two beasts of burden employed by him, and one cart or wagon; the
tools and implements of a mechanic or artisan necessary to carry on his trade; the instruments and chests
of a surgeon, physician, surveyor, and dentist; the
law libraries of an attorney and counsellor; the cabin

or dwelling of a miner, and his pick, rocker, wheelbarrow, and other implements necessary to carry on mining operations; two oxen, two horses or two mules and their harness, and one cart or wagon of the cartman, hackman, or teamster; and one horse with vehicle and harness and other equipments used by a physician, surgeon, or minister of the gospel in making his professional visits; and all arms and accoutrements required by law to be kept by any person.

I never could appreciate the wisdom of that legislation which would allow a poor debtor to be stripped of all needed articles of his household and of the implements by which alone he could earn the means of supporting himself and family and of ultimately discharging his obligations. It has always seemed to me that an exemption from forced sale of a limited amount of household and kitchen furniture of the debtor, and of the implements used in his trade or profession, was not only the dictate of humanity, but of sound policy.

I also incorporated a provision into the Civil Practice Act respecting suits for mining claims, which was the foundation of the jurisprudence respecting mines in the country. The provision was that in actions before magistrates for such claims, evidence should be admitted of the usages, regulations, and customs prevailing in the vicinity, and that such usages, regulations, and customs, when not in conflict with the constitution and laws of the State, or of the United States, should govern the decision of the action. At this time suits for mining claims, the mines being confessedly on the property of the United States, were brought upon an alleged forcible or unlawful detainer. This rule, thus for the first time adopted by legislative enactment, was soon extended to actions for such claims in all courts, and has since been adopted in all the States and Territories west of the Rocky Mountains and substantially by the legislation of Congress. Simple as the provision is, it solved a difficult problem.

I also advocated and aided the passage of the Homestead Exemption Bill. That bill was introduced by Mr. G. D. Hall, a member from El Dorado, and now a resident of San Francisco. It provided for an exemption of the homestead to the value of $5,000. An effort was made to reduce the amount to $3,000, and I think I rendered some aid in defeating this reduction, which has always been to me a source of great gratification.

I also secured the passage of an act concerning attorneys and counsellors-at-law, in which I incorporated provisions that rendered it impossible for any judge to disbar an attorney in the arbitrary manner in which Judge Turner had acted towards me, without notice of the charges against him and affording him an opportunity to be heard upon them.

I also introduced a bill creating the counties of Nevada and Klamath, the provisions of which were afterwards incorporated into a general bill which was passed, dividing the State into counties and establishing the seats of justice therein, and by which also the county of Placer was created.

I drafted and secured the passage of an act concerning county sheriffs, in which the duties and responsibilities of those officers, not only in the execution of process and the detention of prisoners, but as keepers of the county jail, were declared and defined ; also an act concerning county recorders, in which the present system of keeping records was adopted. This latter act, though drawn by me, was introduced by Mr. Merritt, of Mariposa, but he does not hesitate to speak publicly of my authorship of it. I also prepared a bill concerning divorces, which was reported from the Judiciary Committee as a substitute for the one presented by Mr. Carr, of San Francisco, and was passed. In this act, aside from the ordinary causes of adultery, and consent obtained by force or fraud, for which divorces are granted, I made extreme cruelty and habitual intemperance, wilful desertion of either husband or wife for a period of two years, and wilful neglect of the husband to provide for the wife the common necessaries of life, having the ability to provide the same, for a period of three years, also causes of divorce. I also drew the charters of the cities of Marysville, Nevada, and Monterey, which were adopted—that of Monterey being reported by the Judiciary Committee as a substitute for one introduced by a member from that district. Other bills drawn or supported by me were passed, the provisions of which are still retained in the laws of the State.

But notwithstanding all this, when I turned my face towards Marysville I was, in a pecuniary sense, ruined. I had barely the means to pay my passage home. My ventures, after my expulsion from the bar, in June, 1850, had proved so many maelstroms into which the investments were not only drawn but swallowed up. My affairs had got to such a pass that before I left Marysville for the Legislature I felt it to be my duty to transfer all my real property to trustees to pay my debts, and I did so. And now when I stepped upon the landing in Marysville my whole available means consisted of eighteen and three-quarter cents, and I

owed about eighteen thousand dollars, the whole of
which bore interest at the rate of ten per cent. a
month. I proceeded at once to the United States
Hotel, kept by a Mr. Peck, who had known me in the
days of my good fortune. "My dear Mr. Peck," I
said, "will you trust me for two weeks' board?"
"Yes," was the reply, "and for as long as you want."
"Will you also send for my trunks on the steamer,
for I have not the money to pay the carman." "Certainly," the good man added, and so the trunks were
brought up. On the next day I looked around for
quarters. I found a small house, thirty feet by sixteen, for an office, at eighty dollars a month, and took
it. It had a small loft or garret, in which I placed a
cot that I had purchased upon credit. Upon this cot
I spread a pair of blankets, and used my valise for a
pillow. I secured a chair without a back for a wash-
stand, and with a tin basin, a pail, a piece of soap, a
toothbrush, a comb, and a few towels, I was rigged
out. I brought myself each day the water I needed
from a well near by. I had an old pine table and a
cane-bottomed sofa, and with these and the bills which
had passed the Legislature, corrected as they became
laws, and the statutes of the previous session, I put
out my sign as an attorney and counsellor-at-law, and
began the practice of my profession.

Soon afterwards I found my name mentioned as a
candidate for the State Senate. The idea of returning to the Legislature as a Senator pleased me. The
people of the county seemed to favor the suggestion.
Accordingly I made a short visit to neighboring precincts, and finding my candidacy generally approved
I went to work to make it successful. At the election
of delegates to the county convention, which was to

nominate candidates, a majority was returned in my
favor. Several of them being unable to attend the
convention, which was to be held at Downieville, a
distance of about seventy miles from Marysville, sent
me their proxies made out in blank to be filled with
the name of any one whom I might designate. To
one supposed friend I gave ten proxies, to another
five, and to a third two. When the members met,
just previous to the assembling of the convention, it
was generally conceded that I had a majority of the
delegates. But I had a new lesson in manipulation
to learn. Just before the opening of the convention
my supposed friend, who had the ten proxies, was
approached by the other side, and by promises to give
the office of sheriff to his partner—an office supposed
to be worth thirty thousand a year—his ten votes
were secured for my opponent. The one to whom I
had given five proxies was promised for those votes
the county judgeship. So when the convention voted,
to my astonishment and that of my friends, fifteen of
my proxies were cast for my opponent, Joseph C.
McKibbin, afterwards a member of Congress, who
acted so fearlessly when the Kansas question came up.
I was accordingly beaten by two votes.

For the moment I was furious, and hunted up the
man who had held my ten proxies, and had been se-
duced from my support. When I found him in the
room of the convention, I seized him and attempted
to throw him out of the window. I succeeded in getting half his body out, when bystanders pulled me
back and separated us. This was fortunate for both
of us; for just underneath the window there was a
well or shaft sunk fifty feet deep. The following
morning I left Downieville, returned to my office and

loft at Marysville, and gave my attention to the practice of the law. My business soon became very large; and, as my expenses were moderate, within two years and a half I paid off all my indebtedness, amounting with the accumulations of interest to over thirty-eight thousand dollars. Part of this amount was paid by a surrender of the property mortgaged, or a sale of that previously assigned, but the greater part came from my earnings. I paid every creditor but one in full; to each I gave his pound of flesh, I mean his interest, at ten per cent. a month. I never asked one of them to take less than the stipulated rate. The exceptional creditor was Mr. Berry, a brother lawyer, who refused to receive more than five per cent. a month on a note he held for $450. By this time I had become so much interested in my profession as to have no inclination for office of any kind. On several occasions I was requested by influential party leaders to accept a nomination for the State Senate, but I refused. I am inclined to think that I had for some time a more lucrative practice than any lawyer in the State, outside of San Francisco. No such fees, however, were paid in those days as have been common in mining cases since the discovery of the silver mines of Nevada and the organization of great corporations to develop them.

The Bar of Marysville during this period, and afterwards while I remained in that city—which was until October, 1857—was a small, but a very able body of men. Many of its members have since attained distinction and held offices of honor and trust. Richard S. Mesick, who settled there in 1851, became a State Senator, and after his removal to Nevada, a District Judge of that State. He ranks now among the ablest lawyers of the Coast. Charles H. Bryan, who settled there the same year, was an eloquent speaker, and in his forensic contests gave great trouble to his opponent whenever he got at the jury. He was on the Supreme Court of the State for a short period, under the appointment of Governor Bigler. Jesse O. Goodwin, of whom I have already spoken, settled in Marysville in 1850. He was a ready speaker, and sometimes rose to genuine eloquence. He was distinguished in criminal cases. As already stated, he was elected District Attorney in 1850, and afterwards became County Judge, and is now State Senator. Gabriel N. Swezy, who settled there in 1850, was learned in his profession, and quick of apprehension. Few lawyers could equal him in the preparation of a brief. He afterwards at different times represented the county in the Assembly and the Senate of the State. William Walker, who afterwards figured so conspicuously in the filibustering expeditions to Nicaragua, and was called by his followers " the grey-eyed man of destiny," had an office in Marysville in 1851 and '52. He was a brilliant speaker, and possessed a sharp but not a very profound intellect. He often perplexed both court and jury with his subtleties, but seldom convinced either. John V. Berry, who came to Marysville from the mines in 1851, was a fine lawyer, deeply read in the law of adjudged cases. He died in 1853 from poison given to him in mistake by a druggist. Edward D. Wheeler, who came there in 1850, and Thomas B. Reardon, who came in 1853, were both men of strong minds. Mr. Wheeler represented Yuba County at one time in the Senate, and is now the District Judge of the Nineteenth District, at San Francisco. He is regarded as among the ablest and best of the State Judges. Mr. Reardon has been a District Judge for some years in the Fourteenth District, greatly respected by the profession for his ability and learning. Isaac S. Belcher, who came to Marysville at a later period—in 1855, I believe—was noted for his quiet manners and studious habits. He has since been District Judge, and has worthily filled a seat on the bench of the Supreme Court of the State, where he was greatly respected by his associates and members of the bar. Edward C. Marshall, the brilliant orator, who at one time represented the State in Congress, had his office in Marysville in 1855 and '56. He occasionally appeared in court, though he was generally occupied in politics, and in his case, as in nearly all others, the practice of the law and the occupation of politics did not always move harmoniously together.

Charles E. Filkins, afterwards County Judge; Charles Lindley, afterwards also County Judge and one of the Code Commissioners; Henry P. Haun, the first County Judge, and afterwards appointed to the United States Senate by Governor Weller; N. E. Whitesides, afterwards a member of the Legislature from Yuba, and Speaker of the House; F. L. Hatch, now County Judge of Colusa; George Rowe, afterwards Treasurer of the County; and Wm. S. Belcher, who afterwards rendered good service to the public as a School Commissioner, also practiced at the Marysville bar with success.

Charles E. DeLong, afterwards a member of the State Senate, and our Minister to Japan, and Henry K. Mitchell, afterwards a nominee of the Democrats for the U. S. Senate in Nevada, were just getting a good position at the bar when I left, and gave evidence of the ability which they afterwards exhibited.

Others might be named who held fine positions in the profession.

These mentioned show a bar of great respectability, and I may add that its members were, with few exceptions, gentlemen of general information and courteous manners. The litigation which chiefly occupied them and gave the largest remuneration related to mines and mining claims. The enforcement of mortgages and collection of debts was generally—by me, at least—entrusted to clerks, unless a contest was made upon them.

There was one case which I recall with pleasure, because of the result obtained in face of unconcealed bribery on the other side. The subject of the suit was the right to a " placer " mine in Yuba River, at Park's Bar. Its value may be estimated from the fact that within two or three weeks after the decision of the case, the owners took from the mine over ninety thousand dollars in gold dust. This suit was brought before a justice of the peace, and was for an alleged forcible entry and detainer, a form of action generally adopted at the time for the recovery of mining claims, because the title to the lands in which the mines were found was in the United States. It was prosecuted as a purely possessory action. The constable whose duty it was to summon the jurors had received the sum of two hundred dollars to summon certain parties, named by the other side. This fact was established beyond controversy by evidence placed in my hands. And whilst I was in bed in one of the tents or canvas sheds at the Bar, which the people occupied in the absence of more substantial buildings, I heard a conversation in the adjoining room—I could not help hearing it, as it was carried on without any at-

tempt at concealment, and the room was only separated from me by the canvas—between one of the
jurors and one of the opposite party, in which the
juror assured the party that it was "all right," and
he need not worry as to the result of the suit; his side
would have the verdict; the jury were all that way.
On the next day, when the case was summed up, the
saloon in which the trial was had was crowded with
spectators, most of whom were partisans of the other
side. I addressed the jury for over three hours, and
after having commented upon the evidence at length
and shown conclusively, as I thought, that my client
was entitled to a verdict, I said substantially as follows: "Gentlemen, we have not endeavored to influence your judgment except by the evidence; we have
not approached you secretly and tried to control your
verdict; we have relied solely upon the law and the
evidence to maintain our rights to this property. But
the other side have not thus acted; they have not
been content that you should weigh only the evidence; they have endeavored to corrupt your minds
and pervert your judgments; they have said that you
were so low and debased that although you had with
uplifted hands declared that so might the ever-living
God help you, as you rendered a verdict according to
the evidence, you were willing, to please them, to decide against the evidence, and let perjury rest on your
souls. I know that you [pointing to one of the ju-
rors] have been approached. Did you spurn the
wretch away who made a corrupt proposal to you, or
did you hold counsel, sweet counsel with him? I
know that you [pointing to another juror] talked over
this case with one of the other side at the house on
the hill last night, for I overheard the conversation—

the promise made to you and your pledge to him. In the canvas houses here all rooms are as one; the words uttered in one are voices in all. You did not dream that any but you two were in the tent; but I was there and overheard the foul bargain."

At this thrust there was great excitement, and click, click, was heard all through the room, which showed a general cocking of pistols; for every one in those days went armed. I continued : " There is no terror in your pistols, gentlemen ; you will not win your case by shooting me ; you can win it only in one way—by evidence showing title to the property ; you will never win it by bribery or threats of violence. I charge openly attempted bribery, and if what I say be not true, let the jurors speak out now from their seats. Attempted bribery, I say—whether it will be success-ful bribery, will depend upon what may occur here-after. If, after invoking the vengeance of Heaven upon their souls should they not render a verdict according to the evidence, the jurors are willing to sell their souls, let them decide against us."

This home-thrust produced a great sensation. It was evident that the jury were disturbed. When the case was submitted to them, they were absent only a few minutes. They returned a verdict in our favor. Some of them afterwards came to me and admitted that they had been corruptly approached, but added that they were not low enough to be influenced in their verdict in that way. "Of course not," I replied ; though I had little doubt that it was only the fear of exposure which forced them to do right.

I have said that in those days everyone went armed ; it would be more correct to say that this was true in the mining regions of the State and when travelling.

I, myself, carried a Derringer pistol and a Bowie-knife until the Summer of 1854, though of course out of sight. I did so by the advice of Judge Mott, of the District Court, who remarked that, though I never abused a witness or a juror, or was discourteous to any one in court, there were desperate men in the country, and no one could know to what extremity they might go, as I would not be deterred by any considerations from the discharge of my whole duty to my clients. So, until the Summer of 1854, I carried weapons. And yet they were not such provocatives of difficulty as some of our Eastern friends are accustomed to think. On the contrary, I found that a knowledge that they were worn generally created a wholesome courtesy of manner and language.

I continued to occupy my small office and slept in its loft through the Summer and Fall of 1851, and felt quite contented with them. Twice I was summarily dislodged, being threatened by a fire on the other side of the street. On one occasion a most ludicrous incident occurred, which I cannot recall without a smile. A little after midnight we were aroused, on the occasion referred to, by a loud thumping at our door, accompanied by a cry of "fire." My loft was shared with three others, and at the cry we all leaped from our cots and two of our number seizing whatever was convenient and portable carried it out of the house to a distance of about one hundred yards, where gathered a multitude of people, fleeing before the flames with all sorts of baggage, trunks, chairs, beds, and utensils of every kind which they had brought from their houses. I hastily threw the papers of sundry suits and a dozen law books, recently purchased, into a box, and with the assistance of the other occupant of my loft, carried it off. Just as we reached the crowd, a pair of young grizzly bears which the owner had kept in a cage near by were let loose, and they came towards us growling in their peculiar way. At their sight, there was a general *stampede* of men, women, and children, in all directions. Boxes and everything else portable were instantly dropped, and such an indiscriminate flight was never before seen except from a panic in battle.

THE BARBOUR DIFFICULTY.

When the bill of 1851, dividing the State into new judicial districts, became a law, there were several candidates for the office of Judge of the Tenth Judicial District, which comprised the counties of Yuba, Nevada, and Sutter. Henry P. Haun, the County Judge of Yuba, was one candidate; John V. Berry, a lawyer of the same county, was another; and Gordon N. Mott, a lawyer of Sutter County, was a third. My first choice was Berry; but, finding that he had very little chance, I gave what influence I had in favor of Mr. Mott, and he received from the Governor the appointment of Judge of the new district.

In the Summer of 1851, the Governor issued his proclamation for the Fall elections, and, among others, for an election to fill the office of Judge of the Tenth District. I had supposed—and there were many others who agreed with me—that Judge Mott's term under his appointment would continue until the election of 1852. But there being some doubts about the matter and the Governor having issued his proclamation for an election, candidates were nominated by the conventions; and at the ensuing election one of them, William T. Barbour, a lawyer of Nevada County, received a majority of the votes cast and was declared elected. When he came, however, to demand the office, Judge Mott expressed his opinion that there had been no vacancy to be filled and declined to surrender. This led to a suit between them. The question involved being exclusively one of law, an agreed case was made up and presented to the Supreme Court, and that tribunal decided in favor of Barbour. A report of the case is given in the 3d California Reports, under the title of People, ex rel. Barbour, vs. Mott.

In the case I appeared as counsel for Judge Mott and argued his cause. This offended Judge Barbour, and he gave free expression to his displeasure. Afterwards, when his term for the vacancy was about to expire and a new election was to be held, he presented himself as a candidate for a second term. It was my opinion that he was not qualified for the position, and I therefore recommended my friends to vote for his opponent. For some weeks previous to the election I was absent from the district; but I returned two days before it was to take place and at once took a decided part against Barbour and did all I could to defeat him. This action on my part, in connection with my previous zeal in behalf of Judge Mott, led Barbour to make some very bitterly vituperative remarks about me, which being reported to me, I called on him for an explanation. Some harsh words passed between us at the interview. The result was that Barbour refused to make any explanation but gave me a verbal challenge to settle our difficulties in the usual way among gentlemen. I instantly accepted it and designated Judge Mott as my friend.

In half an hour afterwards Judge Mott was called upon by Mr. Charles S. Fairfax as the friend of Barbour, who stated that Barbour had been challenged by me, and that his object in calling upon Mott was to arrange the terms of a hostile meeting. Mott answered that he understood the matter somewhat differently; that the challenge, as he had been in-

formed, came from Barbour, and that I, instead of
being the challenging, was the accepting party. Fairfax, however, insisted upon his version of the affair ;
and upon consulting with Mott, I waived the point
and accepted the position assigned me. Fairfax then
stated that Barbour, being the challenged party, had
the right to choose the weapons and the time and
place of meeting; to all of which Mott assented.
Fairfax then said that, upon consultation with his
principal, he had fixed the time for that evening; the
place, a room twenty feet square, describing it; the
weapons, Colt's revolvers and Bowie-knives ; that the
two principals so armed were to be placed at opposite
sides of the room with their faces to the wall; that
they were to turn and fire at the word, then advance
and finish the conflict with their knives. Mott answered that the terms were unusual, unprecedented,
and barbarous, and that he could not consent to them.
Fairfax admitted that they were so ; but replied that
they were those Barbour had prescribed. He would,
however, see Barbour and endeavor to obtain a modi-
fication of them. Soon afterwards he reported that
Barbour still insisted upon the terms first named and
would not agree to any other.

When Mott reported the result of his conference
with Fairfax, I at once said that Barbour was a
coward and would not fight at all. I knew perfectly
well that such terms could come only from a bully.
I saw that it was a game of bluff he was playing.
So I told Mott to accept them by all means. Mott
accordingly called on Fairfax and accepted the terms
as proposed, and gave notice that I would be on hand
and ready at the time and place designated. This
being reported to Barbour, Fairfax soon afterwards

made his appearance with a message that his principal would waive the Bowie-knives; and not long afterwards he came a second time with another message that it would not do to have the fight in the room designated, because the firing would be heard outside and attract a crowd. In accordance with my instructions, Mott assented to all the modifications proposed, and it was finally agreed that the meeting should take place the next morning in Sutter County. I was to take a private conveyance, and Barbour was to take one of the two daily stages that ran to Sacramento. At a specified place we were to leave our conveyances and walk to a retired spot, which was designated, where the hostile meeting was to take place.

The next morning, accordingly, I took a carriage, and with my friend Judge Mott drove down to the appointed place. After we had been there some time the first stage appeared and stopped. Soon after the second stage appeared and stopped, and Judge Barbour and Mr. Fairfax got out. But instead of proceeding to the designated place, Barbour declared that he was a judicial officer, and as such could not engage in a duel. At the same time he would take occasion to say that he would protect himself, and, if assaulted, would kill the assailant. With these words, leaving Fairfax standing where he was, he walked over to the first stage, and mounting rode on to Sacramento. Seeing Fairfax standing alone on the ground I sent word to him that I would be happy to give him a place in my carriage—an invitation which he accepted, and we then drove to Nicolaus, where we breakfasted, and thence returned to Marysville.*

---

* See letter of Judge Mott detailing the particulars of the affair; Exhibit H, in Appendix.

The conduct of Barbour on the ground, after his fierce and savage terms at the outset, produced a great deal of merriment and derision; and some very sharp squibs appeared in the newspapers. One of them gave him great annoyance, and he inquired for its author. I told the editor of the paper in which it appeared that if it was necessary to protect the writer, to give my name, although I did not write it, or know beforehand that it was to be written.

On the following morning, whilst in front of my office gathering up kindling-wood for a fire, and having my arms full—for each man was his own servant in those days—Barbour came up and, placing a cocked navy revolver near my head, cried out, "Draw and defend yourself." As I had not observed his approach I was taken by surprise, but turning on him I said, "You infernal scoundrel, you cowardly assassin—you come behind my back and put your revolver to my head and tell me to draw; you haven't the courage to shoot; shoot and be damned." There were at least ten witnesses of this scene; and it was naturally supposed that having advanced so far he would go farther; but as soon as he found I was not frightened, he turned away and left me. It is impossible to express the contempt I felt for him at that moment for his dastardly conduct, a feeling which the spectators shared with me, as they have since often stated.[*]

I do not give these details as having any importance in themselves; but they illustrate the semi-barbarous condition of things in those early days, and by comparison show out of what our existing condition has been evolved, and how far we have advanced. I

* See Exhibit I, in Appendix.

give them also for the reason that Barbour afterwards wrote a letter to Turner, which the latter published, referring to the affair, in which he boasted of having given me a " whipping." How far his boast was warranted the above facts show.

For a long time afterwards he expressed his bitterness towards me in every possible way. He did not take Turner's plan of expelling me from the bar; but he manifested his feelings by adverse rulings. In such cases, however, I generally took an appeal to the Supreme Court, and in nearly all of them procured a reversal. The result was that he suddenly changed his conduct and commenced ruling the other way. While this was his policy, there was hardly any position I could take in which he did not rule in my favor. At last I became alarmed lest I should lose my cases in the appellate court by winning them before him.

About a year afterwards he sent one of his friends to ask me if I was willing to meet him half-way— stating that my conduct in court had always been courteous, and he was satisfied that he had done me injustice. I answered that I was always willing to meet any one half way, but in this case it must be without explanations for the past. This condition was accepted ; accordingly we met, and taking a glass of wine, I said, " Here is to an act of oblivion, but no explanations." For a long time no allusion was made by either to the old difficulties. But at last he insisted upon telling me how tales had been brought to him, and how they exasperated him ; and he expressed great regret for what had taken place ; and to make amends, as far as he was able, for what he had written about me, he sent me the following letter :

" MARYSVILLE, *Dec.* 22, 1856.

" Hon. S. J. FIELD.

"DEAR SIR: On yesterday I learned through our mutual friend Charles S. Fairfax, Esq., that Judge W. R. Turner has recently issued a publication which contains a letter of mine, written him some four years ago. I have not been able to procure a copy of this publication, and I have entirely forgotten the language used ; in truth I do not remember to have written him on the subject of yourself or otherwise ; but I suppose I must have done so, and have given expressions of opinion that I have long since ceased to entertain, and to invectives that I have no disposition to justify. You will recall that, at the time referred to, there unfortunately existed between us feelings of deep hostility ; and I may at the time have used harsh terms indicative of my then feelings, which I regret and do not now approve, if they are as represented by others.

" Judge Turner has taken an unwarranted liberty in publishing the letter, be it of what character it may. He never requested my permission for this purpose, nor did I know that it was his intention.

" Trusting that this explanation may be satisfactory, I remain,

" Very respectfully yr. obt. servant,

" WM. T. BARBOUR."

He ever afterwards, as occasion offered, spoke of me in the highest terms as a gentleman and lawyer. My resentment accordingly died out, but I never could feel any great regard for him. He possessed a fair mind and a kindly disposition, but he was vacillating and indolent. Moreover, he loved drink and low company. He served out his second term and afterwards went to Nevada, where his habits became worse, and he sunk so low as to borrow of his acquaintances from day to day small sums—one or two dollars at a time—to get his food and lodging. He died from the effects of his habits of intemperance.

In stating the result of the intended hostile meeting with him, I mentioned that when he proceeded on his way to Sacramento, he left his second, Mr. Fairfax, standing alone on the ground, and that I invited the latter to take a seat in my carriage. From this time the intercourse between Mr. Fairfax and myself became more frequent than it had been previously, and a friendship followed which continued as long as he lived. He was not sparing in his censure of the conduct of his principal, whilst his language was complimentary of mine. In a few months I became quite intimate with him, and I found him possessed of a noble and chivalric spirit. With great gentleness of manner, he had the most intrepid courage. His fidelity to his friends and devotion to their interests attached them strongly to him. He was beloved by all who knew him. No man in the State was more popular. He represented the county of Yuba in the Legislature two or three times, and at one session was Speaker of the Assembly. When the land office at Marysville was established in 1855, he was appointed Register; and in 1856, he was elected Clerk of the Supreme Court of the State. It was my good fortune to aid him in securing both of these positions. At my suggestion, Mr. McDougal, a Member of Congress from California, urged the establishment of the land office, and obtained for him the appointment of Register. In 1856, when he sought the clerkship of the Supreme Court of the State, I became a delegate from Yuba County to the State Convention, and made his nomination for that office my special object, and with the aid of the rest of the delegation, succeeded in obtaining it.

Two or three incidents which I will relate will illustrate the character of the man. It was either in the

session of 1854 or 1855, I forget which, that a petition was presented to the Assembly of California on
the part of some of the colored people of the State,
requesting that the laws then in force, which excluded
them from being witnesses in cases where a white
person was a party, might be repealed so as to allow
them to testify in such cases. At that time there was
a great deal of feeling throughout the country on the
subject of slavery, and any attempt to legislate in
behalf of the colored people was sure to excite opposition, and give rise to suggestions that its promoter
was not sound on the slavery question. The presentation of the petition accordingly stirred up angry
feelings. It created a perfect outburst of indignation,
and some one moved that the petition should be
thrown out of the window; and the motion was
passed almost unanimously. If I recollect aright,
there was but a single vote in the negative. I was
standing by Mr. Fairfax when he was informed of the
proceeding. He at once denounced it, and said, in
energetic terms—"This is all wrong—the petition
should have been received. If my horse or my dog
could in any way express its wishes to me I would
listen to it. It is a shame that a petition from any
one, black or white, should not be received by the
Legislature of the State, whether it be granted or
not." I was greatly impressed at that time with the
manliness of this expression in a community which
looked with suspicion on any movement in favor of
extending any rights to the colored race.

On another occasion, some years afterwards, when
I was Judge of the Supreme Court of the State and
he was the clerk of the court, there was a good deal of
complaint against Harvey Lee, the reporter of the

court, who was appointed to the office by Governor Weller. I believe that Lee was instrumental, but of this I am not certain, in getting a law passed which took the appointment of the reporter from the court and gave it to the Governor. He was an inferior lawyer, and, of course, had very little practice. The appointment, therefore, to which a fair salary was attached, was eagerly sought by him. His reports, however, were so defective that an effort was made by the judges to get the law repealed and have the appointment restored to the court. This led to a bitter feeling on his part towards the judges, and in a conversation with Mr. Fairfax he gave vent to it in violent language. Mr. Fairfax resented the attack and an altercation ensued, when Lee, who carried a sword-cane, drew the sword and ran it into Fairfax's body. Fortunately it entered the chest above the heart. Withdrawing the sword Lee made a second lunge at Fairfax, which the latter partially avoided so as to receive only a flesh wound in the side. By this time Fairfax had drawn his pistol and covered the body of Lee, as he was raising his sword for a third thrust. Lee, seeing the pistol, stepped back and threw up his arms exclaiming, " I am unarmed "—though he had only that moment withdrawn his sword from the body of Fairfax, and it was then dripping with blood. " Shoot the damned scoundrel," cried the latter's friend, Samuel B. Smith, then standing by his side. But Fairfax did not shoot. Looking at Lee, whose body was covered with his pistol, while the blood was trickling from his own person, he said, " You are an assassin! you have murdered me! I have you in my power! your life is in my hands! " And gazing on him, he added, " But for the sake of your poor sick wife and children I will spare you." He thereupon uncocked his pistol and handed it to his friend, into whose arms he fell fainting. He had known the wife of Lee when a young girl; and, afterwards, in speaking of the affair to a friend, he said, "I thought my wife would be a widow before sundown, and I did not wish to leave the world making another." All California rang with the story of this heroic act. It has its parallel only in the self-abnegation of the dying hero on the battle-field, who put away from his parched lips the cup of water tendered to him, and directed that it be given to a wounded soldier suffering in agony by his side, saying, "His need is greater than mine."

During the war his sympathies, as was the case with most Southerners in California, were with his people in Virginia. He told me on one occasion that he could not but wish they would succeed; but, he said; "Though I am a Virginian by birth, I have adopted California, and whilst I live in a State which has taken her stand with the Northern people, I cannot in honor do anything, and I will not, to weaken her attachment to the Union. If my health were good I should leave the State and return to Virginia and give my services to her; but, as that is impossible, I shall remain in California, and, whilst here, will not be false to her by anything I do or say."

These incidents, better than any elaborate description, illustrate the character of the man. He was a lineal descendant of the great Fairfax family which has figured so conspicuously in the history of England and of Virginia. He was its tenth Baron in a direct line. But notwithstanding the rank of his family he was a republican in his convictions. He loved his country and its institutions. He was himself more noble than his title. He came East to attend the National Democratic Convention in 1868 at the head of the delegates from California. After the Convention, he spent some months among his friends and relatives at the old family residence in Maryland. At this time the seeds of consumption, which had long been lurking in his system, began to be developed, and he was taken down with a severe illness which proved fatal. He became so ill as to be unable to walk, and was conveyed to Baltimore to procure the best medical attendance; and there he died on the 4th of April, 1869, in the arms of his devoted wife, who had come from California to be with him in his last hours. His body was brought to Washington and interred within sight of the Capitol, near Rock Creek Church, in which his ancestors had worshipped.

I have mentioned that when Fairfax was stabbed by Lee he fell into the arms of Mr. Samuel B. Smith. This gentleman I had known slightly before my difficulty with Judge Barbour; but the intimacy which sprung up between Fairfax and myself, after that affair, brought me more in contact with Mr. Smith, who was his constant companion. Mr. Smith came to California from New Jersey in 1849, and passed through some stirring scenes during that and the following year. He came with Mr. John S. Hagar, who was afterwards State Senator, District Judge, and United States Senator, and was engaged with him in the mines in the winter of 1849–'50. In 1850 he settled in Sutter County; and in the fall of 1852 was elected State Senator from that county. Having become more intimately acquainted with him after he was elected Senator, I requested him to introduce a bill into the Legislature, revising and amending the one which I had originally drawn concerning the courts and judicial officers of the State; and he cheerfully consented to do so, and took great interest in securing its passage. Indeed, it was through his influence that the bill became a law. Many circumstances threw us together after that, and I learned to appreciate his manly character, his generous disposition, and his great devotion to his friends. Finally, in the fall of 1854, we agreed to form a partnership after my return from the Eastern States, which I then proposed to visit. After the Barbour affair the course of my professional life was much the same as that of any other lawyer. My business was large and I gave to it my unremitting attention. In 1854 I determined to go East to see my parents and brothers and sisters, who had never been out of my mind a single day since I left them in 1849. Accordingly, I went East, and after passing a few months with them I returned to California in January, 1855. After that I continued to practice my profession, with Mr. Smith as my partner, until the spring of 1857, though during this period he went to Washington as Commissioner of the State to obtain from Congress the payment of moneys expended by her in suppressing the hostilities of Indians within her borders, and was absent several months. In April of that year we dissolved our partnership. A few months afterwards I was nominated for the bench of the Supreme Court of the State, and was elected by a large majority. There were two candidates besides myself for the position, and 93,000 votes were polled. Of these I received a majority of 36,000 over each of my opponents, and 17,000 over

them both together.* The term to which I was elected
was for six years, commencing January 1st, 1858. In
September, 1857, Hugh C. Murray, then Chief Justice,
died, and Associate Justice Peter H. Burnett was appointed to fill the vacancy. This left the balance of
Judge Burnett's term of service to be filled, and I
was urged by the Governor of the State to accept his
appointment to it, as it was for less than three months,
and immediately preceded my own term. At first I
refused, as I desired to revisit the East; but being
assured by the judges that taking the place need not
prevent my intended visit, I accepted the appointment, and on the 13th of October, 1857, took my seat
on the bench.

---

* The exact vote was as follows :

For myself...............................	55,216
For Nathaniel Bennett.............	18,944
For J. P. Ralston......................	19,068
Total vote....................	93,228
Majority over Bennett...............	36,272
Majority over Ralston................	36,148
Majority over both...................	17,204

The day following my acceptance of the Governor's
appointment to the Supreme Court of the State, I
returned to Marysville to close my business before
taking up my residence in Sacramento, where the
court held its sessions. I had gone to Sacramento
to argue some cases before the court when the appointment was tendered to me; and, of course, did
not expect to remain there very long. In a few days
I arranged my affairs at Marysville and then removed
permanently to Sacramento. I left Marysville with
many regrets. I had seen it grow from a collection
of tents with a few hundred occupants to a town of
substantial buildings with a population of from eight
to ten thousand inhabitants. From a mere landing
for steamers it had become one of the most important
places for business in the interior of the State. When
I left, it was a depot of merchandise for the country
lying north and east of it; and its streets presented
a scene of bustle and activity. Trains of wagons and
animals were constantly leaving it with goods for the
mines. Its merchants were generally prosperous;
some of them were wealthy. Its bankers were men
of credit throughout the State. Steamers plied daily
between it and Sacramento, and stages ran to all
parts of the country and arrived every hour. Two
daily newspapers were published in it. Schools were
opened and fully attended. Churches of different de-
nominations were erected and filled with worshippers.

Institutions of benevolence were founded and supported. A provident city government and a vigorous police preserved order and peace. Gambling was suppressed or carried on only in secret. A theatre was built and sustained. A lecture-room was opened and was always crowded when the topics presented were of public interest. Substantial stores of brick were put up in the business part of the city; and convenient frame dwellings were constructed for residences in the outskirts, surrounded with plats filled with trees and flowers. On all sides were seen evidences of an industrious, prosperous, moral, and happy people, possessing and enjoying the comforts, pleasures, and luxuries of life. And they were as generous as they were prosperous. Their hearts and their purses were open to all calls of charity. No one suffering appealed to them in vain. No one in need was turned away from their doors without having his necessities relieved. It is many years since I was there, but I have never forgotten and I shall never forget the noble and generous people that I found there in all the walks of life.

The Supreme Court of the State then consisted of three members, the senior in commission being the Chief Justice. David S. Terry was the Chief Justice and Peter H. Burnett was the Associate Justice. Both of these gentlemen have had a conspicuous career in California, and of both I have many interesting anecdotes which would well illustrate their characters and which at some future day I may put upon paper. They were both men of vigorous minds, of generous natures and of positive wills; but in all other respects they differed as widely as it was possible for two extremes. Mr. Terry had the virtues and prejudices of men of the extreme South in those days. His contact and larger experience since with men of the North have no doubt modified many of those prejudices, and his own good sense must have led him to alter some of his previous judgments. Probably his greatest regret is his duel with Mr. Broderick, as such encounters, when they terminate fatally to one of the parties, never fail to bring life-long bitterness to the survivor. A wiser mode of settling difficulties between gentlemen has since been adopted in the State; but those who have not lived in a community where the duel is practiced cannot well appreciate the force of the public sentiment which at one time existed, compelling a resort to it when character was assailed.

Mr. Burnett was one of the early settlers in Oregon, and had held positions of honor and trust there before settling in California. He came here soon after the discovery of gold, took an interest in public affairs, and was elected the first Governor of the State, when the constitution was adopted.

Judge Terry resigned his office in September, 1859, when he determined to send a challenge to Mr. Broderick, and I succeeded him as Chief Justice; and W. W. Cope, of Amador, was elected to fill the vacant place on the bench. I was absent from the State at the time, or I should have exerted all the power I possessed by virtue of my office to put a stop to the duel. I would have held both of the combatants to keep the peace under bonds of so large an amount as to have made them hesitate about taking further steps; and in the meantime I should have set all my energies to work, and called others to my aid, to bring about a reconciliation. I believe I should have adjusted the difficulty.

Mr. Cope, who filled the vacant place on the bench, possessed a superior mind and a genial nature. He made an excellent Judge. He studiously examined every case and carefully prepared his opinions. He remained on the bench until January, 1864, when the new constitutional amendments, reorganizing the court, went into effect. He is now in practice in San Francisco, and has a large clientage.

Judge Burnett continued in office until the election of his successor in the fall of 1858. His successor was Joseph G. Baldwin, a lawyer of distinction and a gentleman of literary reputation. He was the author of "The Flush Times of Alabama and Mississippi," and of "Party Leaders." The first is a work full of humor and a great favorite in the section of the country whose "times" it portrays with such spirit and glee as to excite roars of laughter in the reader. The latter is a thoughtful history of the character and influence upon the country of Jefferson, Hamilton, Jackson, Clay, and Randolph. His portraitures present these men in the fullness and freshness of living beings, whom we see and hear, and whose power we feel.

My friendship for Mr. Baldwin commenced long before he came to the bench, and it afterwards warmed into the attachment of a brother. He had a great and generous heart; there was no virtue of humanity of which he did not possess a goodly portion. He was always brimful of humor, throwing off his jokes, which sparkled without burning, like the flashes of a rocket. There was no sting in his wit. You felt as full of merriment at one of his witticisms, made at your expense, as when it was played upon another. Yet he was a profound lawyer, and some of his opinions are models of style and reasoning. He remained on the bench until January, 1862, when he was succeeded by Edward Norton, of San Francisco. This gentleman was the exemplar of a judge of a subordinate court. He was learned, patient, industrious, and conscientious; but he was not adapted for an appellate tribunal. He had no confidence in his own unaided judgment. He wanted some one upon whom to lean. Oftentimes he would show me the decision of a tribunal of no reputation with apparent delight, if it corresponded with his own views, or with a shrug of painful doubt, if it conflicted with them. He would look at me in amazement if I told him that the decision was not worth a fig; and would appear utterly bewildered at my waywardness when, as was sometimes the case, I refused to look at it after hearing by what court it was pronounced.

It is not my purpose to speak of my own career on the Bench of the Supreme Court of California. It is only for reminiscences of my previous life that you, Mr. Hittell, have asked.* I am tempted, however, to hand to you a letter of Judge Baldwin, my associate for over three years, in which he presents, in terms exaggerated by his friendship, the result of my labors there.†

There is only one scene to which I wish to refer.

About a year and a half after I went upon the bench, a contested election case came up from Trinity County. It appeared that Judge Turner, who had been sent to

---

* These sketches were in the main dictated to a short-hand writer at the request of Mr. Theodore H. Hittell, of San Francisco.

† The letter is printed at the end of this narrative, at page 111.

the district composed of the counties of Trinity and
Klamath, by the act concerning the courts and judicial officers of the State, at the end of his term offered
himself for re-election as Judge of that district.
When the vote was counted there appeared to be a
majority of one against him, and his opponent was
declared elected. He instituted a contest for the
office, and, being defeated in the court below, appealed to the Supreme Court. He then became very
much exercised over his appeal, because I was one of
the Justices. There were not wanting persons who,
out of sheer malice, or not comprehending any higher
motives of conduct than such as governed themselves,
represented that I would improve the opportunity to
strike him a blow.

When his case came on for hearing, I left the
bench to my associates, Judges Terry and Baldwin,
and they decided in his favor. At this action of mine
Turner was amazed. It was something wholly unexpected and surprising to him. Soon after the decision he sent one of his friends, named Snowden, to
know if I would speak to him if he should make the
first advance. I answered that under no circumstances would I ever consent to speak to him ; that
he had done me injuries which rendered any intercourse with him impossible ; that the world was wide
enough for us both, and he must go his own way.
This answer Snowden communicated to him. The
next morning he stationed himself at the foot of the
stairway leading up to the Supreme Court rooms,
which was on the outside of the building, and, as I
passed up, he cried out ; "I am now at peace with all
the world ; if there is any man who feels that I have
done him an injury, I am ready to make him amends."

I turned and looked at him for a moment, and then passed on without saying a word. On the following morning he took the same position and repeated substantially the same language. I stopped and gazed at him for a moment, and then passed on in silence. This was the last time I saw him. He returned to Trinity, and held his office for the balance of his term, six years, under the decision of the Supreme Court, and was re-elected in 1863. But his character and habits unfitted him for a judicial position. He was addicted to gambling and drinking, and he consorted with the lowest characters; and the same tyrannical temper and conduct which he had exhibited towards me in Marysville, were displayed in his new district. Accordingly measures were taken by citizens of Trinity to secure his impeachment by the Legislature. Mr. Westmoreland, a member of the Assembly from that county in 1867 offered a resolution for the appointment of a committee to inquire whether articles of impeachment should be presented against him for high crimes and misdemeanors, with power to send for persons and papers and report articles if warranted by the evidence. In offering the resolution Mr. Westmoreland charged, that during the time Turner had held the office of District Judge he had been grossly tyrannical; that he had imprisoned citizens, depriving them of their liberty without process of law; that he had neglected and refused to perform the duties incumbent upon him by statute; that by a standing rule he allowed no witness to be called in a case unless he was subpœnaed and in attendance on the first day of the term; that he had used the power of his position for the furtherance of his own ends of private hate; that he was an habitual drunkard, with rare intervals of sobriety, and had upon occasions come into the court-room to sit upon the trial of causes so intoxicated as to be unable to stand, and had fallen helplessly upon the floor, whence he had been removed by officers of the court; that upon one occasion, when engaged in a trial, he had in the presence of jurors, witnesses, and other persons attending the court, deliberately gone out of the court-room and openly entered a house of ill-fame near by ; and that by his disgraceful conduct he had become a burden upon the people of that district too grievous to be borne. These things Mr. Westmoreland stated he stood prepared to prove, and he invoked the interposition of the Legislature to protect the people of the Eighth Judicial District who were suffering from the deportment and conduct of this officer. The resolution was passed. Finding that articles of impeachment would be presented against him, Turner resigned his office. After this his habits of drinking became worse, and he was sent to the Asylum for Inebriates, where he died

In thinking over my difficulties with Turner at this distant day, there is nothing in my conduct which I in the least regret. Had I acted differently; had I yielded one inch, I should have lost my self-respect and been for life an abject slave. There was undoubtedly an unnecessary severity of language in two or three passages of my answers to his attacks; and some portion of my answer in court to his order to show cause why I should not be re-expelled from the bar might better have been omitted. I have since learned that one is never so strong as when he is calm, and never writes so forcibly as when he uses the simplest language. My justification in these par-

ticulars, if they require any, must be found in the
savage ferocity with which I was assailed, the brutal
language applied to my character and conduct, and
the constant threats made of personal violence. Malignity and hate, with threats of assassination, followed me like a shadow for months. I went always
armed for protection against assault. I should have
been less or more than man had I preserved at all
times perfect calmness either in my language or conduct.

In the contest with this man I was cheered by the
support of the best men of the State. But of all of
them no one aided me so much, and so freely, as the
editor of the Marysville Herald, Mr. Robert H. Taylor, a gentleman still living, in the full strength of his
intellect, and honored and trusted as a learned member
of the legal profession in Nevada. May length of years
and blessings without number attend him.

Here my narrative of "Personal Experiences" must
for the present end. I could have given you, Mr.
Hittell, more interesting matter. I could have given
you sketches of Fremont, Halleck, Gwin, Broderick,
Weller, Geary, Sherman, Bigler, McDougal, Bennett,
Heydenfeldt, Murray, and others, with many striking
anecdotes illustrative of their characters. They were
all remarkable men, and the history of their lives
would be full of interest and instruction. I could
have related the story of the Vigilance Committees
of 1851 and 1856, and shown how the men of order
and virtue acquired and maintained ascendency over
the irregular and disorderly elements of society. I
could have told you of the gradual development of

the industries of the State until her yearly products have become one of the marvels of the world. I could have described the wild excitement produced by the supposed discoveries of gold in boundless quantities on Fraser River; and the later but more substantial movement upon the development of the silver mines of Nevada. I could have recounted the efforts made in 1860 and 1861 to keep the State in the Union against the movements of the Secessionists, and the communications had with President Lincoln by relays of riders over the Plains. I could have described the commencement, progress, and completion of the Pacific railroad, and the wonderful energy and unfailing resolution of its constructors. I could have told you stories without number, full of interest, of the Judges of California, State and Federal, who preceded me on the bench, and of members of the profession; of Hastings, Bennett, Lyons, Wells, Anderson, Heydenfeldt, and Murray, of the State Supreme Court; of Hoffman and McAllister of the Federal bench; of Robinson, Crittenden, Randolph, Williams, Yale, McConnell, Felton, and others of the Bar, now dead, and of some who are at its head, now living; composing as a whole a bar not exceeded in ability, learning, eloquence, and literary culture by that of any other State of the Union. But you asked me merely for personal reminiscences of occurrences at Marysville and during the days preceding my going there. I will, therefore, postpone until another occasion a narrative which I think will be more interesting than anything I have here related.

THE CAREER OF JUDGE FIELD ON THE SUPREME BENCH
OF CALIFORNIA, BY JUDGE JOSEPH G. BALDWIN, HIS
ASSOCIATE FOR THREE YEARS.

[*From the Sacramento Union, of May* 6, 1863.]

"THE resignation by Judge Field of the office of
Chief Justice of the Supreme Court of California, to
take effect on the 20th instant, has been announced.
By this event the State has been deprived of the ablest
jurist who ever presided over her courts. Judge
Field came to California from New York in 1849, and
settled in Marysville. He immediately commenced
the practice of law and rose at once to a high position
at the local bar, and upon the organization of the
Supreme Court soon commanded a place in the first
class of the counsel practicing in that forum. For
many years, and until his promotion to the bench, his
practice was as extensive, and probably as remunerative, as that of any lawyer in the State. He served
one or two sessions in the Legislature, and the State
is indebted to him for very many of the laws which
constitute the body of her legislation.* In 1857 he
was nominated for Judge of the Supreme Court for a
full term, and in October of the same year was appointed by Governor Johnson to fill the unexpired
term of Justice Heydenfeldt, resigned. He immediately entered upon the office, and has continued ever
since to discharge its duties. Recently, as the reader

* He was in the Legislature only one session.

knows, he was appointed, by the unanimous request of our delegation in Congress, to a seat upon the Bench of the Supreme Court of the United States, and was confirmed, without opposition, by the Senate.

"Like most men who have risen to distinction in the United States, Judge Field commenced his career without the advantages of wealth, and he prosecuted it without the factitious aids of family influence or patronage. He had the advantage, however—which served him better than wealth or family influence—of an accomplished education, and careful study and mental discipline. He brought to the practice of his profession a mind stored with professional learning, and embellished with rare scholarly attainments. He was distinguished at the bar for his fidelity to his clients, for untiring industry, great care and accuracy in the preparation of his cases, uncommon legal acumen, and extraordinary solidity of judgment. As an adviser, no man had more the confidence of his clients, for he trusted nothing to chance or accident when certainty could be attained, and felt his way cautiously to his conclusions, which, once reached, rested upon sure foundations, and to which he clung with remarkable pertinacity. Judges soon learned to repose confidence in his opinions, and he always gave them the strongest proofs of the weight justly due to his conclusions.

"When he came to the bench, from various unavoidable causes the calendar was crowded with cases involving immense interests, the most important questions, and various and peculiar litigation. California was then, as now, in the development of her multiform physical resources. The judges were as much pioneers of law as the people of settlement. To be sure something had been done, but much had yet to be accomplished; and something, too, had to be undone of that which had been done in the feverish and anomalous period that had preceded. It is safe to say that, even in the experience of new countries hastily settled by heterogeneous crowds of strangers from all countries, no such example of legal or judicial difficulties was ever before presented as has been illustrated in the history of California. There was no general or common source of jurisprudence. Law was to be administered almost without a standard. There was the civil law, as adulterated or modified by Mexican provincialism, usages, and habitudes, for a great part of the litigation; and there was the common law for another part, but *what that was* was to be decided from the conflicting decisions of any number of courts in America and England, and the various and diverse considerations of policy arising from local and other facts. And then, contracts made elsewhere, and some of them in semi-civilized countries, had to be interpreted here. Besides all which may be added that large and important interests peculiar to the State existed —mines, ditches, etc.—for which the courts were compelled to frame the law, and make a system out of what was little better than chaos.

" When, in addition, it is considered that an unprecedented number of contracts, and an amount of business without parallel, had been made and done in hot haste, with the utmost carelessness; that legislation was accomplished in the same way, and presented the crudest and most incongruous materials for construction; that the whole scheme and organization of the government, and the relation of the departments to each other, had to be adjusted by judicial construction —it may well be conceived what task even the ablest jurist would take upon himself when he assumed this office. It is no small compliment to say that Judge Field entered upon the duties of this great trust with his usual zeal and energy, and that he leaves the office not only with greatly increased reputation, but that he has raised the character of the jurisprudence of the State. He has more than any other man given tone, consistency, and system to our judicature, and laid broad and deep the foundation of our civil and criminal law. The land titles of the State—the most important and permanent of the interests of a great commonwealth—have received from his hand their permanent protection, and this alone should entitle him to the lasting gratitude of the bar and the people.

" His opinions, whether for their learning, logic, or diction, will compare favorably, in the judgment of some of our best lawyers, with those of any judge upon the Supreme Bench of the Union. It is true what he has accomplished has been done with labor ; but this is so much more to his praise, for such work was not to be hastily done, and it was proper that the time spent in perfecting the work should bear some little proportion to the time it should last. We know it has been said of Judge Field that he is too much of a 'case lawyer,' and not sufficiently broad and comprehensive in his views. This criticism is not just. It is true he is reverent of authority, and likes to be sustained by precedent ; but an examination of his opinions will show that, so far from being a timid copyist, or the passive slave of authority, his rulings rest upon clearly defined principles and strong common sense.

"He retires from office without a stain upon his ermine. Millions might have been amassed by venality. He retires as poor as when he entered, owing nothing and owning little, except the title to the respect of good men, which malignant mendacity cannot wrest from a public officer who has deserved, by a long and useful career, the grateful appreciation of his fellow-citizens. We think that we may safely predict that, in his new place, Justice Field will fulfil the sanguine expectations of his friends."

J. G. B.

SAN FRANCISCO, *May* 1, 1863.

In 1855 a circuit court for California was created by Congress, and clothed with the ordinary jurisdiction of the several circuit courts of the United States. Hon. M. Hall McAllister was appointed its judge. In January, 1863, he resigned and my appointment as his successor was recommended by our Senators. They telegraphed me what they had done, and I replied that I could not accept the place, that I preferred to remain Chief Justice of the Supreme Court of the State than to be a judge of an inferior federal court, but that if a new justice were added to the Supreme Court of the United States, I would accept the office if tendered to me. Notwithstanding this reply my appointment was urged, and I was nominated by the President. The Senators have since told me that they pressed my nomination from a belief that another justice would soon be added to the Supreme Court, and that the appointment would be made from the Pacific States, and that if I were circuit judge it would more likely be tendered to me than to any one else.

The interests of those States were so great, and from the character of their land titles, and their mines of gold and silver, were in some respects so different from those of the Eastern States, that it was deemed important to have some one familiar with them on the Supreme Bench of the United States. Accordingly, while my nomination for circuit judge was pending before the Senate, a bill providing for an additional justice of the Supreme Court, and making the Pacific States a new circuit, was introduced into both Houses of Congress, and on the last day of the session, March 3d, 1863, it became a law. Soon after the adjournment of Congress, the entire delegation from the Pacific States united in recommending my appointment to the new office. The delegation then consisted of four Senators and four Members of the House, of whom five were Democrats and three Republicans; all of them were Union men. I was accordingly nominated by the President, and the nomination was unanimously confirmed by the Senate. My commission was signed on the 10th of March, 1863, and forwarded to me. I did not, however, take the oath of office and enter upon its duties until the 20th of May following. At the time I received the commission there were many important cases pending in the Supreme Court of California, which had been argued when only myself and one of the associate justices were present. I thought that these cases should be disposed of before I resigned, as otherwise a reargument of them would be required, imposing increased expense and delay upon the parties. I therefore sent my resignation as Chief Justice to the Governor, to take effect on the 20th of May. I selected that day, as I believed the cases argued could

be decided by that time, and because it was the birth-
day of my father. I thought it would be gratifying
to him to know that on the eighty-second anniversary
of his birth his son had become a Justice of the Supreme Court of the United States. Accordingly on
that day I took the oath of office.*

---

* Although I had informed the Attorney-General of my action
and delay in taking the oath of office, the salary of the office
was sent to me from the date of my commission, March 10th,
1863. I immediately deposited with the sub-treasurer at San
Francisco, to the credit of the United States, the proportion
for the time between that date and the 20th of May, and informed the Secretary of the Treasury of the deposit, enclosing
to him the sub-treasurer's receipt.

ANNOYANCES OF MY JUDICIAL LIFE.

AFTER the narrative of my Personal Reminiscences
was completed, I concluded to dictate an account of
some strange annoyances to which I had been subjected in the course of my judicial life. The account
will have an interest to those of my friends for whom
the Reminiscences were printed, and it is intended for
their perusal alone.

WHEN I went on the bench, I not only entertained
elevated notions of the dignity and importance of the
judicial office, but looked forward confidently to the
respect and honor of the community from a faithful
discharge of its duties.   I soon discovered, however,
that there would be but little appreciation for conscientious labor on the bench, except from a small number
of the legal profession, until after the lapse of years.
For the heavy hours of toil which the judges endured,
for the long examination which they gave to voluminous records, for their nights of sleeplessness passed
in anxious thought to ascertain what was true and
right amidst a mass of conflicting evidence and doubtful principles, the public at large appeared to have
little thought and less consideration.   The cry of disappointment over frustrated schemes of cupidity and
fraud was sufficient for the time to drown all other
expressions of judgment upon the action of the court.

The unsettled condition of the land titles of the
State gave occasion to a great deal of litigation and
was for a long time the cause of much bad feeling towards the judges who essayed to administer impartial
justice.   When California was acquired the population was small and widely scattered.   To encourage
colonization, grants of land in large quantities, varying from one to eleven leagues, had been made to set-

tlers by the Mexican government. Only small tracts were subjected to cultivation. The greater part of the land was used for grazing cattle, which were kept in immense herds. The grants were sometimes of tracts with defined boundaries, and sometimes of places by name, but more frequently of specified quantities within boundaries embracing a greater amount. By the Mexican law, it was incumbent upon the magistrates of the vicinage to put the grantees in possession of the land granted to them; and for that purpose to measure off and segregate the quantity designated. Owing to the sparseness of the population there was little danger of dispute as to boundaries, and this segregation in the majority of cases had been neglected before our acquisition of the country. From the size of the grants and the want of definite boundaries, arose nearly all the difficulties and complaints of the early settlers. Upon the discovery of gold, immigrants from all parts of the world rushed into the country, increasing the population in one or two years from a few thousand to several hundred thousand. A large number crossed the plains from the Western States, and many of them sought for farming lands upon which to settle. To them a grant of land, leagues in extent, seemed a monstrous wrong to which they could not be reconciled. The vagueness, also, in many instances, of the boundaries of the land claimed gave force and apparent reason to their objections. They accordingly settled upon what they found unenclosed or uncultivated, without much regard to the claims of the Mexican grantees. If the land upon which they thus settled was within the tracts formerly occupied by the grantees with their herds, they denied the validity of grants so large in extent. If the boundaries

designated enclosed a greater amount than that specified in the grants, they undertook to locate the supposed surplus.   Thus, if a grant were of three leagues
within boundaries embracing four, the immigrant
would undertake to appropriate to himself a portion
of what he deemed the surplus; forgetting that other
immigrants might do the same thing, each claiming
that what he had taken was a portion of such surplus,
until the grantee was deprived of his entire property.

When I was brought to consider the questions to
which this condition of things gave rise, I assumed at
the outset that the obligations of the treaty with
Mexico were to be respected and enforced.   This
treaty had stipulated for the protection of all rights
of property of the citizens of the ceded country;
and that stipulation embraced inchoate and equitable
rights, as well those which were perfect.   It was not
for the Supreme Court of California to question the
wisdom or policy of Mexico in making grants of such
large portions of her domain, or of the United States
in stipulating for their protection.   I felt the force of
what Judge Grier had expressed in his opinion in the
case of The United States vs. Sutherland, in the 19th
of Howard, that the rhetoric which denounced the
grants as enormous monopolies and princedoms might
have a just influence when urged to those who had a
right to give or refuse; but as the United States had
bound themselves by a treaty to acknowledge and
protect all *bona-fide* titles granted by the previous
government, the court had no discretion to enlarge or
contract such grants to suit its own sense of propriety
or to defeat just claims, however extensive, by stringent technical rules of construction to which they were
not originally subjected.   Since then, while sitting on

the Bench of the Supreme Court of the United States,
I have heard this obligation of our government to
protect the rights of Mexican grantees stated in the
brilliant and powerful language of Judge Black. In
the Fossat case, referring to the land claimed by one
Justo Larios, a Mexican grantee, he said: "The land
we are claiming never belonged to this government.
It was private property under a grant made long before our war with Mexico. When the treaty of Gua-
dalupe Hidalgo came to be ratified—at the very moment when Mexico was feeling the sorest pressure that
could be applied to her by the force of our armies, and
the diplomacy of our statesmen—she utterly refused
to cede her public property in California unless upon
the express condition that all private titles should be
faithfully protected. We made the promise. The
gentleman sits on this bench who was then our Minister there.* With his own right hand he pledged
the sacred honor of this nation that the United States
would stand over the grantees of Mexico and keep
them safe in the enjoyment of their property. The
pledge was not only that the government itself would
abstain from all disturbance of them, but that every
blow aimed at their rights, come from what quarter
it might, should be caught upon the broad shield of
our blessed Constitution and our equal laws."

"It was by this assurance thus solemnly given that
we won the reluctant consent of Mexico to part with
California. It gave us a domain of more than impe-
rial grandeur. Besides the vast extent of that country, it has natural advantages such as no other can
boast. Its valleys teem with unbounded fertility, and
its mountains are filled with inexhaustible treasures

* Mr. Justice Clifford.

of mineral wealth. The navigable rivers run hundreds of miles into the interior, and the coast is indented with the most capacious harbors in the world. The climate is more healthful than any other on the globe: men can labor longer with less fatigue. The vegeta- tion is more vigorous and the products more abun- dant ; the face of the earth is more varied, and the sky bends over it with a lovelier blue. ———— That was what we gained by the promise to protect men in the situation of Justo Larios, their children, their alienees, and others claiming through them. It is impossible that in this nation they will ever be plundered in the face of such a pledge."—(2 Wallace, 703.)

Actuated by this principle—that fidelity to a nation's pledge is a sacred duty, and that justice is the high- est interest of the country, I endeavored, whenever the occasion presented itself, and my associates heartily co-operated with me, to protect the Mexican grantees. Their grants contained a stipulation for the possession of the lands granted, inasmuch as they were subject to the conditions of cultivation and oc- cupancy, and a failure to comply with the conditions was considered by the tribunals of the United States as a most material circumstance in the determination of the right of the grantees to a confirmation of their claims. I held, therefore, with the concurrence of my associates, that the grantees, whether they were to be considered as having a legal or an equitable right to the lands, were entitled to their possession until the action of the government upon their claims, and, there- fore, that they could recover in ejectment. And when the grant was not a mere float, but was of land within defined boundaries, which embraced a greater quantity than that specified in it, with a provision that the surplus should be measured off by the government, I held that until such measurement the grantee could hold the whole as against intruders, and until then he was a tenant in common with the government. As I said in one of my opinions, speaking for the court, until such measurement no individual could complain, much less could he be premitted to determine in advance, that any particular locality would fall within the supposed surplus, and thereby justify its forcible seizure and detention by himself. "If one person could in this way appropriate a particular parcel to himself, all persons could do so ; and thus the grantee, who is the donee of the government, would be stripped of its bounty for the benefit of those who were not in its contemplation and were never intended to be the recipients of its favors." *

These views have since met with general assent in California and have been approved by the Supreme Court of the United States.† But at that time they gave great offence to a large class, and the judges were denounced in unmeasured terms as acting in the interests of monopolists and land-grabbers.   Even now, when the wisdom and justice of their action are seen and generally recognized, words of censure for it are occasionally whispered through the Press.   Persons sometimes seem to forget that to keep the plighted faith of the nation, to preserve from reproach its fair fame, where its honor is engaged, is one of the highest duties of all men in public life.

The action of the court as to the possession of the public lands of the United States met with more

---

* Cornwall vs. Culver, 16 Cal., 429.

† Van Reynegan vs. Bolton, 95 U. S., 33,

favor. The position of the people of California with respect to the public lands was unprecedented. The discovery of gold brought, as already stated, an immense immigration to the country. The slopes of the Sierra Nevada were traversed by many of the immigrants in search of the precious metals, and by others the tillable land was occupied for agricultural purposes. The title was in the United States, and there had been no legislation by which it could be acquired. Conflicting possessory claims naturally arose, and the question was presented as to the law applicable to them. As I have mentioned in my Narrative of Reminiscences, the Legislature in 1851 had provided that in suits before magistrates for mining claims, evidence of the customs, usages, and regulations of miners in their vicinage should be admissible, and, when not in conflict with the Constitution and laws of the United States, should govern their decision, and that the principle thus approved was soon applied in actions for mining claims in all courts. In those cases it was considered that the first possessor or appropriator of the claim had the better right as against all parties except the government, and that he, and persons claiming under him, were entitled to protection. This principle received the entire concurrence of my associates, and was applied by us, in its fullest extent, for the protection of all possessory rights on the public lands. Thus, in Coryell vs. Cain, I said, speaking for the court: "It is undoubtedly true, as a general rule, that the claimant in ejectment must recover upon the strength of his own title, and not upon the weakness of his adversary's, and that it is a sufficient answer to his action to show title out of him and in a third party. But this general rule has, in this State, from the anomalous condition of things arising from the peculiar character of the mining and landed interests of the country, been, to a certain extent, qualified and limited. The larger portion of the mining lands within the State belong to the United States, and yet that fact has never been considered as a sufficient answer to the prosecution of actions for the recovery of portions of such lands. Actions for the possession of mining claims, water privileges, and the like, situated upon the public lands, are matters of daily occurrence, and if the proof of the paramount title of the government would operate to defeat them, confusion and ruin would be the result. In determining controversies between parties thus situated, this court proceeds upon the presumption of a grant from the government to the first appropriator of mines, water privileges, and the like. This presumption, which would have no place for consideration as against the assertion of the rights of the superior proprietor, is held absolute in all those controversies. And with the public lands which are not mineral lands, the title, as between citizens of the State, where neither connects himself with the government, is considered as vested in the first possessor, and to proceed from him."—(16 Cal., p. 572.)

The difficulties attendant upon any attempt to give security to landed possessions in the State, arising from the circumstances I have narrated, were increased by an opinion, which for some time prevailed, that the precious metals, gold and silver, found in various parts of the country, whether in public or private lands, belonged to the State by virtue of her sovereignty. To this opinion a decision of the Supreme Court of the State, made in 1853, gave great potency. In Hicks vs. Bell, decided that year, the court came to that conclusion, relying upon certain decisions of the courts of England recognizing the right of the Crown to those metals. The principal case on the subject was that of The Queen vs. The Earl of Northumberland, reported in Plowden. The counsel of the Queen in that case gave, according to our present notions, some very fanciful reasons for the conclusion reached, though none were stated in the judgment of the court. There were three reasons, said the counsel, why the King should have the mines and ores of gold and silver within the realm, in whatsoever land they were found : " The first was, in respect to the excellency of the thing, for of all things which the soil within this realm produces or yields, gold and silver are the most excellent, and of all persons in the realm, the King is, in the eye of the law, most excellent. And the common law, which is founded upon reason, appropriates everything to the person whom it best suits, as common and trivial things to the common people, things of more worth to persons in a higher and superior class, and things most excellent to those persons who excel all others ; and because gold and silver are the most excellent things which the soil contains, the law has appointed them (as in reason it ought) to the person who is most excellent, and that is the King.———The second reason was, in respect of the necessity of the thing. For the King is the head of the Weal-public and the subjects are his members ; and the office of the King, to which the law has appointed him, is to preserve his subjects ; and their preservation consisted in two things, viz., in an army to defend them againt hostilities, and in good laws. And an army cannot be

had and maintained without treasure, for which reason some authors, in their books, call treasure the sinews of war; and, therefore, inasmuch as God has created mines within this realm, as a natural provision of treasure for the defence of the realm, it is reasonable that he who has the government and care of the people, whom he cannot defend without treasure, should have the treasure wherewith to defend them.————
The third reason was, in respect of its convenience to the subjects in the way of mutual commerce and traffic. For the subjects of the realm must, of necessity, have intercourse or dealing with one another, for no individual is furnished with all necessary commodities, but one has need of the things which another has, and they cannot sell or buy together without coin.————And if the subject should have it (the ore of gold or silver) the law would not permit him to coin it, nor put a print or value upon it, for it belongs to the King only to fix the value of coin, and to ascertain the price of the quantity, and to put the print upon it, which being done, the coin becomes current for so much as the King has limited.————
So that the body of the realm would receive no benefit or advantage if the subject should have the gold and silver found in mines in his land; but on the other hand, by appropriating it to the King, it tends to the universal benefit of all the subjects in making their King able to defend them with an army against all hostilities, and when he has put the print and value upon it, and has dispersed it among his subjects, they are thereby enabled to carry on mutual commerce with one another, and to buy and sell as they have occasion, and to traffic at their pleasure. Therefore, for these reasons, viz., for the excel-

lency of the thing, and for the necessity of it, and the convenience that will accrue to the subjects, the common law, which is no other than pure and tried reason, has appropriated the ore of gold and silver to the King, in whatever land it be found."

The Supreme Court of the State, without considering the reasons thus assigned in the case in Plowden, adopted its conclusion ; and as the gold and silver in the British realm are there held to belong to the Crown, it was concluded, on the hypothesis that the United States have no municipal sovereignty within the limits of the State, that they must belong in this country to the State. The State, therefore, said the court, "has solely the right to authorize them " (the mines of gold and silver) " to be worked; to pass laws for their reg iation ; to license miners ; and to affix such terms and conditions as she may deem proper to the freedom of their use. In the legislation upon this subject she has established the policy of permitting all who desire it to work her mines of gold and silver, with or without conditions, and she has wisely provided that their conflicting claims shall be adjudicated by the rules and customs which may be established by bodies of them working in the same vicinity."—(3 Cal., 220.)

The miners soon grasped the full scope of this decision, and the lands of private proprietors were accordingly invaded for the purpose of mining as freely as the public lands. It was the policy of the State to encourage the development of the mines, and no greater latitude in exploration could be desired than was thus sanctioned by the highest tribunal of the State. It was not long, however, before a cry came up from private proprietors against the invasion of their possessions which the decision had permitted; and the court was compelled to put some limitation upon the enjoyment by the citizen of this right of the State. Accordingly, within two years afterwards, in Stoakes vs. Barrett, (5 Cal., 37,) it held that although the State was the owner of the gold and silver found in the lands of private individuals as well as in the public lands, "yet to authorize an invasion of private property in order to enjoy a public franchise would require more specific legislation than any yet resorted to."

The spirit to invade other people's lands, to which the original decision gave increased force against the intention of its authors, could not be as easily repressed as it was raised in the crowd of adventurers, who filled the mining regions. Accordingly, long before I went on the bench, the right to dig for the precious metals on the lands of private individuals was stoutly asserted under an assumed license of the State. And afterwards, in the case of Biddle Boggs vs. The Merced Mining Co., which came before the court in 1859, where the plaintiff claimed under a patent of the United States, issued upon the confirmation of a Mexican grant, the existence of this license was earnestly maintained by parties having no connection with the government, nor any claim of title to the land. Its existence was, however, repudiated by the court, and speaking for it in that case I said : " There is gold in limited quantities scattered through large and valuable districts, where the land is held in private proprietorship, and under this pretended license the whole might be invaded, and, for all useful purposes, destroyed, no matter how little remunerative the product of the mining. The entry might be made at all seasons, whether the land was under cultivation or not, and without reference to its condition, whether covered with orchards, vineyards, gardens, or otherwise. Under such a state of things, the proprietor would never be secure in his possessions, and without security there would be little development, for the incentive to improvement would be wanting. What value would there be to a title in one man, with a right of invasion in the whole world? And what property would the owner possess in mineral land—the same being in fact to him poor and valueless just in proportion to the actual richness and abundance of its products? There is something shocking to all our ideas of the rights of property in the proposition that one man may invade the possessions of another, dig up his fields and gardens, cut down his timber, and occupy his land, under the pretence that he has reason to believe there is gold under the surface, or if existing, that he wishes to extract and remove it."

At a later day the court took up the doctrine, that the precious metals belonged to the State by virtue of her sovereignty, and exploded it. The question arose in Moore vs. Smaw, reported in 17th California, and in disposing of it, speaking for the court, I said: "It is undoubtedly true that the United States held certain rights of sovereignty over the territory which is now embraced within the limits of California, only in trust for the future State, and that such rights at once vested in the new State upon her admission into the Union. But the ownership of the precious metals found in public or private lands was not one of those rights. Such ownership stands in no different relation to the sovereignty of a State than that of any other property which is the subject of barter and sale. Sovereignty is a term used to express the supreme political authority of an independent State or Nation. Whatever rights are essential to the existence of this authority are rights of sovereignty. Thus the right to declare war, to make treaties of peace, to levy taxes, to take private property for public uses, termed the right of eminent domain, are all rights of sovereignty, for they are rights essential to the existence of supreme political authority. In this country, this authority is vested in the people, and is exercised through the joint action of their federal and State governments. To the federal government is delegated the exercise of certain rights or powers of sovereignty ; and with respect to sovereignty, rights and powers are synonymous terms ; and the exercise of all other rights of sovereignty, except as expressly prohibited, is reserved to the people of the respective States, or vested by them in their local governments. When we say, therefore, that a State of the Union is sovereign, we only mean that she possesses supreme political authority, except as to those matters over which such authority is delegated to the federal government, or prohibited to the States ; in other words, that she possesses all the rights and powers essential to the existence of an independent political organization, except as they are withdrawn by the provisions of the Constitution of the United States. To the existence of this political authority of the State—this qualified sovereignty, or to any part of it—the ownership of the minerals of gold and silver found within her limits is in no way essential. The minerals do not differ from the great mass of property, the ownership of which may be in the United States, or in individuals, without affecting in any respect the political jurisdiction of the State. They may be acquired by the State, as any other property may be, but when thus acquired she will hold them in the same manner that individual proprietors hold their property, and by the same right; by the right of ownership, and not by any right of sovereignty."

And referring to the argument of counsel in the case in Plowden, I said that it would be a waste of time to show that the reasons there advanced in support of the right of the Crown to the mines could not avail to sustain any ownership of the State in them. The State takes no property by reason of " the excellency of the thing," and taxation furnishes all requisite means for the expenses of government. The convenience of citizens in commercial transactions is undoubtedly promoted by a supply of coin, and the right of coinage appertains to sovereignty. But the exercise of this right does not require the ownership of the precious metals by the State, nor by the federal government, where this right is lodged under our system, as the experience of every day demonstrates.

I also held that, although under the Mexican law the gold and silver found in land did not pass with a grant of the land, a different result followed, under the common law, when a conveyance of land was made by an individual or by the government. By such conveyance everything passed in any way connected with the land, forming a portion of its soil or fixed to its surface.

The doctrine of the right of the State by virtue of her sovereignty to the mines of gold and silver perished with this decision. It was never afterwards seriously asserted. But for holding what now seems so obvious, the judges were then grossly maligned as acting in the interest of monopolists and land owners, to the injury of the laboring class.

The decisions, however, which caused for the time the greatest irritation, and excited the bitterest denunciation of the judges, related to the titles to land in the city of San Francisco, though in the end they proved to be of incalculable benefit. Upon the acquisition of California, there was a Mexican Pueblo upon the site of the city. The term *pueblo* is aptly translated by the English word *town*. It has all the vagueness of that term, and is equally applicable to a settlement of a few individuals at a particular place, or to a regularly organized municipality. The *Pueblo* of San Francisco was composed of a small population ; but, as early as 1835, it was of sufficient importance to have an *Ayuntamiento* or Town Council, composed of alcaldes and other officers, for its government. At the time of our acquisition of the country it was under the government of alcaldes or justices of the peace. By the laws of Mexico, then in force, *pueblos* or towns, when once officially recognized as such by the appointment of municipal magistrates, became entitled to four square leagues of land, to be measured off and assigned to them by the officers of the government. Under these laws the city of San Francisco, as successor of the Mexican Pueblo, asserted a claim to such lands, to be measured off from the northern portion of the peninsula upon which the city is situated. And the alcaldes, assuming an authority similar to that possessed by *alcaldes* in other *pueblos*, exercised the power of distributing these municipal lands in small parcels to settlers for building, cultivation, and other uses.

When the forces of the United States took possession of the city, the alcaldes, holding under the Mexican government, were superseded by persons appointed by our military or naval officers having command of the place. With the increase of population which followed the discovery of gold, these magistrates were besieged by applicants for grants of land; and it was refreshing to see with what generous liberality they disposed of lots in the city—a liberality not infrequent when exercised with reference to other people's property. Lots, varying in size from fifty to one hundred varas square, (a measure nearly equal to our yard,) were given away as freely as they were asked, only a small fee to meet necessary charges for preparing and recording the transfers being demanded. Thus, for the lot occupied by the Lick House, and worth now nearly a million, only a few dollars, less I believe than twenty, were paid. And for the lot covered by the Grand Hotel, admitted to be now worth half a million, less than thirty-five dollars were paid.

The authority of the alcaldes to dispose of the lands was questioned by many of the new immigrants, and the validity of their grants denied. They asserted that the land was part of the public property of the United States. Many holding these views gave evidence of the earnestness of their convictions by immediately appropriating to themselves as much vacant land in the city as they could conveniently occupy. Disputes followed, as a matter of course, between claimants under the alcalde grants and those holding as settlers, which often gave rise to long and bitter litigation. The whole community was in fact divided between those who asserted the existence of a *pueblo* having a right to the lands mentioned, and the power of the alcaldes to make grants of them; and those who insisted that the land belonged to the United States.

Early in 1850, after the State government was organized, the Legislature incorporated the City of San Francisco; and, as is usual with municipal bodies not restrained by the most stringent provisions, it contracted more debts than its means warranted, and did not always make provision for their payment at maturity. Numerous suits, therefore, were instituted and judgments were recovered against the city. Executions followed, which were levied upon the lands claimed by her as successor of the *pueblo*. Where the occupants denied the title of the city, they were generally indifferent to the sales by the sheriff. Property of immense value, in some cases many acres in extent, was, in consequence, often struck off to bidders at a merely nominal price. Upon the deeds of the officer, suits in ejectment were instituted in great numbers; and thus questions as to the existence of the alleged *pueblo*, and whether, if existing, it had any right to land, and the nature of such right, if any, were brought before the lower courts; and, finally, in a test case—Hart vs. Burnett—they found their way to the Supreme Court of the State. In the meantime a large number of persons had become interested in these sales, aside from the occupants of the land, and the greatest anxiety was manifested as to the decision of the Court. Previous decisions on the questions involved were not consistent; nor had they met the entire approval of the profession, although the opinion prevailed generally that a Mexican pueblo of some kind, owning or having an interest in lands, had existed on the site of the city upon the acquisition of the country, and that such lands, like other property of the city not used for public purposes, were vendible on execution.

In 1855, after the sale in respect to which the test case was made, the Council of the city passed " the Van Ness Ordinance," so called from the name of its author, the object of which was to settle and quiet, as far as practicable, the title of persons occupying land in the city. It relinquished and granted the right and interest of the city to lands within its corporate limits, as defined by the charter of 1851, with certain exceptions, to parties in the actual possession thereof, by themselves or tenants, on or before the first of January, 1855, if the possession were continued to the time of the introduction of the ordinance into the Common Council in June of that year ; or, if interrupted by an intruder or trespasser, it had been or might be recovered by legal process. And it declared that, for the purposes of the act, all persons should be deemed in possession who held titles to land within the limits mentioned, by virtue of a grant made by the authorities of the pueblo, including alcaldes among them, before the 7th of July, 1846,—the day when the jurisdiction over the country is deemed to have passed from Mexico to the United States,—or by virtue of a grant subsequently made by those authorities, if the grant, or a material portion of it, had been entered in a proper book of record deposited in the office or custody of the recorder of the county of San Francisco on or before April 3d, 1850. This ordinance was approved by an act of the Legislature of the State in March, 1858, and the benefit of it and of the confirmatory act was claimed by the defendant in the test case.

That case was most elaborately argued by able and learned counsel. The whole law of Mexico respecting *pueblos*, their powers, rights, and property, and whether, if possessing property, it was subject to forced sale, the effect upon such land of the change of sovereignty to the United States, the powers of alcaldes in disposing of the property of these municipalities, the effect of the Van Ness Ordinance, and the confirmatory act of the Legislature, were all discussed with a fullness and learning which left nothing unexplained or to be added. For weeks afterwards the judges gave the most laborious attention to the questions presented, and considered every point and the argument on both sides of it with anxious and painful solicitude to reach a just conclusion. The opinion of the court, prepared by Mr. Justice Baldwin, is without precedent for the exhaustive learning and research it exhibits upon the points discussed. The court held, among other things, that, at the date of the conquest and cession of the country, San Francisco was a pueblo, having the rights which the law of Mexico conferred upon such municipal organizations; that as such pueblo it had proprietary rights to certain lands, which were held in trust for the public use of the city, and were not subject to seizure and sale under execution; that such portions as were not set apart for common use or special purposes could be granted in lots to private persons by its ayuntamiento or by alcaldes or other officers who represented or had succeeded to its powers; that the lands and the trusts upon which they were held, were public and municipal in their nature, and since the organization of the State were under its control and supervision; that the act of the Legislature confirming the Van Ness

Ordinance was a proper exercise of the power of the State, and vested in the possessors therein described, as against the city and State, a title to the lands mentioned ; and that the city held the lands of the pueblo, not legally disposed of by its officers, unaffected by sheriff's sales under executions against her.

This decision was of the greatest importance both to the city and the occupants of land within its limits. The Van Ness Ordinance had reserved from grant for the uses of the city all the lots which it then occupied or had set apart for public squares, streets, sites for school-houses, city hall and other buildings belonging to the corporation, and also such other lots as it might subsequently select for public purposes within certain designated limits. All these were by the decision at once released from any possible claim by virtue of sales on executions. All persons occupying lands not thus reserved were by the decision quieted in their possession, so far as any claim of the city or State could be urged against them. Property to the value of many millions was thereby rescued from the spoiler and speculator, and secured to the city or settler. Peace was given to thousands of homes. Yet for this just and most beneficent judgment there went up from a multitude, who had become interested in the sales, a fierce howl of rage and hate. Attacks full of venom were made upon Judge Baldwin and myself, who had agreed to the decision. No epithets were too vile to be applied to us ; no imputations were too gross to be cast at us. The Press poured out curses upon our heads. Anonymous circulars filled with falsehoods, which malignity alone could invent, were spread broadcast throughout the city, and letters threatening assassination in the streets

or by-ways were sent to us through the mail. The violence of the storm, however, was too great to last.
Gradually it subsided and reason began to assert its
sway. Other words than those of reproach were
uttered; and it was not many months before the
general sentiment of the people of the city was with
the decision. A year did not elapse before the great
good it had conferred upon the city and settler was
seen and appreciated. Since then its doctrines have
been repeatedly re-affirmed. They have been approved by the Supreme Court of the United States;
and now no one doubts their soundness.

After that decision there was still wanting for the
complete settlement of titles in the city the confirmation by the tribunals of the United States of her
claim to the lands. The act of Congress of March 3d,
1851, creating the Board of Land Commissioners,
provided that all claims to land in California, by
virtue of any right or title derived from the Spanish
or Mexican government, should be presented to the
board for examination and adjudication. Accordingly,
the city of San Francisco, soon after the organization
of the board, in 1852, presented her claim for four
square leagues as successor of the *pueblo*, and asked
for its confirmation. In December, 1854, the board
confirmed the claim for a portion of the four square
leagues, but not for the whole; the portion confirmed
being embraced within the charter limits of 1851.
The city was dissatisfied with this limitation, and appealed from the decision of the Commissioners to the
District Court of the United States. An appeal was
also taken by the United States, but was subsequently
withdrawn. The case remained in the District Court
without being disposed of until September, 1864,

nearly ten years, when, under the authority of an act of Congress of July 1st of that year, it was transferred to the Circuit Court of the United States.

Whilst the case was pending in the District Court, the population of the city had increased more than four-fold; and improvements of a costly character had been made in all parts of it. The magnitude of the interests which had thus grown up demanded that the title to the land upon which the city rested should be in some way definitely settled. To expedite this settlement, as well as the settlement of titles generally in the State, was the object of the act of July 1st, 1864. Its object is so stated in its title. It was introduced by Senator Conness, of California, who was alive to everything that could tend to advance the interests of the State. He felt that nothing would promote its peace and prosperity more than giving security to its land titles, and he labored earnestly to bring about that result. In framing the act, he consulted me, and at my suggestion introduced sections four, five, and seven, which I drafted and gave to him, but without the exception and proviso to the fifth section, which were added at the request of the Commissioner of the Land Office.* The fourth section authorized the District Court to transfer to the Circuit Court cases pending before it arising under the act of March 3d, 1851, affecting the title to lands within the corporate limits of a city or town, and provided that in such cases both the District and Circuit Judges might sit. By the fifth section, all the right and title of the United States to the land within the corporate limits of the city, as defined by its charter of 1851, were relinquished and granted to the city and its

---

* See Exhibit J, in Appendix.

successors for the uses and purposes specified in the
Van Ness Ordinance. The exceptions incorporated
at the suggestion of the Commissioner of the Land
Office related to parcels of land previously or then
occupied by the United States for military, naval, or
other public purposes, and such other parcels as might
be subsequently designated for such purposes by the
President within one year after the return to the land
office of an approved plat of the exterior limits of the
city. The holders of grants from the authorities of
the *pueblo* and the occupants of land within the limits
of the charter of 1851 were thus quieted in their possessions. But as the claim of the city was for a much
greater quantity, the case for its confirmation was still
prosecuted. Under the fourth section it was transferred to the Circuit Court, as already stated ; and it
was soon afterwards brought to a hearing. On the
30th of October, 1864, it was decided. For some
reason I do not now recall, the District Judge was
unable to sit with me, and the case was, therefore,
heard before me alone. I held that a pueblo of some
kind existed at the site of the present city of San
Francisco upon the cession of the country ; that as
such it was entitled to the possession of certain lands
to the extent of four square leagues ; and that the
present city had succeeded to such rights, following,
in these particulars, the decision which had previously
been made in the case of Hart vs. Burnett, by the
Supreme Court of the State, in which I had participated. I accordingly decided that the city was
entitled to have her claim confirmed to four square
leagues of land, subject to certain reservations. But
I also added that the lands to which she was entitled
had not been given to her by the laws of the former

government in absolute property with full right of disposition and alienation, but to be held in trust for the benefit of the whole community, with such powers of use, disposition, and alienation as had been or might thenceforth be conferred upon her or her officers for the execution of the trust. The trust character of the city's title was expressed in the decree of confirmation. The decision was rendered on the 30th of October, 1864, as stated, and a decree was soon afterwards entered; but as a motion was made for a re-hearing, the control over it was retained by the Circuit Court until May of the following year. Upon the suggestion of counsel, it was then modified in some slight particulars so as to limit the confirmation to land above ordinary high water mark, as it existed at the date of the acquisition of the country, namely, the 7th of July, 1846. On the 18th of May, 1865, the decree was finally settled and entered. Appeals from it were prosecuted to the Supreme Court both by the United States and by the city; by the United States from the whole decree, and by the city from so much of it as included certain reservations in the estimate of the quantity of land confirmed.

In October following I proceeded as usual to Washington to attend the then approaching term of the Supreme Court, and thought no more of the case until my attention was called to it by a most extraordinary circumstance. Just before leaving San Francisco Mr. Rulofson, a photographer of note, requested me to sit for a photograph, expressing a desire to add it to his gallery. I consented, and a photograph of a large size was taken. As I was leaving his rooms he observed that he intended to make some pictures of a small size from it, and would send me a few copies.

On the morning of the 13th of January following
(1866), at Washington, Mr. Delos Lake, a lawyer of
distinction in California, at one time a District Judge
of the State, and then District Attorney of the United
States, joined me, remarking, as he did so, that the
arrival of the California steamer at New York had
been telegraphed, and he hoped that I had received
some letters for him, as he had directed his letters to
be forwarded to my care.   I replied that when I left
my room my messenger had not brought my mail ;
but if he would accompany me there we would probably find it.   Accordingly, we proceeded to my room,
where on the centre-table lay my mail from California,
consisting of a large number of letters and papers.
Among them I noticed a small package about an inch
and a half thick, three inches in breadth, and three
and a half in length.   It was addressed as follows,
the words being printed :

Per steamer.	[Three postage stamps.] Hon. STEPHEN J. FIELD, Washington, D. C.

It bore the stamp of the San Francisco post-office
upon the address.   My name had evidently been cut
from the California Reports, but the words " Washington, D. C.," and " Per steamer," had been taken
from a newspaper.   The slips were pasted on the
package.   On the opposite side were the words in
print :

From

GEO. H. JOHNSON'S

Pioneer Gallery,

645 and 649 Clay street,

SAN FRANCISCO.

As I took up the package I remarked that this must come from Rulofson;—no, I immediately added, Rulofson has nothing to do with the Pioneer Gallery. It then occurred to me that it might be a present for my wife, recollecting at the moment that the mail came by the steamer which sailed from San Francisco about Christmas time. It may be, I said to myself, a Christmas present for my wife. I will open it just far enough to see, and, if it be intended for her, I will close it and forward it to New York, where she was at the time. I accordingly tore off the covering and raised the lid just far enough to enable me to look inside. I was at once struck with the black appearance of the inside. "What is this, Lake?" I said, addressing myself to my friend. Judge Lake looked over my shoulder into the box, as I held it in my hand, and at once exclaimed, "It is a torpedo. Don't open it." I was startled by the suggestion, for the idea of a torpedo was the last thing in the world to occur to me. I immediately laid the package on the sill of the window, where it was subjected to a careful inspection by us both, so far as it could be made with the lid only an eighth of an inch open.

Soon afterwards Judge Lake took the package to the Capitol, which was directly opposite to my rooms, and to the office of the Clerk of the Supreme Court, and showed it to Mr. Broom, one of the deputies.

They dipped the package into water and left it to
soak for some minutes. They then took it into the
carriage way under the steps leading to the Senate
Chamber, and shielding themselves behind one of the
columns, threw the box against the wall. The blow
broke the hinge of the lid and exposed the contents.
A murderous contrivance it was ;—a veritable infernal
machine! Twelve cartridges such as are used in a
common pistol, about an inch in length, lay imbedded
in a paste of some kind, covered with fulminating
powder, and so connected with a bunch of friction
matches, a strip of sand-paper, and a piece of linen
attached to the lid, that on opening the box the
matches would be ignited and the whole exploded.
The package was sent to the War Department, and
the following report was returned, giving a detailed
description of the machine :

WASHINGTON ARSENAL, *Jan.* 16, 1866.

Gen. A. B. Dyer, *Chief of Ordnance, Washington, D. C.*

SIR : Agreeably to your instructions, I have examined the
explosive machine sent to this arsenal yesterday. It is a small
miniature case containing twelve copper cartridges, such as
are used in a Smith & Wesson pocket pistol, a bundle of sen-
sitive friction matches, a strip of sand-paper, and some fulminating powder. The cartridges and matches are imbedded in
common glue to keep them in place. The strip of sand-paper
lies upon the heads of the matches. One end has been thrown
back, forming a loop, through which a bit of thread evidently
passed to attach it to the lid of the case. This thread may be
seen near the clasp of the lid, broken in two. There are two
wire staples, under which the strip of sand-paper was intended
to pass to produce the necessary pressure on the matches.
The thread is so fixed that the strip of sand-paper could be
secured to the lid after it was closed.

The whole affair is so arranged that the opening of the lid
would necessarily ignite the matches, were it not that the lower

end of the strip has become imbedded in the glue, which prevents it from moving. That the burning of the matches may explode the cartridges, there is a hole in each case, and all are covered with mealed powder.

One of the cartridges has been examined and found to contain ordinary grain powder. Two of the cartridges were exploded in a closed box sent herewith. The effect of the explosion was an indentation on one side of the box.

Very respectfully, your obedient servant,

J. G. BENTON,
Major of Ord. and Bvt. Col. Comdg.

Between the outside covering and the box there were two or three folds of tissue-paper—placed there, no doubt, to prevent the possibility of an explosion from the stamping at the post office, or the striking against other packages during the voyage from San Francisco to New York.

On the inside of the lid was pasted a slip cut from a San Francisco paper, dated October 31st, 1864, stating that on the day previous I had decided the case of the City against the United States, involving its claim to four square leagues of land, and giving the opening lines of my opinion.

The Secretary of War, Mr. Stanton, immediately telegraphed in cypher to General Halleck, then in command in San Francisco, to take active measures to find out, if possible, the person who made and sent the infernal machine. General Halleck put the detectives of his department on the search. Others employed detectives of the San Francisco police—but all in vain. Suspicions were excited as to the complicity of different parties, but they were never sustained by sufficient evidence to justify the arrest of any one. The instrument, after remaining in the hands of the detectives in San Francisco for nearly two years, was returned to me and it is now in my possession.*

It has often been a matter of wonder to me how it was that some good angel whispered to me not to open the box. My impetuous temperament would naturally have led me to tear it open without delay. Probably such hesitation in opening a package directed to me never before occurred, and probably never will again. Who knows but that a mother's prayer for the protection of her son, breathed years before, was answered then? Who can say that her spirit was not then hovering over him and whispering caution in his ear? That I should on that occasion have departed from my usual mode of action is strange—passing strange.

As already stated, the fifth section of the act of Congress of July 1st, 1864, which granted the interest of the United States to the lands within the charter limits of 1851 to the city and its successors in trust for the benefit of possessors under the Van Ness Ordinance, among other things provided for certain reservations to be subsequently made by the President, within one year after an approved plat showing the exterior limits of the city had been filed in the land office. No such map was filed nor were any reservations made. The case on appeal in the meantime was not reached in the Supreme Court, and was not likely to be for a long period. Ascertaining from General Halleck that the Secretary of War would not recommend any further reservations to be made from the municipal lands, and that probably none would

* See Exhibit K, in Appendix.

be made, I drew a bill to quiet the title of the city to all the lands embraced within the decree of confirmation, and gave it to Senator Conness, who being ready, as usual, to act for the interests of the city, immediately took charge of it and secured its passage in the Senate. In the House Mr. McRuer, Member of Congress from California, took charge of it, and with the assistance of the rest of the delegation from the State, procured its passage there. It was signed by the President and became a law on the 8th of March, 1866. By it all the right and title of the United States to the land covered by the decree of the Circuit Court were relinquished and granted to the city, and the claim to the land was confirmed, subject, however, to certain reservations and exceptions ; and upon trust that all the land not previously granted to the city, should be disposed of and conveyed by the city to the parties in the bona fide actual possession thereof, by themselves or tenants, on the passage of the act, in such quantities, and upon such terms and conditions, as the Legislature of the State of California might prescribe, except such parcels thereof as might be reserved and set apart by ordinance of the city for public uses.

Not long afterwards both the appeals to the Supreme Court were dismissed by stipulation of parties. The litigation over the source of title to lands within the limits of the city, not disposed of by independent grants of the government previous to the acquisition of the country, was thus settled and closed. The title of the city rests, therefore, upon the decree of the Circuit Court entered on the 18th day of May, 1865, and this confirmatory act of Congress. It has been so adjudged by the Supreme Court of the United

States.—(See Townsend vs. Greely, 5 Wall., 337 ; Grisar vs. McDowell, 6 Wall., 379.)

The title of the city being settled, the municipal authorities took measures, under the provisions of the confirmatory act, to set apart lands for school-houses, hospitals, court-house buildings, and other public purposes, and through their exertions, instigated and encouraged by Mr. McCoppin, the accomplished and efficient Mayor of the city at that time, the Ocean Park, which looks out upon the Pacific Ocean and the Golden Gate, and is destined to be one of the finest parks in the world, was set apart and secured to the city for all time. As the grounds thus taken were, in many instances, occupied by settlers, or had been purchased from them, an assessment was levied by the city and sanctioned by the Legislature upon other lands conveyed to the occupants, as a condition of their receiving deeds from the city ; and the money raised was applied to compensate those whose lands had been appropriated.

THE irritations and enmities created by the civil
war did not end with the cessation of active hostilities.
They were expressed whenever any acts of the military
officers of the United States were called in question ;
or any legislation of the States or of Congress in hostility to the insurgents was assailed; or the validity
of the " Reconstruction Acts " was doubted. And
they postponed that cordial reconciliation which all
patriotic men earnestly desired.

The insurrection was overthrown after a contest
which, for its magnitude and the number and courage
of the belligerents, was without a parallel in history.
The immense loss of life and destruction of property
caused by the contest, and the burden of the enormous
debt created in its prosecution, left a bitterness in the
hearts of the victors which it was difficult to remove.
The assassination of Mr. Lincoln added intensity to
the feeling. That act of a madman, who had conceived
the idea that he might become in our history what
Brutus was in the history of Rome, the destroyer of
the enemy of his country, was ascribed to a conspiracy
of leading Confederates. The proclamation of the
Secretary of War, offering a reward for the arrest of
parties charged with complicity in the act, gave support to this notion. The wildest stories, now known
to have had no foundation, were circulated and obtained ready credence among the people of the North,
already wrought up to the highest pitch of excitement.

They manifested, therefore, great impatience when a doubt was cast upon the propriety or validity of the acts of the government, or of its officers, which were taken for the suppression of the rebellion or " the reconstruction " of the States ; and to question their validity was almost considered proof of hostility to the Union.

By those who considered the union indissoluble, except by the common consent of the people of the several States, the organization known as the Confederate States could only be regarded as unlawful and rebellious, to be suppressed, if necessary, by force of arms. The Constitution prohibits any treaty, alliance, or confederation by one State with another, and it declares on its face that it is the supreme law of the land. The Confederate government, therefore, could only be treated by the United States as the military representative of the insurrection against their authority. Belligerent rights were accorded to its armed forces in the conduct of the war, and they thus had the standing and rights of parties engaged in lawful warfare. But no further recognition was ever given to it, and when those forces were overthrown its whole fabric disappeared. But not so with the insurgent States which had composed the Confederacy. They retained the same form of government and the same general system of laws, during and subsequent to the war, which they had possessed previously. Their organizations as distinct political communities were not destroyed by the war, although their relations to the central authority were changed. And their acts, so far as they did not impair or tend to impair the supremacy of the general government, or the rights of citizens of the loyal States, were valid and binding.

All the ordinary authority of government for the protection of rights of persons and property, the enforcement of contracts, the punishment of crime, and the due order of society, continued to be exercised by them as though no civil war had existed.

There was, therefore, a general expectation throughout the country, upon the cessation of actual hostilities, that these States would be restored to their former relations in the Union as soon as satisfactory evidence was furnished to the general government that resistance to its authority was overthrown and abandoned, and its laws were enforced and obeyed. Some little time might elapse before this result would clearly appear. It was not expected that they would be immediately restored upon the defeat of the armies of the Confederacy, nor that their public men, with the animosities of the struggle still alive, would at once be admitted into the councils of the nation, and allowed to participate in its government. But whenever it was satisfactorily established that there would be no renewal of the struggle and that the laws of the United States would be obeyed, it was generally believed that the restoration of the States would be an accomplished fact.

President Johnson saw in the institution of slavery the principal source of the irritation and ill-feeling between the North and the South, which had led to the war. He believed, therefore, that its abolition should be exacted, and that this would constitute a complete guaranty for the future. At that time the amendment for its abolition, which had passed the two Houses of Congress, was pending before the States for their action. He was of opinion, and so expressed himself in his first message to Congress,

that its ratification should be required of the insurgent States on resuming their places in the family of
the Union ; that it was not too much, he said, to ask
of them " to give this pledge of perpetual loyalty and
peace." " Until it is done," he added, " the past, however much we may desire it, will not be forgotten.
The adoption of the amendment re-unites us beyond
all power of disruption. It heals the wound that is
still imperfectly closed ; it removes slavery, the element which has so long perplexed and divided the
country ; it makes of us once more a united people,
renewed and strengthened, bound more than ever to
mutual affection and support."

It would have been most fortunate for the country
had this condition been deemed sufficient and been
accepted as such. But the North was in no mood for
a course so simple and just. Its leaders clamored
for more stringent measures, on the ground that they
were needed for the protection of the freedmen, and
the defeat of possible schemes for a new insurrection.
It was not long, therefore, before a system of measures was adopted, which resulted in the establishment
at the South of temporary governments, subject to
military control, the offices of which were filled chiefly
by men alien to the States and indifferent to their
interests. The misrule and corruption which followed
are matters of public history. It is no part of my
purpose to speak of them. I wish merely to refer to
the state of feeling existing upon the close of the
civil war as introductory to what I have to say of the
unfriendly disposition manifested at the North towards the Supreme Court and some of its members,
myself in particular.

Acts of the military officers, and legislation of some

of the States and of Congress, during and immediately succeeding the war, were soon brought to the
consideration of the Court. Its action thereon was
watched by members of the Republican party with
manifest uneasiness and distrust. Its decision in the
Dred Scott case had greatly impaired their confidence
in its wisdom and freedom from political influences.
Many of them looked upon that decision as precipi-
tating the war upon the country, by the sanction it
gave to efforts made to introduce slavery into the
Territories ; and they did not hesitate to express
their belief that the sympathies of a majority of the
Court were with the Confederates. Intimations to
that effect were thrown out in some of the journals
of the day, at first in guarded language, and afterwards more directly, until finally it came to be generally believed that it was the purpose of the Court,
if an opportunity offered, to declare invalid most of
the legislation relating to the Southern States which
had been enacted during the war and immediately
afterwards. Nothing could have been more unjust
and unfounded. Many things, indeed, were done
during the war, and more after its close, which could
not be sustained by any just construction of the limitations of the Constitution. It was to be expected
that many things would be done in the heat of the
contest which could not bear the examination of
calmer times. Mr. Chief Justice Chase expressed
this fact in felicitous language when speaking of his
own change of views as to the validity of the provision of law making government notes a legal tender,
he said : " It is not surprising that amid the tumult
of the late civil war, and under the influence of apprehensions for the safety of the Republic almost

universal, different views, never before entertained
by American statesmen or jurists, were adopted by
many. The time was not favorable to considerate
reflection upon the constitutional limits of legislative
or executive authority. If power was assumed from
patriotic motives, the assumption found ready justification in patriotic hearts. Many who doubted yielded
their doubts ; many who did not doubt were silent.
Those who were strongly averse to making government notes a legal tender felt themselves constrained
to acquiesce in the views of the advocates of the
measure. Not a few who then insisted upon its
necessity, or acquiesced in that view, have, since the
return of peace, and under the influence of the calmer
time, reconsidered this conclusion, and now concur
in those which we have just announced."

Similar language might be used with reference to
other things done during the war and afterwards,
besides making government notes a legal tender. The
Court and all its members appreciated the great difficulties and responsibilities of the government, both in
the conduct of the war, and in effecting an early restoration of the States afterwards, and no disposition was
manifested at any time to place unnecessary obstacles
in its way. But when its measures and legislation
were brought to the test of judicial judgment there
was but one course to pursue, and that was to apply
the law and the Constitution as strictly as though no
war had ever existed. The Constitution was not one
thing in war, and another in peace. It always spoke
the same language, and was intended as a rule for all
times and occasions. It recognized, indeed, the possibility of war, and, of course, that the rules of war
had to be applied in its conduct in the field of military

operations. The Court never presumed to interfere there, but outside of that field, and with respect to persons not in the military service within States which adhered to the Union, and after the war in all the States, the Court could not hesitate to say that the Constitution, with all its limitations upon the exercise of executive and legislative authority, was, what it declares on its face to be, the supreme law of the land, by which all legislation, State and federal, must be measured.

The first case growing out of the acts of military officers during the war, which attracted general attention and created throughout the North an uneasy feeling, was the Milligan case, which was before the Court on habeas corpus. In October, 1864, Milligan, a citizen of the United States and a resident of Indiana, had been arrested by order of the military commander of the district and confined in a military prison near the capital of the State. He was subsequently, on the 21st of the same month, put on trial before a military commission convened at Indianapolis, in that State, upon charges of: 1st. Conspiring against the government of the United States; 2d. Affording aid and comfort to the rebels against the authority of the United States; 3d. Inciting insurrection; 4th. Disloyal practices; and 5th. Violations of the laws of war; and was found guilty and sentenced to death by hanging. He had never been in the military service; there was no rebellion in Indiana; and the civil courts were open in that State and in the undisturbed exercise of their jurisdiction. The sentence of the military commission was affirmed by the President, who directed that it should be carried into immediate execution. The condemned thereupon presented a petition to the Circuit Court of the United States in Indiana for a writ of habeas corpus, praying to be discharged from custody, alleging the illegality of his arrest and of the proceedings of the military commission. The judges of the Circuit Court were divided in opinion upon the question whether the writ should be issued and the prisoner be discharged, which, of course, involved the jurisdiction of the military commission to try the petitioner. Upon a certificate of the division the case was brought to the Supreme Court at the December term of 1865. The case has become historical in the jurisprudence of the country, and it is unnecessary to state the proceedings at length. Suffice it to say that it was argued with great ability by eminent counsel—consisting of Mr. Joseph E. McDonald, now U. S. Senator from Indiana, Mr. James A. Garfield, a distinguished member of Congress, Mr. Jeremiah S. Black, the eminent jurist of Pennsylvania, and Mr. David Dudley Field, of New York, for the petitioner; and by Mr. Henry Stanbery, the Attorney-General, and Gen. B. F. Butler, for the government. Their arguments were remarkable for learning, research, ability, and eloquence, and will repay the careful perusal not only of the student of law, but of all lovers of constitutional liberty. Only a brief synopsis of them is given in the report of the case in 4th Wallace. The decision of the Court was in favor of the liberty of the citizen. Its opinion was announced by Mr. Justice Davis, and it will stand as a perpetual monument to his honor. It laid down in clear and unmistakable terms the doctrine that military commissions organized during the war, in a State not invaded nor engaged in rebellion, in which the federal courts were open and in the undisturbed ex-

ercise of their judicial functions, had no jurisdiction
to try a citizen who was not a resident of a State in
rebellion, nor a prisoner of war, nor a person in the
military or naval service; and that Congress could
not invest them with any such power ; and that in
States where the courts were thus open and undisturbed the guaranty of trial by jury contained in the
Constitution was intended for a state of war as well
as a state of peace, and is equally binding upon rulers
and people at all times and under all circumstances.

This decision was concurred in by Justices Nelson,
Grier, Clifford, and myself, then constituting, with
Justice Davis, a majority of the Court. At this day
it seems strange that its soundness should have been
doubted by any one, yet it was received by a large
class—perhaps a majority of the Northern people—
with disfavor, and was denounced in unmeasured
terms by many influential journals. It was cited as
conclusive evidence of the hostility of the Court to
the acts of the government for the suppression of the
rebellion. The following, taken from the *Daily Chronicle* of January 14th, 1867, a journal of Washington,
edited by Mr. Forney, then Secretary of the Senate,
is a fair sample of the language applied to the decision :

" The opinion of the Supreme Court on one of the most mo-
mentous questions ever submitted to a judicial tribunal, has
not startled the country more by its far reaching and calami-
tous results, than it has amazed jurists and statesmen by the
poverty of its learning and the feebleness of its logic. It has
surprised all, too, by its total want of sympathy with the spirit
in which the war for the Union was prosecuted, and, necessarily,
with those great issues growing out of it, which concern not
only the life of the Republic, but the very progress of the race,
and which, having been decided on the battle-field, are now

sought to be reversed by the very theory of construction which led to rebellion."

At the same term with the Milligan case the test-oath case from Missouri was brought before the Court and argued. In January, 1865, a convention had assembled in that State to amend its constitution. Its members had been elected in November previous. In April, 1865, the constitution, as revised and amended, was adopted by the convention, and in June following by the people. Elected, as the members were, in the midst of the war, it exhibited throughout traces of the animosities which the war had engendered. By its provisions the most stringent and searching oath as to past conduct known in history was required, not only of officers under it, but of parties holding trusts and pursuing avocations in no way connected with the administration of the government. The oath, divided into its separate parts, contained more than thirty distinct affirmations touching past conduct, and even embraced the expression of sympathies and desires. Every person unable to take the oath was declared incapable of holding, in the State, " any office of honor, trust, or profit under its authority, or of being an officer, councilman, director, or trustee, or other manager of any corporation, public or private, now existing or hereafter established by its authority, or of acting as a professor or teacher in any educational institution, or in any common or other school, or of holding any real estate or other property in trust for the use of any church, religious society, or congregation."

And every person holding, at the time the amended constitution took effect, any of the offices, trusts, or positions mentioned, was required, within sixty days

thereafter, to take the oath ; and, if he failed to comply with this requirement, it was declared that his
office, trust, or position should *ipso facto* become
vacant.

No person, after the expiration of the sixty days,
was permitted, without taking the oath, "to practice as
an attorney or counsellor-at-law," nor, after that period
could "any person be competent as a bishop, priest,
deacon, minister, elder, or other clergyman, of any religious persuasion, sect, or denomination, to teach, or
preach, or solemnize marriages."

Fine and imprisonment were prescribed as a punishment for holding or exercising any of "the offices,
positions, trusts, professions, or functions" specified,
without having taken the oath; and false swearing or
affirmation in taking it was declared to be perjury,
punishable by imprisonment in the penitentiary.

Mr. Cummings of Missouri, a priest of the Roman
Catholic Church, was indicted and convicted in one of
the Circuit Courts of that State, of the crime of teach-
ing and preaching as a priest and minister of that religious denomination without having first taken the oath
thus prescribed, and was sentenced to pay a fine of
five hundred dollars and to be committed to jail until
the same was paid. On appeal to the Supreme Court
of the State the judgment was affirmed, and the case
was brought on a writ of error to our court. It was
there argued with great learning and ability by Mr.
Montgomery Blair, of Washington, Mr. David Dudley
Field, of New York, and Mr. Reverdy Johnson, of
Maryland, for Mr. Cummings ; and by Mr. G. P.
Strong and Mr. John B. Henderson, of Missouri, the
latter then United States Senator for the State.

It was evident, after a brief consideration of the

case, that the power asserted by the State of Missouri to exact this oath for past conduct from parties, as a condition of their continuing to pursue certain professions, or to hold certain trusts, might, if sustained, be often exercised in times of excitement to the oppression, if not ruin, of the citizen. For, if the State could require the oath for the acts mentioned, it might require it for any other acts of one's past life, the number and character of which would depend upon the mere will of its legislature. It might compel one to affirm, under oath, that he had never violated the ten commandments, nor exercised his political rights except in conformity with the views of the existing majority. Indeed, under this kind of legislation, the most flagrant wrongs might be committed and whole classes of people deprived, not only of their political, but of their civil rights.

It is difficult to speak of the whole system of expurgatory oaths for past conduct without a shudder at the suffering and oppression they were not only capable of effecting but often did effect. Such oaths have never been exacted in England, nor on the Continent of Europe ; at least I can recall no instance of the kind. Test-oaths there have always been limited to an affirmation on matters of present belief, or as to present disposition towards those in power. It was reserved for the ingenuity of legislators in our country during the civil war to make test-oaths reach to past conduct.

The Court held that enactments of this character, operating, as they did, to deprive parties by legislative decree of existing rights for past conduct, without the formality and the safeguard of a judicial trial, fell within the inhibition of the Constitution against the passage of bills of attainder. In depriving parties of existing rights for past conduct, the provisions of the constitution of Missouri imposed, in effect, a punishment for such conduct. Some of the acts for which such deprivation was imposed were not punishable at the time; and for some this deprivation was added to the punishments previously prescribed, and thus they fell under the further prohibition of the Constitution against the passage of an *ex post facto* law. The decision of the Court, therefore, was for the discharge of the Catholic priest. The judgment against him was reversed, and the Supreme Court of Missouri was directed to order the inferior court by which he was tried to set him at liberty.

Immediately following the case of Cummings that of *Ex-parte* Garland was argued, involving the validity of the iron-clad oath, as it was termed, prescribed for attorneys and counsellors-at-law by the act of Congress of January 24th, 1865. Mr. A. H. Garland, now United States Senator from Arkansas, had been a member of the Bar of the Supreme Court of the United States before the civil war. When Arkansas passed her ordinance of secession and joined the Confederate States, he went with her, and was one of her representatives in the Congress of the Confederacy. In July, 1865, he received from the President a full pardon for all offences committed by his participation, direct or implied, in the rebellion. At the following term of the Court he produced his pardon and asked permission to continue to practice as an attorney and counsellor without taking the oath required by the act of Congress, and the rule of the Court made in conformity with it, which he was unable to take by reason of the offices he had held under the Confederate government. The application was argued by Mr. Matthew H. Carpenter, of Wisconsin, and Mr. Reverdy Johnson, of Maryland, for the petitioner—Mr. Garland and Mr. Marr, another applicant for admission, who had participated in the rebellion, filing printed arguments—and by Mr. Speed, of Kentucky, and Mr. Henry Stanbery, the Attorney-General, on the other side. The whole subject of expurgatory oaths was discussed, and all that could be said on either side was fully and elaborately presented.

The Court in its decision followed the reasoning of the Cummings case and held the law invalid, as applied to the exercise of the petitioner's right to practice his profession ; that such right was not a mere indulgence, a matter of grace and favor, revocable at the pleasure of the Court, or at the command of the legislature ; but was a right of which the petitioner could be deprived only by the judgment of the Court for moral or professional delinquency. The Court also held that the pardon of the petitioner released him from all penalties and disabilities attached to the offence of treason committed by his participation in the rebellion, and that, so far as that offence was concerned, he was placed beyond the reach of punishment of any kind. But to exclude him by reason of that offence—that is, by requiring him to take an oath that he had never committed it—was to enforce a punishment for it notwithstanding the pardon ; and that it was not within the constitutional power of Congress thus to inflict punishment beyond the reach of executive clemency.

I had the honor to deliver the opinion of the Court in these cases—the Cummings case and the Garland case. At the present day both opinions are generally admitted to be sound, but when announced they were received by a portion of the Northern Press with apparent astonishment and undisguised condemnation. It is difficult to appreciate at this day the fierceness with which the majority of the Court was assailed. That majority consisted of Justices Wayne, Nelson, Grier, Clifford, and myself. I was particularly taken to task, however, as it was supposed—at least I can only so infer from the tone of the Press—that because I had been appointed by Mr. Lincoln, I was under some sort of moral obligation to support all the measures taken by the States or by Congress during the war. The following, respecting the opinion in the Garland case, from the editor of the *Daily Chronicle*, of Washington, to the *Press*, of Philadelphia, under date of January 16, 1867, is moderate in its language compared with what appeared in many other journals :

"Dred Scott Number Three has just been enacted in the Supreme Court of the United States, Justice Field, of California, taking the leading part as the representative of the majority decision against the constitutionality of the iron-clad test-oath, to prevent traitors from practicing before that high tribunal. I understand it takes the ground that, as the law is a living or profession, the oath cannot be insisted upon to take that living away, and that the President's pardon restores all such rights. The country has been repeatedly admonished that such a decision would be made about this time ; nevertheless, a very considerable sensation was created when it was officially enunciated. All these movements are but preparations for a counter-revolution in the interest of slavery and treason."———"I learn that the opinion of Justice Field against the test-oath, like that against military trials in time of war, goes outside of the immediate case in issue, and indulges in a fierce onslaught upon test-oaths in general. If so, it will only add another reason for such a reorganization as will prevent the judges in the last resort from becoming the mere agents of party, or the mere defenders of rebellion. The adage constantly quoted, yet never out of fashion, that ' Whom the Gods wish to destroy they first make mad,' is having a pointed illustration in these successive judicial assaults upon the rights of the people. Although the Supreme Judges hold for life, there is at once precedent, necessity, and law for such a change in the present system as will in a short time make it a fearless interpreter of republican institutions, instead of the defender and apologist of treason."

The decisions were announced on the 14th of January, 1867. On the 22d of the month, Mr. Boutwell, from Massachusetts, introduced a bill into the House far more stringent in its provisions than the act of Congress just declared invalid. It was a pitiable exhibition of hate and vengeance against all persons who had been engaged, directly or indirectly, in the rebellion. It declared that no person who had been thus engaged should be permitted to act as an attorney and counsellor in any courts of the United States; and made it the duty of the judges, when it was suggested in open court, or when they had reason to believe that any person was thus debarred, to enquire and ascertain whether he had been so engaged, and if the court was of opinion that such was the fact, he was to be excluded. The court was thus, upon the suggestion of any one, to be turned into a tribunal for the summary trial of the accused without the ordinary safeguards for the protection of his rights. In introducing it Mr. Boutwell, referring to the decision of the Court, said that—

" If there be five judges upon the bench of the highest tribunal who have not that respect for themselves to enact rules, and to enforce proper regulations, by which they will protect themselves from the contamination of conspirators and traitors against the government of the country, then the time has already arrived when the legislative department of the government should exercise its power to declare who shall be officers of the government in the administration of the law in the courts of the Union; and this bill is for that purpose."

And he called for the previous question upon it. In subsequently advocating its passage, he said :

" I say here upon my responsibility, with reference to the recent decision of the Supreme Court, that it is an offence to the dignity and respectability of the nation that this tribunal, under the general authority vested in it under the Constitution and laws, does not protect itself from the contamination of rebels and traitors, until the rebellion itself shall be suppressed and those men shall be restored to their former rights as citizens of the country."

This language was used in 1867, and the last gun of the war had been fired in May, 1865. It showed the irritation of violent partisans of the North against the Court because it gave no sanction to their vindictive and proscriptive measures.

The bill was passed, under a suspension of the rules, by a vote of 111 to 40.*

The Reconstruction Acts, so-called—that is, " An act to provide for the more efficient government of the rebel States," of March 2d, 1867, and An act of the 23d of the same month, supplementary to the former—were at once attacked, as may well be supposed, as invalid, unconstitutional, and arbitrary measures of the government; and various steps were taken at an early day to bring them to the test of judicial examination and

---

* Congressional Globe, 39th Congress, 2d Session, Part I., pp. 646–649.

When the bill reached the Senate it was referred to the Judiciary Committee, and by them to a sub-committee of which Mr. Stewart, Senator from Nevada, was chairman. He retained it until late in the session, and upon his advice, the committee then recommended its indefinite postponement. The bill was thus disposed of.

arrest their enforcement. Those acts divided the late insurgent States, except Tennessee, into five military districts, and placed them under military control to be exercised until constitutions, containing various provisions stated, were adopted and approved by Congress, and the States declared to be entitled to representation in that body. In the month of April following the State of Georgia filed a bill in the Supreme Court, invoking the exercise of its original jurisdiction, against Stanton, Secretary of War, Grant, General of the Army, and Pope, Major-General, assigned to the command of the Third Military District, consisting of the States of Georgia, Florida, and Alabama ; to restrain those officers from carrying into effect the provisions of those acts. The bill set forth the existence of the State of Georgia as one of the States of the Union ; the civil war in which she, with other States forming the Confederate States, had been engaged with the government of the United States; the surrender of the Confederate armies in 1865, and her submission afterwards to the Constitution and laws of the Union; the withdrawal of the military government from Georgia by the President as Commander-in-Chief of the Army of the United States ; the re-organization of the civil government of the State under his direction and with his sanction ; and that the government thus re-organized was in the full possession and enjoyment of all the rights and privileges, executive, legislative, and judicial, belonging to a State in the Union under the Constitution, with the exception of a representation in the Senate and House of Representatives. The bill alleged that the acts were designed to overthrow and annul the existing government of the State, and to erect another and a different government in its place, unauthorized by the Constitution and in defiance of its guarantees; that the defendants, acting under orders of the President, were about to set in motion a portion of the army to take military possession of the State, subvert her government, and subject her people to military rule. The presentation of this bill and the argument on the motion of the Attorney-General to dismiss it produced a good deal of hostile comment against the Judges, which did not end when the motion was granted. It was held that the bill called for judgment upon a political question, which the Court had no jurisdiction to entertain.*

Soon afterwards the validity of the Reconstruction Acts was again presented in the celebrated McArdle case, and in such a form that the decision of the question could not well be avoided. In November, 1867, McArdle had been arrested and held in custody by a military commission organized in Mississippi under the Reconstruction Acts, for trial upon charges of (1) disturbance of the public peace; (2) inciting to insurrection, disorder, and violerce; (3) libel; and (4) impeding reconstruction. He thereupon applied to the Circuit Court of the United States for the District of Mississippi for a writ of habeas corpus, in order that he might be discharged from his alleged illegal imprisonment. The writ was accordingly issued, but on the return of the officer showing the authority under which the petitioner was held, he was ordered to be remanded. From that judgment he appealed to the Supreme Court. Of course, if the Reconstruction Acts were invalid, the petitioner could not be held, and he was entitled to his discharge. The case excited great interest throughout

* 6th Wallace, 50.

the country. Judge Sharkey and Robert J. Walker, of Mississippi, David Dudley Field and Charles O'Connor, of New York, and Jeremiah S. Black, of Pennsylvania, appeared for the appellant; and Matthew H. Carpenter, of Wisconsin, Lyman Trumbull, of Illinois, and Henry Stanbery, the Attorney-General, appeared for the other side. The hearing of it occupied four days, and seldom has it been my fortune during my judicial life, now (1877) of nearly twenty years, to listen to arguments equal in learning, ability, and eloquence. The whole subject was exhausted. As the arguments were widely published in the public journals, and read throughout the country, they produced a profound effect. The impression was general that the Reconstruction Acts could not be sustained; that they were revolutionary and destructive of a republican form of government in the States, which the Constitution required the Federal government to guarantee. I speak now merely of the general impression. I say nothing of the fact, as the Court never expressed its opinion in judgment. The argument was had on the 2d, 3d, 4th, and 9th of March, 1868, and it ought to have been decided in regular course of proceedings when it was reached on the second subsequent consultation day, the 21st. The Judges had all formed their conclusions, and no excuse was urged that more time was wanted for examination. In the meantime an act was quietly introduced into the House, and passed, repealing so much of the law of February 5th, 1867, as authorized an appeal to the Supreme Court from the judgment of the Circuit Court on writs of *habeas corpus*, or the exercise of jurisdiction on appeals already taken. The President vetoed the bill, but Congress passed it over his veto, and it became a law on the 27th of the month.* Whilst it was pending in Congress the attention of the Judges was called to it, and in consultation, on the 21st they postponed the decision of the case until it should be disposed of. It was then that Mr. Justice Grier wrote the following protest, which he afterwards read in Court:

In re } McArdle. }   PROTEST OF MR. JUSTICE GRIER.

This case was fully argued in the beginning of this month. It is a case that involves the liberty and rights not only of the appellant, but of millions of our fellow-citizens. The country and the parties had a right to expect that it would receive the immediate and solemn attention of this Court. By the postponement of the case we shall subject ourselves, whether justly or unjustly, to the imputation that we have evaded the performance of a duty imposed on us by the Constitution, and waited for legislation to interpose to supersede our action and relieve us from our responsibility. I am not willing to be a partaker either of the eulogy or opprobrium that may follow; and can only say:

     " Pudet hæc opprobria nobis,
        Et dici potuisse; et non potuisse repelli." †

                        R. C. GRIER.

I am of the same opinion with my brother Grier, and unite in his protest.

                        FIELD, J.

After the passage of the repealing act, the case was continued; and at the ensuing term the appeal was dismissed for want of jurisdiction.—(7 Wall., 506.)

The record had been filed early in the term, and, as

---

* 15 Stats. at Large, 44.

† "It fills us with shame that these reproaches can be uttered, and cannot be repelled." The words are found in Ovid's Metamorphoses, Book I., lines 758–9. In some editions the last word is printed *refelli.*

the case involved the liberty of the citizen, it was advanced on the calendar on motion of the appellant. From that time until its final disposition the Judges were subjected to close observation, and most of them to unfriendly comment. Their every action and word were watched and canvassed as though national interests depended upon them. I was myself the subject of a most extraordinary exhibition of feeling on the part of members of the lower house of Congress, the immediate cause of which was a circumstance calculated to provoke merriment. Towards the close of January, 1868, I was invited to a dinner given by Mr. Samuel Ward to the Secretary of the Treasury, Mr. McCullough. It was understood that the dinner was to be one of unusual excellence, and that gentlemen of distinction in Congress would be present. As some of the invited guests desired to go to New York on the same evening, the hour was fixed at five. A distinguished party assembled at that time at the rooms of Welcker, a noted restaurateur in Washington. Our host, Mr. Ward, was a character deserving of special notice. He had been a member of the noted firm of bankers, Prime, Ward & King, of New York ; and afterwards represented our government in Brazil. He was an accomplished linguist, familiar with several languages, ancient and modern. He was a profound mathematician, and had read, without the assistance of Bowditch's translation, Laplace's celebrated work, the "Mécanique Céleste." He passed most of his time during the sessions of Congress in Washington, looking after the interests of bankers and others in New York, as they might be affected by pending legislation. Though called "King of the Lobby," he had little of the character of the lobbyist. He was a gentleman in manners and education, and as such he always drew the company of gentlemen to his entertainments. On the occasion mentioned, some of the brightest spirits of Congress were present. As we took our seats at the table I noticed on the menu a choice collection of wines, Johannisberg among others. The dinner was sumptuous and admirably served. Our host saw that the appropriate wine accompanied the successive courses. As the dinner progressed, and the wine circulated, the wit of the guests sparkled. Story and anecdote, laughter and mirth abounded, and each guest seemed joyous and happy. At about eight song had been added to other manifestations of pleasure. I then concluded that I had better retire. So I said to my host, that if he would excuse me, I would seek the open air ; and I left.

Just at this moment Mr. Rodman M. Price, formerly Governor of New Jersey, made his appearance and exclaimed, " How is this ? I was invited to dinner at eight "—producing his card of invitation. " Look again," said Ward, " and you will see that your eight is a five." And so it was. " But never mind," said Ward ; " the dinner is not over. Judge Field has just left. Take his seat." And so Price took my place. He had been travelling in the Southern States, and had been an observer of the proceedings of various State conventions then in session to frame constitutions under the Reconstruction Acts, which he termed " Congo Conventions." To the amusement of the party he gave an account of some curious scenes he had witnessed in these conventions ; and wound up one or two of his stories by expressing his opinion that the whole reconstruction measures would soon be "smashed up "

and sent to "kingdom come" by the Supreme Court.
The loud mirth and the singing attracted the attention
of news-hunters for the Press—item gatherers in the
rooms below. Unfortunately one of these gentlemen
looked into the banquet-hall just as Price had pre-
dicted the fate of the reconstruction measures at the
hands of the Supreme Court. He instantly smelt
news, and enquired of one of the waiters the name
of the gentleman who had thus proclaimed the action
of the Court. The waiter quietly approached the seat
of the Governor, and, whilst he was looking in another
direction, abstracted the card near his plate which
bore my name. Here was, indeed, a grand item for
a sensational paragraph. Straightway the newsgath-
erer communicated it to a newspaper in Washington,
and it appeared under an editorial notice. It was
also telegraphed to a paper in Baltimore. But it was
too good to be lost in the columns of a newspaper.
Mr. Scofield, a member of Congress from Pennsylvania, on the 30th of January, 1868, asked and obtained unanimous consent of the House to present
the following preamble and resolution :

"Whereas it is editorially stated in the *Evening Express*,
a newspaper published in this city, on the afternoon of Wednesday, January 29, as follows : 'At a private gathering of
gentlemen of both political parties, one of the Justices of the
Supreme Court spoke very freely concerning the reconstruction measures of Congress, and declared in the most positive
terms that all those laws were unconstitutional, and that the
Court would be sure to pronounce them so. Some of his
friends near him suggested that it was quite indiscreet to
speak so positively ; when he at once repeated his views in a
more emphatic manner ; ' and whereas several cases under said
reconstruction measures are now pending in the Supreme
Court : Therefore, be it—

" *Resolved*, That the Committee on the Judiciary be directed to enquire into the truth of the declarations therein contained, and report whether the facts as ascertained constitute such a misdemeanor in office as to require this House to present to the Senate articles of impeachment against said Justice of the Supreme Court; and that the committee have power to send for persons and papers, and have leave to report at any time."

An excited debate at once sprung up in the House, and in the course of it I was stated to be the offending Justice referred to. Thereupon the members for California vouched for my loyalty during the war. Other members wished to know whether an anonymous article in a newspaper was to be considered sufficient evidence to authorize a committee of the House to enquire into the private conversation of members of the Supreme Court. The mover of the resolution, Mr. Scofield, declared that he knew nothing of the truth of the statement in the paper, but deemed it sufficient authority for his action, and moved the previous question on the resolution. Several of the members protested against the resolution, declaring that it was unworthy of the House to direct an investigation into the conduct of a judicial officer upon a mere newspaper statement. But it was of no use. The resolution was adopted by a vote of 97 to 57—34 not voting. Some members, indeed, voted for its passage, stating that it was due to myself that I should be vindicated from the charge implied in the debate ; the force of which reason I have never been able to appreciate.

The resolution was evidently intended to intimidate me, and to act as a warning to all the Judges as to what they might expect if they presumed to question the wisdom or validity of the reconstruction measures of Congress. What little effect it had on me my subsequent course in the McArdle case probably showed to the House. I had only one feeling for the movement—that of profound contempt; and I believe that a similar feeling was entertained by every right-thinking person having any knowledge of the proceeding.

The facts of the case soon became generally known, and created a good deal of merriment in Washington. But all through the country the wildest stories were circulated. Communications of a sensational character relating to the matter were published in the leading journals. Here is one which appeared in the New York *Evening Post* from its correspondent:

" It is the intention of the committee to examine the matter thoroughly, and in view of this a large number of witnesses have been summoned to appear on Friday.

"The friends of Justice Field are endeavoring to hush the matter up, and, if possible, to avert an investigation; but in this they will be disappointed, for the members of the Judiciary Committee express themselves firmly determined to sift the case, and will not hesitate to report articles of impeachment against Justice Field if the statements are proved."

Other papers called for the strictest scrutiny and the presentation of articles of impeachment, representing that I was terribly frightened by the threatened exposure. So for months I was amused reading about my supposed terrible excitement in anticipation of a threatened removal from office. But, as soon as the author of the objectionable observations was ascertained, the ridiculous nature of the subsequent proceedings became manifest. The Chairman of the Judiciary Committee, Mr. Wilson, of Iowa, occupied a seat next to me at Mr. Ward's dinner, and knew, of course, that, so far as I was concerned, the whole story was without foundation. And so he said to his associates on the Judiciary Committee.

Near the close of the session—on June 18th, 1868—
the committee were discharged from the further consideration of the resolution, and it was laid on the
table—a proceeding which was equivalent to its indefinite postponement.

The amusing mistake which gave rise to this episode
in the lower house of Congress would be unworthy of
the notice I have taken of it, except that it illustrates
the virulent and vindictive spirit which occasionally
burst forth for some time after the close of the war,
and which, it is to be greatly regretted, is not yet
wholly extinguished.

THE MOULIN VEXATION.

Soon after my appointment to the Bench of the U. S. Supreme Court, I had a somewhat remarkable experience with a Frenchman by the name of Alfred Moulin. It seems that this man, sometime in the year 1854 had shipped several sacks of onions and potatoes on one of the mail steamers, from San Francisco to Panama. During the voyage the ship's store of fresh provisions ran out, and the captain appropriated the vegetables, and out of this appropriation originated a long and bitter prosecution, or rather persecution, on the part of Moulin, who proved to be not only one of the most malignant, but one of the most persevering and energetic men I have ever known.

Upon the return of the steamer from Panama to San Francisco, Moulin presented himself at the steamship company's office, and complained, as he properly might, of the appropriation of his property, and demanded compensation. The company admitted his claim and expressed a willingness to make him full compensation; but when it came to an adjustment of it, Moulin preferred one so extravagant that it could not be listened to. The property at the very most was not worth more than one or two hundred dollars, but Moulin demanded thousands; and when this was refused, he threatened Messrs. Forbes and Babcock, the agents of the company, with personal violence. These threats he repeated from time to time for two or three years, until at length becoming annoyed and alarmed by his fierce manner, they applied to the police court and had him bound over to keep the peace.

Notwithstanding he was thus put upon his good behavior, Moulin kept continually making his appearance and reiterating his demands at the steamship company's office. Forbes and Babcock repeatedly told him to go to a lawyer and commence suit for his claim; but Moulin refused to do so, saying that he could attend to his own business as well as, and he thought better than, any lawyer. At length, to get rid of further annoyance, they told him he had better go to New York and see Mr. Aspinwall, the owner of the vessel, about the matter; and to enable him to do so, gave him a free ticket over the entire route from San Francisco to that city.

Upon arriving in New York, Moulin presented himself to Mr. Aspinwall and asked that his claim should be allowed. Mr. Aspinwall said that he knew nothing about his claim and that he did not want to be bothered with it. Moulin still insisted, and Mr. Aspinwall told him to go away. Moulin thereupon became excited, said he was determined to be paid, and that he would not be put off. He thereupon commenced a regular system of annoyance. When Mr. Aspinwall started to go home from his office, Moulin walked by his side along the street. When Aspinwall got into an omnibus, Moulin got in also; when Aspinwall got out, Moulin got out too. On the following morning, when Aspinwall left his residence to go to his office, Moulin was on hand, and taking his place, marched along by his side as before. If Aspinwall hailed an omnibus and got in, Moulin got in at the same time. If Aspinwall got out and hailed a private carriage, Moulin got out and hailed another carriage, and ordered the driver to keep close to Mr. Aspinwall's carriage. In fact, wherever Aspinwall went Moulin went also, and it seemed as if nothing could tire him out or deter him from his purpose.

At length Mr. Aspinwall, who had become nervous from the man's actions, exclaimed, " My God, this man is crazy; he will kill me ; " and calling him into the office, asked him what he wanted in thus following and persecuting him. Moulin answered that he wanted pay for his onions and potatoes. Aspinwall replied, " But I don't know anything about your onions and potatoes; how should I? Go back to my agents in California, and they will do what is right. I will direct them to do so." "But," said Moulin, " I have no ticket to go to California ; " and thereupon Aspinwall gave him a free ticket back to San Francisco. Moulin departed, and in due course of time again presented himself to Forbes and Babcock, in San Francisco. At the re-appearance of the man, they were more annoyed than ever ; but finally managed to induce him to commence a suit in the United States District Court. When the case was called, by an understanding between his lawyer and the lawyer of the steamship company, judgment was allowed to be entered in Moulin's favor for four hundred and three dollars and a half, besides costs. The amount thus awarded greatly exceeded the actual value of the onions and potatoes appropriated. It was thought by the defendant that on the payment of so large a sum, the whole matter would be ended. But Moulin was very far from being satisfied. He insisted that the judgment ought to have been for three thousand and nine hundred dollars, besides interest, swelling the amount to over six thousand dollars, and applied to Judge Hoffman of the District Court to set it aside. But as the judgment had been rendered for the full value of the property taken, as admitted by his lawyer, the Judge declined to interfere. This was in 1861.

In 1863 I received my appointment as Judge of the Supreme Court of the United States, and was assigned to the circuit embracing the district of California. Moulin then appealed to the Circuit Court from the judgment in his favor, and at the first term I held, a motion was made to dismiss the appeal. I decided that the appeal was taken too late, and dismissed it. Moulin immediately went to Mr. Gorham, the clerk of the court, for a copy of the papers, insisting that there was something wrong in the decision. Gorham asked him what he meant, and he replied that I had no right to send him out of court, and that there was something wrong in the matter, but he could not tell exactly what it was. At this insinuation, Gorham told him to leave the office, and in such a tone, that he thought proper to go at once and not stand upon the order of his going. The following year, after Mr. Delos Lake had been appointed United States District Attorney, Moulin went to his office to complain of Gorham and myself; but Lake, after listening to his story, told him to go away. Two or three years afterwards he again presented himself to Lake and demanded that Judge Hoffman, Gorham, and myself should be prosecuted. Lake drove him a second time from his office ; and thereupon he went before the United States Grand Jury and complained of all four of us. As the grand jury, after listening to his story for a while, dismissed him in disgust, he presented himself before their suc-

cessors at a subsequent term and complained of
them. From the Federal Court he proceeded to the
State tribunals; and first of all he went to the County
Court of San Francisco with a large bundle of papers
and detailed his grievances against the United States
judges, clerks, district attorney and grand jury.
Judge Stanley, who was then county judge, after
listening to Moulin's story, told the bailiff to take
possession of the papers, and when he had done so,
directed him to put them into the stove, where they
were soon burned to ashes. Moulin then complained
of Stanley. At the same time, one of the city newspapers, the "Evening Bulletin," made some comments upon his ridiculous and absurd proceedings,
and Moulin at once sued the editors. He also
brought suit against the District Judge, District Attorney and his assistant, myself, the clerk of the
court, the counsel against him in the suit with the
steamship company and its agents, and numerous
other parties who had been connected with his various legal movements. And whenever the United
States Grand Jury met, he besieged it with narra-
tives of his imaginary grievances; and, when they
declined to listen to him, he complained of them.
The courts soon became flooded with his voluminous
and accumulated complaints against judges, clerks,
attorneys, jurors, editors, and, in fact, everybody who
had any connection with him, however remote, who
refused to listen to them and accede to his demands.
By this course Moulin attracted a good deal of attention, and an inquiry was suggested and made as
to whether he was *compos mentis.* The parties who
made the inquiry reported that he was not insane,
but was actuated by a fiendish malignity, a love of

notoriety and the expectation of extorting money by blackmail. For years—indeed until September, 1871 —he continued to besiege and annoy the grand juries of the United States courts with his imaginary grievances, until he became an intolerable nuisance. His exemption from punishment had emboldened him to apply to the officers of the court—the judges, clerks, and jurors—the most offensive and insulting language. Papers filled with his billingsgate were scattered all through the rooms of the court, on the desks of the judges, and on the seats of jurors and spectators. It seemed impossible, under existing law, to punish him, for his case did not seem to fall within the class of contempts for which it provided. But in September of 1871 his insolence carried him beyond the limits of impunity. In that month he came to the United States Circuit Court. where Judge Sawyer (then United States Circuit Judge) and myself were sitting, and asked that the grand jury which was about to be discharged might be detained; as he proposed to have us indicted for corruption, and commenced reading a long string of vituperative and incoherent charges of criminal conduct. The proceeding was so outrageous that we could not overlook it. We accordingly adjudged him guilty of contempt, fined him five hundred dollars, and ordered him to be committed to prison until the fine should be paid. Whilst in prison, and not long after his commitment, he was informed that upon making a proper apology for his conduct, he would be discharged. Instead, however, of submitting to this course, he commenced writing abusive articles to the newspapers, and sending petitions to the Legislature charging us with arbitrary and criminal conduct. His articles were of such a character as to create quite erroneous impressions of our action. The newspapers, not waiting to ascertain the facts, at first took sides with him and assailed us. These attacks, of course, had no effect upon the man's case; but, after he had remained in prison for several weeks, on understanding that his health was infirm, and being satisfied that he had been sufficiently punished, we ordered his discharge.

THE HASTINGS MALIGNITY.

WHILST the Moulin matter was in progress, an individual by the name of William Hastings was practising before the United States Courts. He had been, as I am told, a sailor, and was then what is known as a "sailor's lawyer." He was a typical specimen of that species of the profession called, in police court parlance, "shysters." He was always commencing suits for sailors who had wrongs to redress, and particularly for steerage passengers who complained that they had not had sufficient accommodations and proper fare. He generally took their cases on speculation, and succeeded very often in forcing large sums from vessels libelled, as he was generally careful to bring his actions so as to arrest the vessels on the eve of their departure, when the payment of a few hundred dollars was a much cheaper mode of proceeding for the captains than detention even for a few days.

But in one of his suits in the United States District Court, in the year 1869, brought for a steerage passenger against a vessel from Australia, the captain declined to be blackmailed and defended himself. When the matter came on for hearing, Hastings was found to have no cause of action, and the case was thereupon dismissed by Judge Hoffman. Hastings then appealed to the United States Circuit Court, and that court affirmed the judgment of the District Court. This happened as I was about leaving for Europe; and I left supposing that I had heard the last of the case.

During my absence, Hastings moved Judge Hoffman, of the United States District Court, from whose decision the appeal had been taken, to vacate the decision of the United States Circuit Court. This, of course, Judge Hoffman refused. Hastings thereupon made a motion that my decision should be set aside, on the ground that it was rendered by fraud and corruption. When Judge Hoffman became aware of the charges thus made, he was indignant and immediately cited Hastings before him to show cause why he should not be disbarred and punished for contempt. Hastings refused to make any explanation or withdraw his offensive language; and thereupon Judge Hoffman expelled him from the bar and ordered his name to be stricken from the roll of attorneys. I was then absent in Europe, and knew nothing whatever of the proceedings.

About this time Mr. George W. Julian, a member of Congress from Indiana, came to California and pretended to be a great friend of the settlers. He obtained the confidence of that large class of the community, and especially of those who were known as the Suscol claimants. These were the men who, upon the rejection by the United States Supreme Court of the so-called Suscol grant, in Napa and Solano Counties, rushed in and squatted upon the most valuable land in the State. The title to this land had previously been considered as good as any in California; it had been held valid by the local tribunals, and also by the Board of Land Commissioners and by the District Court of the United States. On the strength of these confirmations the land had been divided into farms, upon which, besides cultivated fields, there were numerous orchards, vineyards, gardens, and two cities, each of which had been the capital of the State. The farms and city lots had been sold, in good faith, to purchasers at full value. But when the question came before the United States Supreme Court, and it appeared that the grant had been made to General Vallejo, in consideration of military services, and for moneys advanced to the Mexican government, and not for colonization purposes, it was held that there was no authority under the Mexican laws for such a disposition of the public domain, and that the grant was, therefore, invalid. At the same time Judge Grier filed a dissenting opinion, in which he expressed a hope that Congress would not allow those who had purchased in good faith from Vallejo, and expended their money in improving the land, to be deprived of it. Congress at once acted upon the suggestion thus made and passed an act allowing the grantees of Vallejo to purchase the lands occupied by them at a specified sum per acre. Mr. John B. Frisbie, Vallejo's son-in-law, who had bought and sold large quantities, took immediate steps to secure himself and his grantees by purchasing the lands and obtaining patents for them. In the meanwhile the squatters had located themselves all over the property; most of them placing small shanties on the land in the nighttime, near the houses, gardens, and vineyards, and on cultivated fields of the Vallejo grantees. They then filed claims in the Land Office as pre-emptioners, under the general land laws of the United States, and insisted that, as their settlements were previous to the act of Congress, their rights to the land were secure. In this view Julian, when he came to California, encouraged them, and, as was generally reported and believed, in consideration of a portion of

the land to be given to him in case of success, undertook to defend their possessions.*

When Frisbie applied, under the provisions of the
act of Congress, for a patent to the land, a man named
Whitney, one of the squatters, protested against its
issue, on the ground that under the pre-emption laws
he, Whitney, having settled upon the land, had acquired a vested right, of which Congress could not
deprive him. But the Land Department took a different view of the matter and issued the patent to Frisbie. Whitney thereupon commenced a suit against
Frisbie in the Supreme Court of the District of Columbia to have him declared a trustee of the land thus
patented, and to compel him, as such trustee, to execute a conveyance to the complainant. The Supreme
Court of the District of Columbia decided the case in
favor of Whitney, and ordered Frisbie to execute a
conveyance; but on appeal to the Supreme Court the
decision was reversed; and it was held that a pre-
emptioner did not acquire any vested right as against
the United States by making his settlement, nor until he had complied with all the requirements of the
law, including the payment of the purchase-money;
and that until then Congress could reserve the land
from settlement, appropriate it to the uses of the government, or make any other disposition thereof which
it pleased. The court, therefore, adjudged that the
Suscol act was valid, that the purchasers from Vallejo
had the first right of entry, and that Frisbie was accordingly the owner of the land purchased by him.
Soon after the decision was rendered Julian rose in
his seat in the House of Representatives and de-

---

* See Exhibit L, in Appendix.

nounced it as a second Dred Scott decision, and applied to the members of the court remarks that were
anything but complimentary. It so happened that
previous to this decision a similar suit had been decided in favor of Frisbie by the Supreme Court of California, in which a very able and elaborate opinion was
rendered by the Chief Justice. I did not see the
opinion until long after it was delivered, and had nothing whatever to do with it; but in some way or other,
utterly inexplicable to me, it was rumored that I had
been consulted by the Chief Justice with respect to
that case, and that the decision had been made through
my instrumentality. With this absurd rumor Hastings, after he had been disbarred by Judge Hoffman,
went on to Washington. There he joined Julian;
and after concocting a long series of charges against
Judge Hoffman and myself, he placed them in Julian's
hands, who took charge of them with alacrity. The
two worthies were now to have their vengeance—
Hastings for his supposed personal grievances and
Julian for the Suscol decision, which injured his
pocket.

These charges on being signed by Hastings were
presented to Congress by Julian; and at his request
they were referred to the Judiciary Committee. That
committee investigated them, considered the whole
affair a farce, and paid no further attention to it. But
the next year Mr. Holman, of Indiana, who succeeded
Julian, the latter having failed of a re-election, re-
introduced Hastings' memorial at Julian's request
and had it referred to the Judiciary Committee, with
express instructions to report upon it. Hastings
appeared for the second time before that committee
and presented a long array of denunciatory statements,

in which Judge Hoffman, myself, and others were charged with all sorts of misdemeanors. The committee permitted him to go to any length he pleased, untrammelled by any rules of evidence; and he availed himself of the license to the fullest extent. There was hardly an angry word that had been spoken by a disappointed or malicious litigant against whom we had ever decided, that Hastings did not rake up and reproduce; and there was hardly an epithet or a term of vilification which he did not in some manner or other manage to lug into his wholesale charges. As a specimen of his incoherent and wild ravings, he charged that "the affairs of the federal courts for the District of California were managed principally in the interests of foreign capitalists and their co-conspirators, and that the judges thereof appeared to be under the control of said foreign capitalists, and that the said courts and the process thereof were being used or abused to deprive the government of the United States and the citizens thereof of the property that legally and equitably belonged to them respectively, and to transfer the same, in violation of law and through a perversion of public justice, to said foreign capitalists and their confederates and co-conspirators, and that nearly the whole of the sovereign powers of the State were under the control and management of said foreign capitalists and their confederates and co-conspirators;" and he alleged that he "was aware of the existence in the United States of a well-organized, oath-bound band of confederated public officials who are in league with the subjects of foreign powers, and who conspire against the peace, prosperity, and best interests of the United States, and who prey upon and plunder the government of

the United States and the city and county governments thereof, and also upon private citizens, and
who now are carrying into practice gigantic schemes
of plunder through fraud, usurpation, and other
villainy, in order to enrich themselves, bankrupt the
nation, and destroy our government, and that their
power is so great that they can and do obstruct the
administration of public justice, corrupt its fountains,
and paralyze to some extent the sovereign powers of
the government of the United States and the people thereof." The Judiciary Committee after having
patiently listened to this rigmarole, absurd and
ludicrous as it was, unanimously reported that Hastings' memorial should be laid upon the table and the
committee discharged from any further consideration
of the subject. The House adopted the report, and,
so far as Congress was concerned, there the matter
dropped. But in the meanwhile it had been telegraphed all over the country that articles of impeachment were pending against the judges, and sensational
newspaper articles appeared in different parts of the
country. Some expressed regret that the conduct of
the judges had been of a character to necessitate such
proceedings. Others said it was not to be wondered
at that the judicial ermine should be soiled in a country of such loose morals as California. Still others
thought it no more than proper to impeach a few of
the judges, in order to teach the remainder of them
a salutary lesson. These articles were paraded in
large type and with the most sensational headings.

When the action of the House on the memorial was
announced, Hastings and Julian became furious. It
then appeared that the only charge which had made
any impression upon the minds of the committee was

that relating to Moulin, the Frenchman. Three, indeed, of the members, (Messrs. Voorhees, of Indiana, Potter, of New York, and Peters, of Maine,) said it was a shame and disgrace that such ridiculous and monstrous twaddle should be listened to for a moment; but a majority considered it their duty, under the order of reference, to hear the matter patiently. They had, therefore, allowed Hastings the widest latitude and listened to everything that his malice could invent.

As a comical conclusion to these extraordinary proceedings, Hastings commenced a suit in the U. S. Circuit Court for the State of New York against the Judiciary Committee for dismissing his memorial. Being a non-resident he was required by that court to give security for costs, and as that was not given the action was dismissed. This result was so distasteful to him that he presented a petition to the Chief Justice of the U. S. Supreme Court, stating that Judge Hunt had too much to do with churches, banks, and rings, and asking that some other judge might be appointed to hold the court. The petition was regarded as unique in its character, and caused a great deal of merriment. But the Chief Justice sent it back, with an answer that he had no jurisdiction of the matter. After this Hastings took up his residence in New York, and at different times worried the judges there by suits against them—Judge Blatchford, among others—generally charging in his peculiar way a conspiracy between them and others to injure him and the rest of mankind.

The above was written upon my dictation in the summer of 1877. In November of that year Hastings again appeared at Washington and applied to a Senator to move his admission to the Supreme Court. The Senator inquired if he was acquainted with any of the Judges, and was informed in reply of that gentleman's proceedings against myself; whereupon the Senator declined to make the motion. Hastings then presented to the House of Representatives a petition to be relieved from his allegiance as a citizen of the United States. As illustrative of the demented character of the man's brain, some portions of the petition are given. After setting forth his admission to the Supreme Court of California as an attorney and counsellor-at-law, and his taking the oath then required, he proceeded to state that on the 6th of November, 1877, he entered the chamber of the Supreme Court of the United States to apply for admission as an attorney and counsellor of that court; that he was introduced by a friend to a Senator, with a request that the Senator would move his admission; that the Senator asked him if he knew a certain Justice of the Supreme Court, and upon being informed that he did, and that his relations with said Justice were not friendly, as he had endeavored to get him impeached, and that the damaging evidence he produced against such Justice had been secreted and covered up by the Judiciary Committee of the House, whom he had accordingly sued, the petition continued as follows: "Whereupon said Senator replied, I have a cause to argue as counsel before this court this morning, and I would, therefore, prefer not to move your admission. Said Senator then and there arose and took his seat in front of the bench of said court; and your petitioner remained in said U. S. Supreme Court until one application for admission was made and granted on motion of one S. P. Nash, of Tweed-Sweeney Ring settlement fame [thereby demonstrating poetic injustice], and until the Chief Justice of the United States—shadow not shade of Selden—called the first case on the docket for that day, and a moment or two after the argument of said cause commenced, your petitioner arose and left the court-room of said United States Supreme Court, (to which the genius of a Marshall and a Story has bid a long farewell,) and as your petitioner journeyed towards his hotel, your petitioner soliloquized thus: 'Senator W—— is evidently afraid of Justice ——, with whom I have had a difficulty, and he possesses neither the manly independence of a freeman, nor moral nor physical courage, and he is, therefore, an improper person (possibly infamous) for such a high and responsible position, and my rights as a citizen are not safe in the keeping of such a poltroon and conniving attorney, and he is probably disqualified to hold the high and responsible office of Senator of the United States—that he improperly accepts fees from clients, possibly in part for the influence which his exalted position as Senator gives him as counsel for parties having cases before the U. S. Supreme Court, and which practice is wholly inconsistent with the faithful, impartial performance of his sworn duty as such Senator ; and by thus accepting fees he has placed himself in a position where his personal interests conflict with the obligations of his oath of office ; while the Justices of the Supreme Court are, I conceive, derelict in the performance of their sworn duty, for permitting such practices to be inaugurated and continued.'

"Cowardice taints the character with moral turpitude; and I believe the facts related above show that said Senator is a coward; at all events he lacks moral courage, and is afraid of the Justices of the United States Supreme Court, whose judge the Senator-attorney of the court becomes in case of trial of any of said Justices by impeachment: surely this is one unclean body incestuously holding illicit commerce with another unclean body, and both become interchangeably soiled, and too impure to touch the spotless robes of the judicial ermine; still, as this government has ceased to be a government of law and justice, and has become a foul and unclean machine of corrupt compromises, carried on by colluding and conniving shyster bartering attorneys, the practice of said Supreme Court of the United States, above referred to, is strictly in accord therewith."

The petition continued in a similar strain, and wound up by asking the passage of a concurrent resolution of the Houses releasing him from his allegiance to the United States!

APPENDIX.

EXHIBIT A.

[From the New York *Evening Post* of November 13th, 1849.]

Among the passengers leaving in the Crescent City to-day is Stephen J. Field, Esq., of this city, brother and late law-partner of D. D. Field, Esq., one of the Commissioners of the Code of Practice.

Mr. Field is on his way to San Francisco, where he proposes to practise his profession, and take up his future residence. If he should realize either the hopes or the expectations of the numerous friends he leaves behind, he will achieve an early and desirable distinction in the promising land of his adoption.

EXHIBIT B.

Mr. William H. Parks, of Marysville, has always asserted that my election as Alcalde was owing to a wager for a dinner made by him with a friend. He was at the time engaged in transporting goods to the mines from the landing at Nye's Ranch on the Yuba River, called Yubaville, and arriving at the latter place whilst the election was going on he made the wager that I would be elected, and voted all his teamsters, numbering eleven, for me. As I had a majority of only nine, he claims that he had the honor of giving me my first office. The claim must be allowed, unless the person with whom he wagered offset this number, or at least some of the teamsters, by votes for my opponent.

After the election Mr. Parks introduced himself to me, and from that time to this he has been a warm and steadfast friend. He afterwards settled in Sutter County, but now resides in Marysville. He has amassed a handsome fortune, and takes an interest in all public affairs. He has represented his county

as a Senator in the Legislature of the State. He is a gentleman of high character and has the confidence and respect of
the community.

My opponent for the office of Alcalde was Mr. C. B. Dodson,
from Illinois. I afterwards met him only once or twice in
California, and knew little of his history. But when I was a
member of the Electoral Commission, in February of this year
(1877), a copy of a paper published in Geneva, Illinois—the
Republican, of the 10th of that month—was sent to me, containing the following account of him, from which it appears
that he, too, has lived a life of strange vicissitudes and stirring
adventure :

REMINISCENCES.

'An account of the various positions of the selected arbitrators says that in 1850 Judge Field was elected Alcalde and Recorder of Marysville, California. Judge Field's competitor for
the position was our townsman, Capt. C. B. Dodson, who was
defeated by nine votes. As there is no doubt that had the
Captain gained the position of Alcalde he would have risen as
his competitor did, to various judicial positions, and finally to
the arbitrator's seat, these nine votes must be considered as
the only reasons why Geneva does not number one of her citizens among the arbitrators for the highest of the world's official
positions. Among the votes polled for our friend Dodson on
that occasion was that of Macaulay, one of the family of the
famous historian of England's greatest days and proudest
times.

The Captain has been a natural and inveterate pioneer, and
few citizens of the State have figured more prominently or
proudly in its early annals. In 1834, forty-three years ago,
Mr. Dodson came to dispute with the aboriginal Pottawatomies
the possession of the Fox River valley. White faces were rare
in those days, and scarcely a squatter's cabin rose among the
Indian lodges. The Captain built the first saw-mill on the
river, and he and Col. Lyon were the hardy spirits about whom
the early settlers clustered for encouragement and advice.

In 1837 he was employed by the government to superintend
the removal of the Indians to Council Bluffs and Kansas, and
their successful emigration, as well as their uniform good will

toward the whites prior to their removal, were largely due to his sagacity and influence among them.

When Capt. Sutter first found the yellow gold gleaming in the dirt of his mill-race, and all the world joined in a mad rush to the mines, the venturesome spirit of Capt. Dodson led him to press forward with the first, and he was a "forty-niner," that pride of the old Californians. In that surging crowd of wild adventurers from the ends of the earth, the Captain was, as he has been among the early pioneers of Illinois, a directing and controlling spirit. Though he failed in his judicial aspirations for Alcalde, and Judge Field succeeded, yet his continued exertions and marked influence caused him to leave a name richly associated with all the early history of Marysville and vicinity.

When the war broke out, Mr. Dodson was among the very first to proffer his services, and he raised the first company of cavalry which went to the front from Kane County.

The Captain is not an old man yet in health and vigor, although an "old settler" in varied and numerous experiences. His name is marked in unmistakable characters on every prominent event of the early settlement of Northern Illinois, and blended and associated with all the pioneer way-marks of California. A friend and companion of all the great Illinoians of the generation which is now passing into old age, he has not yet ceased to be a spirit actively mingling in all the affairs of the present times. But we only started to tell of his contest with Field, not to write an eulogium on the Captain, for here where he is known it is better pronounced in his record, which lies in the memories of his friends.

EXHIBIT C.

Oath of Office as Alcalde.

STATE OF CALIFORNIA, } *ss.*
SACRAMENTO DISTRICT. }

SACRAMENTO CITY, *January 22d*, 1850.

Personally appeared before me Stephen J. Field, First Alcalde of Yubaville, in the District of Sacramento, and made oath that he would discharge the duties of the office of First Alcalde as aforesaid with faithfulness and fidelity to the best of his ability, and that he would support the Constitution of the United States and the constitution of the State of California.

R. A. WILSON,
Judge of 1st Instance, Sacramento District.

EXHIBIT D.

The following are the orders of the District Court mentioned in the Narrative.

Order imprisoning and fining Mr. Field for alleged contempt of court.

DISTRICT COURT, ⎫
EIGHTH JUDICIAL DISTRICT, ⎬
COUNTY OF YUBA. ⎭

At a term of said District Court held at Marysville, county of Yuba, on the 7th of June, 1850. present, Hon. Wm. R. Turner, Judge, the following proceeding was had :

Ordered, That Stephen J. Field be imprisoned forty-eight hours and fined five hundred dollars for contempt of court.

Order expelling Messrs. Field, Goodwin, and Mulford from the bar.

DISTRICT COURT, ⎫
EIGHTH JUDICIAL DISTRICT, ⎬
COUNTY OF YUBA. ⎭

At a term of said court held at Marysville, on the 10th of June, 1850, present, Hon. William R. Turner, Judge, the following proceeding was had :

Whereas, Messrs. Field, Goodwin, and Mulford, having set at defiance the authority of this court, and having vilified the court and denounced its proceedings, the said Field, Goodwin, and Mulford are hereby, by order of the court, expelled from the bar of the same.

Order imprisoning and fining Judge Haun for releasing Mr.
Field from imprisonment upon a writ of habeas corpus, and
directing that the order to imprison Mr. Field be enforced.

DISTRICT COURT,   }
EIGHTH JUDICIAL DISTRICT, }
COUNTY OF YUBA.   }

At a term of said District Court held at Marysville, county of Yuba, on the 10th of June, 1850, present, Hon. Wm. R. Turner, Judge, the following proceeding was had :

Whereas, Judge Haun having, in defiance of the authority of this court, and in violation of the law, obstructed and prevented the execution of an order of this court to imprison Mr. Field for a contempt offered to the court while in session, by releasing the said Field from the custody of the sheriff ; the said Haun is hereby sentenced to forty-eight hours' imprisonment and to pay a fine of fifty dollars.

The sheriff will enforce the order of the court to imprison Mr. Field for forty-eight hours.

EXHIBIT E.

Record of Proceedings in the Court of Sessions, mentioned in the
Narrative.

Court of Sessions of Yuba County.

Met at Marysville, June 10th, A. D. 1850, at 10 o'clock A. M., and was duly opened by R. B. Buchanan, sheriff of the county.

Present, Hon. H. P. Haun, County Judge, F. W. Barnard, Associate Justice.

IN THE MATTER OF }
STEPHEN J. FIELD. } Application for Habeas Corpus.

On the reading of the petition of the applicant, duly authenticated by his oath, it is ordered that the prayer of the petitioner be granted, and that R. B. Buchanan, sheriff of Yuba County, or any person acting under him and having said Field in custody, bring the said Field into court forthwith, to be dealt with according to law.

In pursuance of the above order, the said Field came into court, and proceeded to address the court on the matter touching the cause of his confinement, and while making his remarks, and previous to the close thereof, and while the court was in session, R. B. Buchanan, sheriff of Yuba County, at the head of fifty men, entered the court, and stated that he came there for the purpose and with the intent to seize H. P. Haun, County Judge as aforesaid, and place him in close confinement, under and by virtue of a certain order or decree made by one William R. Turner, Judge of the Eighth Judicial District of the State of California.

The court informed the said Sheriff Buchanan that it was holding its regular term, and that order must be preserved while it was in session. The said Sheriff Buchanan then left the court, whereupon the business before the court was again resumed.

At the expiration of some five minutes, the said R. B. Buchanan, as aforesaid, re-entered the court, and stated that the said H. P. Haun, County Judge as aforesaid, must leave the court and go with him, as he was peremptorily ordered by William R. Turner, the Judge as aforesaid, to arrest the said H. P. Haun and keep him in close confinement for the space of forty-eight hours.

R. B. Buchanan was here notified that he was violating the laws of the land, and that he would be fined if he persisted in disturbing the session of the court. The reply of said Buchanan was " that he could not be trifled with," and immediately seized the said H. P. Haun, County Judge as aforesaid, by the arm, and attempted to drag him from the room while the court was in session. Whereupon a fine of two hundred dollars was then and there imposed upon the said R. B. Buchanan for a contempt of court.

The said R. B. Buchanan then and there called upon the fifty persons ordered out by him as his posse to take hold of the said H. P. Haun, and take him from the court. But the persons in attendance, conceiving the order to arrest the Hon. H. P. Haun to be illegal and unjustifiable, refused to assist the sheriff in the execution of his illegal order. The sheriff then retired, and the court was then adjourned to 3 o'clock P. M.

Court met pursuant to adjournment. Court adjourned to to-morrow morning at 9 o'clock.

I hereby certify the above to be a true transcript of the

record of the proceedings of the Court of Sessions on the 10th day of June, A. D. 1850. Witness E. D. Wheeler, clerk of the Court of Sessions of Yuba County, California, with the seal of the court affixed, this 26th day of December, A. D. 1850.

[L. S.]   E. D. WHEELER, *Clerk.*

The records of the District Court show the following entry made the same day, June 10, 1850 :

" A communication was received from H. P. Haun, stating ' that if he was guilty of obstructing the order of the court in releasing Field, he did it ignorantly, not intending any contempt by so doing.' Whereupon the court ordered that H. P. Haun be released from confinement, and his fine be remitted."

The following is taken from the deposition of Mr. Wheeler, the clerk of the court, before the committee of the Assembly to whom was referred the petition of citizens of Yuba County for the impeachment of Judge Turner :

MARCH 26th, 1851.

E. D. Wheeler,* being duly sworn, says : I reside in Marysville, Yuba County ; I am the county clerk of that county ; I know Wm. R. Turner, judge of the Eighth Judicial District ; I am clerk of his court in and for Yuba County.

Question. Were you in court on the 7th day of June last, when Stephen J. Field was fined by Judge Turner and ordered to be imprisoned ? If so, please to state what took place at that time in court.

Ans. I was in court on the 7th day of June last. A motion was made in a suit (Cameron against Sutter) in which Stephen J. Field was counsel for the defendant, upon which motion a discussion arose among the members of the bar employed in the case.

During the remarks of Mr. Field, Judge Turner said that it was useless to say more, as the mind of the court was made

---

* Mr. Wheeler is at present (1877) District Judge of the Nineteenth District of the State.

up. I think Mr. Field then offered to read from the Statutes,
whereupon Judge Turner ordered him to take his seat, and
that a fine of two hundred dollars be entered up against him,
and that he be imprisoned eight hours or thereabout. Mr.
Field replied, " Very well." Then Judge Turner said, fine him
three hundred dollars and imprison him—I do not remember
the precise time—but think it was twenty-four hours. Mr.
Field made some quiet reply—I think it was " Very well ; "
whereupon the fine was increased to four hundred dollars and
the imprisonment made something longer. I think Mr. Field
said something about his rights at the bar, and I think he
appealed to the members of the bar. Then Judge Turner
became quite furious, and in loud and boisterous language
ordered the fine to be five hundred dollars and the imprisonment to be forty-eight hours, and ordered the sheriff to take
him out of court. He was boisterous, and several times ordered
the sheriff to take him out ; to summon a posse; to summon
the court, and he would turn him out.

Q. Did you see anything disrespectful in the manner, or
hear anything disrespectful in the language of Mr. Field which
occasioned the fine and imprisonment ?

Ans. I did not.

Q. Did Mr. Field, in consequence of the order of Judge
Turner, leave the court-room in company with the deputy
sheriff ?

Ans. He left in company with the deputy sheriff, and I suppose it was in consequence of the order of Judge Turner.

Q. Was the trial of Cameron against Sutter proceeded with
after Mr. Field left ?

Ans. It was.

Q. Who took the place of Mr. Field after he left ?

Ans. John V. Berry, Esq.

Q. Were you in court on the 10th day of June ?

Ans. I was.

Q. Were any members of the bar expelled by Judge Turner
on that day ? And if so, please state who they were and
whether they were in court at the time, and whether or not
the order was made upon a hearing of the parties.

Ans. There were three persons expelled, to wit : S. J. Field,
S. B. Mulford, and J. O. Goodwin. I do not recollect whether

the parties were all in court at the time. I am sure that Mr. Goodwin was in court. There was no hearing had to my knowledge.

Q. After the order imprisoning Mr. Field, on the 7th of June and before the 10th, were any steps taken by Mr. Field to be discharged on a writ of habeas corpus ?

Ans. There were, and Mr. Field was discharged by the Judge of the County of Yuba.

Q. What was done by Judge Turner with Judge Haun, the County Judge, in consequence of his discharging Mr. Field from imprisonment on the writ of habeas corpus ?

Ans. Judge Haun was fined fifty dollars by Judge Turner and ordered to be imprisoned forty-eight hours. This was on the 10th of June, at the same time that the other gentlemen were expelled from the bar.

Q. Did the Court of Sessions of Yuba County hold a session on that day ?

Ans. Yes.

Q. Did you continue in the District Court or did you go to the Court of Sessions ?

Ans. I continued in the District Court.

Q. Who made up the records of the Court of Sessions on that day ?

Ans. F. W. Barnard, one of the associate justices of the court.

Q. Look at this paper and state whether it is a copy of the proceedings of that court on the 10th of June, certified by you as the clerk.

Ans. It is.*

Q. Whilst you were in the District Court on that day did the sheriff of Yuba County give any information to the District Court about the Court of Sessions being in session ?

Ans. He did.

Q. Did Judge Turner give any directions to the sheriff to arrest Judge Haun, notwithstanding he was holding his court ?

Ans. He did, and told the sheriff to put him in irons, if necessary to handcuff him.

Q. Were any directions given about a posse ?

---

* The record of the proceedings is printed above.

Ans. There were. He told the sheriff to summon a posse forthwith and enforce the orders of the court. He addressed two or three professional gamblers present and asked them if they would not join the posse to arrest Judge Haun. Then the excitement became so great that several of the members of the bar requested him to adjourn the court; but before the court adjourned the Judge asked several of the members of the bar to join the posse; but they made excuses, whereupon the court adjourned.

Q. Was the order entered on the records of the District Court expelling Messrs. Field, Goodwin, and Mulford?

Ans. It was.

Q. What day was that order entered?

Ans. On the 10th day of June.

Q. Has that order ever been vacated on the records of the District Court?

Ans. So far as it relates to Mr. Goodwin it has been vacated, but no further.

Q. Has Mr. Field or Mr. Mulford ever been restored to the bar by the District Court since the order of expulsion on the 10th of June?

Ans. No.

EXHIBIT F.

The following is the petition to the Governor mentioned in the Narrative. Of course the Governor possessed no power to suspend a judicial officer from office. But at the time the petition was signed and sent to him the State had not been admitted into the Union, and Congress had not approved of the action of the people in calling a convention and framing a constitution; and it appeared very doubtful whether such approval would be given. There was a general impression that in the meantime the Governor could exercise the power to remove and suspend officers of the State which the former governors under Mexico possessed, or were supposed to possess. The petition, however, is none the less significant, as the expression of the opinions of the people of Marysville upon the conduct of Judge Turner.

To His Excellency Peter H. Burnett, Governor of California.

The undersigned citizens of Marysville, Yuba County, in this State, respectfully request that Your Excellency would suspend William R. Turner, District Judge of the Eighth Judicial District of this State, from his judicial office.

1st. Because the said William R. Turner is grossly incompetent to discharge the duties of a judge, he having exhibited during his judicial career, and particularly during the session of the District Court held at Marysville, in Yuba County, during the present month, ignorance of the most elementary principles of law,—such as to excite the derision of counsel, jurors, witnesses, and persons in attendance upon the court.

2d. Because the said William R. Turner has, during the session of the District Court held at Marysville, exercised the power vested in him as judge, in an arbitrary and tyrannical manner, outraging the rights of counsel, clients, and witnesses.

3d. Because the said William R. Turner has refused to hear counsel on questions of vital importance to the suits of their clients, and in one instance fined and imprisoned counsel for stating in the most respectful manner and in the most respectful language, that he appealed from an order made by him, though such is an acknowledged right of all counsel, and a right given by statute—under pretence that counsel by so doing was guilty of a contempt.

4th. Because the said Wm. R. Turner has trampled upon and spurned with contempt the privilege of the writ of habeas corpus which is guaranteed to all citizens by the Constitution of the United States and by the constitution of the State of California, and fined and imprisoned the Hon. Henry P. Haun, Judge of Yuba County, for the exercise by him of a judicial act in discharging a gentleman from arrest under a writ of habeas corpus.

5th. Because the said William R. Turner, to carry out his arbitrary order to fine and imprison the Hon. Henry P. Haun, Judge of Yuba County, for the exercise of a judicial act, ordered the sheriff of said county with a posse to invade the Court of Sessions of Yuba County while the said court was sitting, and over which the said Haun presided, and to carry off by force the said county judge and put him in close custody.

6th. Because the said William R. Turner ordered the sheriff of Yuba County, with a posse, to force Mr. S. J. Field from the Court of Sessions of said county whilst said Field was before said court on a writ of habeas corpus arguing for his discharge, and the said William R. Turner was informed that the Court of Sessions forbid the sheriff from disturbing the proceedings of the court on the hearing of said writ.

7th. Because the said William R. Turner has, in the exercise of arbitrary power, expelled counsel from the bar for giving their testimony as witnesses on the return of a writ of habeas corpus before the Hon. Henry P. Haun, Judge of the County Court, under pretence that by so doing they were vilifying the court and denouncing its proceedings.

8th. Because the said William R. Turner, during the session of the District Court at Marysville, Yuba County, in the present month, frequently went into Court with revolving pistols upon his person, to the great scandal of the court and of the county.

For the above, and other reasons, your petitioners respectfully request that the said William R. Turner may be suspended from his office, as the further exercise by him of judicial power will destroy all confidence of the community in the administration of justice, and all respect for the tribunals of the country ; and your petitioners will ever pray.

Marysville, June 19th, 1850.

Stephen J. Field, Ira A. Eaton, James S. Green, T. B. Parker, E. W. Judkins, Harrington Osgood, Chas. W. Gleason, Geo. W. Hastat, S. Sartwell, jr., M. S. Ebright, S. C. Stambaugh, P. Steinman, Henry Cuttcher, M. Cunningham, Ed. B. Jefferds, Wm. H. Mitchell, Benj. Barker, H. Cecil & Co., Osbourn & Co., Asa Stearns, John Bennett, jr., J. P. F. Haskell, W. A. Crampton, J. C. Jewett, H. Stenhome, John Parks, Absalom Parks, David Parks, James Imbrie, Alfred Parry, H. C. Ward, Richard McRae, Wm. Johnson, F. Prunean, H. W. Taylor, R. A. Eddy, S. T. Brewster, C. Sala, Dericerpre, M. Donaldson Kinney, R. M. Foltz, Jas. F. Hibbard, Thomas Gaffney, Allen Gries, W. H. Swain, Oben Lacey, E. S. Peck, B. Smith, John Graham, Wm. Kyle, S. C. Tompkins, A. C. Ladd, C. B. Kinnard, Cyrus Crouch, H. H. Welch, Jas. Stuart, Jas. DeBell, Uriah Davis, L. H. Babb & Co., I. B. Purdy, G. Dimon, Henry

J. Williams, D. W. C. Rice, N. Purdy, William K. Coit, James
B. Cushing, Thomas West, S. B. Mulford, J. Ford, Wm. Ford,
Charles A. Van Dorn, Gustavus B. Wright, J. Burlingame, G.
Beaulamy, A. Mace, F. Frossard, C. W. Durkee, John S. Ryder,
Geo. H. Childs, Ezra F. Nye, S. T. Nye, Geo. W. Durkee, John
C. Marks, John L. Carpenter, Leonard Crofford, Robert Lacy,
FrenchPaige, L. A. Allen, James Hughes, J. C. Sargent, Wm. P.
Hoyt, F. L. Reed, J. S. Bell, Henry B. Compton, G. F. Kussel,
Reuben Scott, Warren Drury, Joel F. Whitney, O. C. Gardner,
B. F. Taber, Johnson Thompson, jr., Ganahl & Co., T. W.
Hall, J. Donnel, Wm. Irwin, Wm. W. Nelson, R. H. McCall,
B. G. Bixby, Geo. L. Boswell, Wm. W. Tinker, Robert S.
Baker, N. F. Cooke, Edwards Woodruff, J. N. Briceland, Joseph
F. Emeric, John F. Delong, James Q. Packard, Sibley & Co.,
Boone, Larrow & Co., P. W. Hayes & Co., Geo. C. Gorham,
R. Dunlap, M. Cameron, R. Brown, A. W. Loynes, F. Owradon,
J. W. Turner, P. D. Bailey, James L. Springer, Matthew S.
Smith, Wm. Fulton, John George Smith, Isaiah Porter, Wm.
R. Taylor, John McClellan, R. H. Macy, Charles B. Mitchell,
Thomas R. Anthony, Geo. W. Webster, Daniel M. Shepherd,
M. J. Eavyerberth, Lewis A. Gosey, John Rueyer, Tehan Van
De Wett, Wm. Cassede, G. P. Russell, S. G. Haywood, G. W.
Hopkins, Wm. E. Wightman, E. Ferris, Samuel R. St. John,
A. O. Garrett, D. C. Benham.

EXHIBIT G.

*Letter of Mr. Eaton, by whom the message mentioned in the
Narrative was sent to Judge Turner.*

WEDNESDAY AFTERNOON, *Aug.* 7, 50.

DEAR JUDGE : I have given your message to Turner. He
does not like it much and flared up considerably when I told
him. But it was no use. I have made him understand that
you do not want any personal difficulty with him, but that you
are ready for him, and if he attacks you he will get badly hurt.

I will see you soon and explain. Give him ——. You can always count on me.

Yours truly,

IRA A. EATON.

The Narrative of Reminiscences was sent to a friend in San Francisco, soon after it was printed, and was shown to Gen. A. M. Winn of that city. He was in Marysville in 1850 and also gave Judge Turner to understand the line of conduct I intended to pursue. The following letter has since been received from him.

SAN FRANCISCO, May 10th, '80.

FRIEND FIELD : In looking over the Early Reminiscences of California I was pleased with the faithful recital of your trouble with Judge Turner at Marysville in 1850. Being there about that time I recollect to have met with Judge Turner and found him in a fighting rage, making threats of what he would do on meeting you. Although I have not an exalted opinion of men's courage, when they talk so much about it, I thought he might put his threats into execution and warned you of approaching danger.

The course you pursued was generally approved, and public opinion culminated in your favor. You made many warm friends, though Turner and his friends were the more enraged in consequence of that fact.

With great respect, I am, as ever, your friend,

A. M. WINN.

Hon. STEPHEN J. FIELD,
Washington, D. C.

EXHIBIT H, No. I.*

After the Narrative of Reminiscences was written, the Proceedings of the Assembly of California of 1851, on the petition of citizens of Yuba and Nevada Counties for the impeachment

---

* By mistake, there are two Exhibits H ; they are, therefore, marked No. I, and No. II.

of Judge Turner, were published. Annexed to them was a statement by the editor of the causes of the indefinite postponement of the matter. They are there stated to be : 1st, That it was supposed that I had acquiesced in such a disposition of the case, because by the act concerning the courts of justice and judicial officers, Turner had been sent to the northern portion of the State, where he could do no harm ; 2d, That the legislature did not wish to extend the session for the period which the trial of an impeachment would require: and 3d, That the whole matter had become extremely distasteful to me.

A copy of this statement with the record of the proceedings was sent to the surviving members of the seven, mentioned in the Narrative, who voted for the indefinite postponement of the matter ; and they wrote the replies which are given below as part of this exhibit. They are preceded by a letter from a member, written soon after the vote was taken.

Letter of Mr. Bennett.

HOUSE OF ASSEMBLY,
SAN JOSE, *April* 23d, 1851.

Hon. STEPHEN J. FIELD.

DR. SIR : I take pleasure in adopting this form to explain to you my vote upon the question put to the House in the final disposition of the case for the impeachment of Judge Turner.

Had the House been called for a direct vote upon the question of impeachment, I should certainly have voted for the impeachment ; but finding that some of the members thought the wishes of the citizens of Yuba County had been accomplished by the removal of Judge Turner from your district, and on that account would vote against the impeachment, I thought there was less injustice in postponing the whole matter indefinitely, than in coming to a direct vote. I will also say that it was understood by many members that you would be satisfied with such a disposition.

I am very truly your friend,

F. C. BENNETT.

To the Hon. STEPHEN J. FIELD, *San Jose.*

Letter of Mr. Merritt.

SALT LAKE CITY, UTAH, *May 4th*, 1879.

MY DEAR JUDGE :

Your letter of the 27th of April reached me day before yesterday, and the copy of the proceedings in the matter of the
impeachment of W. R. Turner, on yesterday. The editorial
comments on the case, so far as I am concerned, are exactly
correct. I remember distinctly having voted for the indefinite
postponement of the charges against Turner on the distinct
understanding that you consented to it, or at least acquiesced,
for the reasons :

1st, That Turner, by the passage of the bill concerning
courts of justice, etc., had been sent to a district where he
could do no harm and was out of the way ; 2d, That you did
not desire to extend the session of the Legislature ; and, 3d,
That the whole matter was extremely distasteful and disagree-
able to you. I remember further very distinctly, even after
this great lapse of time, that I was very much astonished when
you told me that I had voted under a misapprehension as to
your views and wishes. It is very certain that Turner would
have been impeached had not a false report, as to your views
and wishes on the subject, been industriously circulated among
the members of the Assembly a short time before the vote was
taken. That report alone saved Turner from impeachment.

Very truly your friend,

SAML. A. MERRITT.

Hon. S. J. FIELD, *Sup. Ct. U. S.*

Letter of Mr. McCorkle.

WASHINGTON CITY, D. C., *May 8th*, 1879.

Hon. S. J. FIELD.

MY DEAR SIR : I have received your note and the printed
record of the " Proceedings of the Assembly of the State of
California of 1851, on the petition of the citizens of Yuba and
Nevada Counties for the impeachment of Wm. R. Turner,
Judge of the Eighth Judicial District of California." The

simple reading of the record recalls vividly to my mind all of the circumstances of the case and enables me to answer your inquiry in regard to the indefinite postponement of the motion to impeach Judge Turner.

A bill introduced by yourself, increasing and changing the numbers of the judicial districts of the State, had passed the Legislature, and became a law some weeks before the motion to impeach Judge Turner was called up. By this law Judge Turner was banished to the Klamath—a region inhabited almost exclusively by savage red-skins, the elk, and grizzly bear, and as Turner was supposed by anthropologists to be a resultant of that mysterious law of generation denominated atavism or reversionary heredity, and bore the impression, in not only the bodily form, but the instincts, passions, manners, and habits of the " cave dwellers " of the rough-stone age, there appeared to be a fitness and adaptation in the new locality and its surroundings to the man, which was at once appreciated and approved by all persons familiar with him, and his conduct and behavior, both on and off the bench.

Under these circumstances the report obtained general credence, that you and your constituents were satisfied with the removal of Judge Turner from the bench of the Eighth Judicial District ; and I have no doubt influenced all or nearly all who voted to indefinitely postpone his impeachment.

As for myself, having a personal knowledge of the truth of the charges made against Judge Turner by the citizens of Yuba and Nevada Counties, I am free to say that no consideration other than that you and your constituents were satisfied with Judge Turner's removal from the Eighth Judicial District, could have induced me to cast my vote for the indefinite postponement of Judge Turner's impeachment.

Do you realize the fact, my dear Judge, that more than a quarter of a century has elapsed since these events transpired ? Though my respect for you as a man, and my admiration for you as a jurist, have increased since we were actors in these scenes ; yet I am frank enough to say to you, that if I had to play my part again, with my increased experience, I would not vote to indefinitely postpone the impeachment of a judge whom I knew to be guilty of the charges made against Judge Turner by yourself and others, *even though the report were true* that you and your constituents were satisfied with his simple removal from your judicial district.

Respectfully and truly yours, &c.,

Jos. W. McCorkle.

Letter of Mr. Bradford.

Springfield, Ill., *May 8th*, 1879.

Judge Field.

My Dear Friend : Yours of the 27th April should have been answered ere this, but before doing so I desired to get all the reminders that I could. I looked carefully over the journal. All that I had recollected in the whole matter was that I had an intense feeling in favor of sustaining your position, and when you informed me that I had voted to dismiss the proceedings I was profoundly astonished. I thought you must be mistaken until I saw the journal. . . . . Some very satisfactory assurance must have been given me that such vote would be satisfactory to you and I only wonder that I did not have the assurance verified. . . . I assume that the Editor is correct in the explanation as given.

Very truly,

J. S. Bradford.

Letter of Mr. Carr.

San Francisco, *May 15th*, 1879.

My Dear Judge : I have received your letter and a printed copy of the record of the proceedings of the Assembly of California of 1851, in the matter of the impeachment of William R. Turner, Judge of the then Eighth Judicial District of the State. In reply, I have to say, that the statement of the Editor as to the vote on the motion to indefinitely postpone the proceedings is correct so far as I am concerned.

It was distinctly understood by me, and to my knowledge by other members of the Assembly, that you had consented to such postponement, it being explained that the postponement was not to be taken as an approval of the Judge's conduct.

On no other ground could the motion have been carried. If the vote had been taken on the charges made, articles of impeachment against the Judge would undoubtedly have been ordered.

Your consent to the postponement was understood to have been given, because of the change in the judicial districts by an act introduced into the Assembly by yourself, under which Judge Turner was sent to a district in the northern part of the State, where there was at the time scarcely any legal business, and which was removed to a great distance from the district in which you resided, and because of the general desire manifested by others to bring the session of the Legislature to a speedy close. The impeachment of the Judge would have necessitated a great prolongation of the session.

No member of the Assembly justified or excused the atrocious and tyrannical conduct of the Judge towards yourself and others.

I am, very truly, yours,

JESSE D. CARR.

Hon. STEPHEN J. FIELD.

EXHIBIT H, No. II.

Letter of Judge Gordon N. Mott giving the particulars of the difficulty with Judge Barbour.

SAN FRANCISCO, *Apr. 28th*, 1876.

Hon. STEPHEN J. FIELD.

DEAR SIR: Your letter of the eleventh instant, in which you requested me to give you, in writing, an account of the affair between yourself and Judge W. T. Barbour, at Marysville in 1853, was duly received.

The facts in relation to that unpleasant affair are as fresh in my memory as if they had happened yesterday; and I give them to you the more willingly for the reason that you incurred the spite and malice of Judge Barbour, by acts of personal and professional kindness to me, which gave him no just or reasonable cause of offence; and though the following statement of facts will place the character of Judge Barbour, now deceased, in a very bad and even ludicrous light, the events in mind are nevertheless a part of the history of our early days in California, and I see no impropriety in complying with your request. The facts are as follows: You and I were walking together along D street in the city of Marysville, when we met Judge Barbour, who, after using some offensive and insolent remarks gave you a verbal challenge to meet him in the way resorted to by gentlemen for the settlement of their personal difficulties. You accepted the challenge instantly, and referred him to me, as your friend, who would act for you in settling the preliminaries of a hostile meeting. In half an hour I was called upon by Hon. Chas. S. Fairfax as the friend of Judge Barbour. He said Judge Barbour had told him that Judge Field had challenged him to mortal combat, and requested him to meet me for the purpose of arranging the terms of the meeting between them. I told Mr. Fairfax at once that such was not my understanding of the matter ; that I was present when the challenge was given by Judge Barbour and accepted by Judge Field. After further consultation with you we agreed that it was better for you to accept the false position in which Judge Barbour seemed determined to place you, and '' to fight it out on that line,'' than longer submit to the insolence and persecution of a bitter and unscrupulous adversary. Mr. Fairfax then claimed, in behalf of Judge Barbour, that, as he was the party challenged, he had the right to the choice of weapons, and the time, place, and manner of the combat ; to which I assented. He then stated that Judge Barbour proposed that the meeting should take place that evening in a room twenty feet square ; that each party was to be armed with a Colt's navy revolver and a *Bowie-knife ;* that they should be stationed at opposite sides of the room, and should fire at the word, and advance at pleasure, and finish the conflict with the knives. I told Mr. Fairfax that the terms proposed by his principal were unusual and inconsistent with the '' code,'' and that I could not consent to them or countenance a conflict so unprecedented and barbarous. Mr. Fairfax agreed with me that Judge Barbour had no right to insist upon the terms proposed, and said that he would consult with him and get him to modify his proposition. Upon doing so he soon returned, and stated that Judge Barbour insisted upon the terms he had proposed as his ultimatum, and requested me to go with him and call on Judge Barbour, which I did. I had now come to the conclusion that Barbour was playing the role of the bravo and bully, and that he did not intend to fight, and resolved on the course that I would pursue with him. Mr. Fairfax and myself then called on Judge Barbour, and I repeated what I had said to Mr. Fairfax, adding that it would be shameful for two gentlemen, occupying such positions as they in society, to fall upon each other with knives like butchers or savages, and requesting him to dispense with the knives, which he still refused to do. I then looked him straight in the eye and said, well, sir, if you insist upon those terms we shall accept. I saw his countenance change instantly. '' His coward lips did from their color fly ; '' and he finally stammered out that he would "waive the knife." Without consulting you, I had determined that if Barbour still insisted upon a conflict with Bowie-knives I would take your place, believing that he would not have any advantage over me in any fight he could make ; and knowing, moreover, that you had involved yourself in the difficulty on my account, I thought it only just for me to do so. But it was demonstrated in the sequel that Barbour was playing the game of bluff, and that he did not intend to fight from the start. It was finally settled, however, that the combat should take place as first proposed, except that pistols only were to be used. Mr. Fairfax and myself then commenced looking about for a room ; but in the meantime the affair had been noised about town and we found it impossible to get one. Mr. Fairfax then, after consulting Judge Barbour, proposed that the meeting should take place the next morning in Sutter County ; to which I assented ; and all the terms and preliminaries were arranged and agreed upon. At that time there were two daily lines of stages leaving Marysville for Sacramento, and you and your friends were to go down the Sacramento road to a point below Bear River in advance of the stages, and I was to select a suitable place for the meeting. Judge Barbour and his friends were to follow us in one of the coaches and I was to hail the driver as he approached the place of meeting. You and your adversary were to be stationed one hundred yards apart, each armed with as many Colt's revolvers as he chose to carry ; to fire upon each other at the word, and to advance at pleasure and finish the conflict. Our party was promptly on the ground according to agreement; and when the first coach came in sight I hailed the driver and found that Judge Barbour and his friends were not aboard, and the coach passed on a little below us and turned out of the road and stopped. Soon after the other coach came in sight, and I again hailed the driver, who stopped the coach, and Judge Barbour instantly jumped out, and in a very excited manner said that he was going forward to the other coach, and called on the passengers "to take notice, that if that d——d rascal" (pointing to you) "attacked him he would kill him." I stepped in front of Judge Barbour and said: Hold! Judge Field will not attack you, sir; remarking at the same time to Mr. Fairfax that this was strange conduct on the part of his friend, and not in accordance with our understanding and agreement; that each party was to bear his portion of the responsibility of the meeting which was to take place between them. Mr. Fairfax appeared both astonished and mortified at the pusillanimous conduct of his principal, who seemed determined to rush forward to the other coach; and I requested him to wait until I could go back and consult you in the matter, for I was afraid that you might possibly be provoked to make the attack. When I returned to you and explained what had been said at the coach, you asked if it would be proper for you to make the attack. I told you most decidedly not; to let the coward go, and he would never annoy or trouble you again. Mr. Fairfax, who possessed a nice sense of honor, and was a gallant and accomplished gentleman, was so disgusted and mortified at the conduct of his principal that he left him and came over and joined our party, and after taking breakfast with us at Nicolaus, returned with us to Marysville, while Judge Barbour went on his way to Sacramento. Thus, what threatened in its inception to be a sanguinary tragedy, ended in a ridiculous farce. The determined and resolute stand which you assumed in this affair with Judge Barbour, saved you from any farther insolence or persecution from men of his class.

This letter has been drawn out to a most tedious length, and yet there are many circumstances connected with our early life and times in Marysville that I would add but for fear of trying your patience.

Please write to me on receipt of this, and tell me how my memory of the facts contained in this letter agrees with yours.

Very respectfully and truly your friend,

GORDON N. MOTT.

EXHIBIT I.

Letter of L. Martin, Esq., the friend of Judge Barbour in his street attack.

MARYSVILLE, *Tuesday, March* 21, '54.

DEAR JUDGE : I was glad to hear a few days ago from our friend Filkins that the trouble between you and Judge Barbour had been settled, and that the hatchet was buried.

I wish now to explain my connection with the assault made upon you about a year ago by Barbour.* You have always appeared to think me in some way implicated in that affair, because I was seen by you at that time not far off from him. The facts are these : Judge Barbour told me the night before that he expected to have a street fight with you, and wanted me to accompany him. I had heard of his conduct in the affair of the intended duel in Sutter County, and knew there was bad blood between you, but I was astonished at his saying there was going to be a difficulty between you in the street. I consented to accompany him, but I supposed of course that you had received notice of his purpose, and that there would be no unfair advantage taken by him. I was, therefore, surprised when I saw you in front of your office with your arms partly filled with small pieces of board, apparently to kindle a fire. Barbour's drawing a pistol upon you under these circumstances, and calling upon you to draw and defend yourself, was not what we call at the South very chivalric. It was not justified by me then, and never has been in any way or manner, and I told him he had acted badly. I was glad to hear you defy him as you did, and dare him to shoot. I reckon he

---

* It was February 21, 1853.

is not very proud of his conduct. I have never approved of
his action, and should never have accompanied him had I
believed or suspected he had not given you notice of his purpose.

  With great respect I am very truly yours,

L. MARTIN.

Hon. JUDGE FIELD.

EXHIBIT J.

*Sections four, five, and seven of the act entitled "An act to ex-
pedite the settlement of titles to lands in the State of California," approved July 1st, 1864.*

SEC. 4. *And be it further enacted*, That whenever the district
judge of any one of the district courts of the United States for
California is interested in any land, the claim to which, under
the said act of March third, eighteen hundred and fifty-one, is
pending before him on appeal from the board of commissioners
created by said act, the said district court shall order the case
to be transferred to the Circuit Court of the United States for
California, which court shall thereupon take jurisdiction and
determine the same. The said district courts may also order
a transfer to the said circuit court of any other cases arising
under said act, pending before them, affecting the title to lands
within the corporate limits of any city or town, and in such
cases both the district and circuit judges may sit.

SEC. 5. *And be it further enacted*, That all the right and title
of the United States to the lands within the corporate limits of
the city of San Francisco, as defined in the act incorporating
said city, passed by the Legislature of the State of California,
on the fifteenth of April, one thousand eight hundred and fifty-
one, are hereby relinquished and granted to the said city and
its successors, for the uses and purposes specified in the ordinance of said city, ratified by an act of the Legislature of the
said State, approved on the eleventh of March, eighteen hundred and fifty-eight, entitled "An act concerning the city of
San Francisco, and to ratify and confirm certain ordinances of
the common council of said city," there being excepted from

this relinquishment and grant all sites or other parcels of lands
which have been, or now are, occupied by the United States
for military, naval, or other public uses, [or such other sites or
parcels as may hereafter be designated by the President of the
United States, within one year after the rendition to the General Land-Office, by the surveyor-general, of an approved plat
of the exterior limits of San Francisco, as recognized in this
section, in connection with the lines of the public surveys :
And provided, That the relinquishment and grant by this act
shall in no manner interfere with or prejudice any bona fide
claims of others, whether asserted adversely under rights derived from Spain, Mexico, or the laws of the United States, nor
preclude a judicial examination and adjustment thereof.]

SEC. 7. *And be it further enacted*, That it shall be the duty
of the Surveyor-General of California, in making surveys of
the private land claims finally confirmed, to follow the decree
of confirmation as closely as practicable whenever such decree
designates the specific boundaries of the claim. But when
such decree designates only the out-boundaries within which
the quantity confirmed is to be taken, the location of such
quantity shall be made, as near as practicable, in one tract and
in a compact form. And if the character of the land, or intervening grants, be such as to render the location impracticable
in one tract, then each separate location shall be made, as near
as practicable, in a compact form. And it shall be the duty of
the Commissioner of the General Land-Office to require a substantial compliance with the directions of this section before
approving any survey and plat forwarded to him.—[13 Stats.
at Large, pp. 333–4.]

That part of the fifth section, which is included within
brackets, was inserted at the suggestion of the Commissioner
of the General Land-Office.

———

*The act entitled "An act to quiet the title to certain lands within
the corporate limits of the city of San Francisco," approved
March 8th, 1866.*

———

*Be it enacted by the Senate and House of Representatives of
the United States of America in Congress assembled*, That all

the right and title of the United States to the land situated within the corporate limits of the city of San Francisco, in the State of California, confirmed to the city of San Francisco by the decree of the Circuit Court of the United States for the Northern District of California, entered on the eighteenth day of May, one thousand eight hundred and sixty-five, be, and the same are hereby, relinquished and granted to the said city of San Francisco and its successors, and the claim of the said city to said land is hereby confirmed, subject, however, to the reservations and exceptions designated in said decree, and upon the following trusts, namely, that all the said land, not heretofore granted to said city, shall be disposed of and conveyed by said city to parties in the bona fide actual possession thereof, by themselves or tenants, on the passage of this act, in such quantities and upon such terms and conditions as the legislature of the State of California may prescribe, except such parcels thereof as may be reserved and set apart by ordinance of said city for public uses : *Provided, however*, That the relinquishment and grant by this act shall not interfere with or prejudice any valid adverse right or claim, if such exist, to said land or any part thereof, whether derived from Spain, Mexico, or the United States, or preclude a judicial examination and adjustment thereof.—[14 Stat. at Large, p. 4.]

EXHIBIT K.

Letter of Judge Lake giving an account of the torpedo.

SAN FRANCISCO, *April* 29, '80.

Honorable STEPHEN J. FIELD.

MY DEAR SIR : In the winter of 1866 I was in Washington attending the United States Supreme Court, and was frequently a visitor at your room.

One morning in January of that year I accompanied you to your room, expecting to find letters from San Francisco, as I had directed that my letters should be forwarded to your care. I found your mail lying on the table. Among other matter addressed to you was a small package, about four inches square, wrapped in white paper, and bearing the stamp of the Pioneer Photographic Gallery of San Francisco. Two printed slips were pasted upon the face of the package and formed the address : Your name, evidently cut from the title-page of the " California Law Reports ; " and " Washington, D. C.," taken from a newspaper. You supposed it to be a photograph, and said as much to me, though from the first you professed surprise at the receipt of it.

You were standing at the window, when you began to open it, and had some difficulty in making the cover yield. When you had removed the cover you raised the lid slightly, but in a moment said to me, " What is this, Lake ? It can hardly be a photograph." A sudden suspicion flashed upon me, and stepping to your side, I exclaimed, " Don't open it ; it means mischief ! "

When I had looked at it more nearly, I said, " It's an infernal machine " or " a torpedo." I carried it over to the Capitol, opposite to your rooms, where Mr. Broom, one of the clerks of the Supreme Court, joined me in the examination of your mysterious looking present. It was put in water, and afterwards we dashed off the lid of the box by throwing it against the wall in the carriage way under the Senate steps. About a dozen copper cartridges were disclosed—those used in a Smith & Wesson pocket pistol, it appeared afterward—six of them lying on each side of a bunch of friction matches in the centre. The sides of the cartridges had been filed through, so that the burning of the matches might explode the cartridges. The whole was kept in place in a bed of common glue, and a strip of sand-paper lying upon the heads of the matches was bent into a loop to receive the bit of thread, whose other end, secured to the clasp of the box, produced that tension and consequent pressure requisite to ignite the matches upon the forcible opening of the lid. To make assurance doubly sure, a paste of fulminating powder and alcohol had been spread around the matches and cartridges.

There was a newspaper slip also glued to the inside of the lid, with words as follows : " Monday, Oct. 31, 1864. The City of San Francisco vs. United States. Judge Field yesterday delivered the following opinion in the above case. It will be read with great interest by the people of this city." Then followed several lines of the opinion. Even that gave no clue to the source of the infernal machine, but from the fact that it was evidently made by a scientific man, and that from its size it must have been passed through the window at the post office, instead of into the letter-box, it was thought [that there was] a sufficiently conspicuous mode of·action to expose the sender of the torpedo to detection. Whoever it may have been took a late vengeance for the decision of the Pueblo case—if such was the veritable motive of the frustrated assassination— as the decision referred to was rendered in 1864. On that account it was conjectured that the contriver of the machine might be some guilty person, who had received sentence from you, and who used the reference to the Pueblo case to divert suspicion from himself.

So far as I know, all efforts to discover the author of the intended mischief have been fruitless.

The box with its contents was sent to the Secretary of War, who directed an examination by the Ordnance Department. General Dyer, then Chief of Ordnance, pronounced it a most cleverly combined torpedo, and exploded one of the cartridges in a closed box, producing a deep indentation upon its sides.

General Dyer added, among other analytical details, that the ball weighed 52 grains.

All the circumstances connected with the reception of the infernal machine were too singular and, at that time, ominous, not to remain vividly impressed upon my memory.

Very truly, your friend,

DELOS LAKE.

EXHIBIT L.

The following is an extract from the Report to the Commissioner of the General Land-Office by the Register and Receiver of the Land-Office in California, to whom the matter of the contests for lands on the Soscol Ranch was submitted for investigation, showing the condition and occupation of the lands previous to the rejection of the grant by the Supreme Court of the United States, and the character of the alleged pre-emption settlements which Julian undertook to defend.

A general report of the facts established by said evidence is briefly as follows : * When the United States government took possession of California, Don Mariana Guadaloupe Vallejo was in the occupancy of the rancho of Soscol, claiming to own it by virtue of the grant from the Mexican nation, which has recently (December term, 1861) been declared invalid by the Supreme Court of the United States. His occupancy was the usual one of the country and in accordance with the primitive habits of the people. He possessed the land by herding stock upon it. General Vallejo, as military commandant of his district, consisting of all Alta California lying north of the bay of San Francisco, was necessarily the leading personage of the country. His influence among the rude inhabitants of the Territory was almost monarchical, and his establishment was in accordance with his influence. His residence at Sonoma was the capital of his commandancy, and the people of the country for hundreds of miles around looked to General Vallejo for advice and assistance in business and for protection and defence in time of trouble. These things are part of the history of California.

He had other ranchos besides that of Soscol, as that at Sonoma, which was devoted to agriculture and residences.

The Soscol he especially devoted to the herding and grazing of stock, for which purpose it was most admirably adapted. Wild oats grew in great luxuriance all over this tract, from the water's edge to the tops of the highest hills, and being sur-

---

* The evidence taken before those officers.

rounded on three sides by the waters of the bays and rivers, required little attention in the way of herdsmen.

On this rancho General Vallejo kept as many as fifteen thousand head of horses and horned cattle running at will, attended only by the necessary vaqueros employed to watch and attend them.

There was no other use to which the land could at that time be devoted. The want of reliable labor and lack of a market both forbade agricultural operations beyond personal or family necessities. It was not practicable then, nor for years after, to put the land to any use other than stock pasturing.

We have, therefore, to report that the possession that General Vallejo had of "Soscol" in 1846 was the usual use and possession of the time and the country, and that it was the best and most perfect use and occupation of which the land was capable.

The rancho was, therefore, reduced to possession by General Vallejo before the Americans took possession of the country.

Soon after the American occupation or conquest, General Vallejo began to sell off portions of the "Soscol," and continued this practice until about the year 1855, at which time he sold the last of it, and does not appear to have had or claimed any interest since.

This sale and consequent dividing the land into small parcels produced its usual effect in the way of improvements.

From 1855 to 1860 the "rancho of Soscol" was almost entirely reduced to absolute and actual possession and control by his vendees, being by them fenced up into fields, surrounded by substantial enclosures, and improved with expensive farm-houses, out-buildings, orchards, and the like, and was cultivated to grain wherever suitable for that purpose.

It had upon it two cities of considerable importance, viz: Benicia and Vallejo, each of which had been at one time the capital of the State of California.

No rural district of California was more highly improved than this, and but a very small portion equal to it.

The title to "Soscol," before its rejection by the United States Supreme Court, was considered the very best in all California. All the really valuable agricultural land in California was held under Mexican grants, and, as a consequence, all had to pass the ordeal of the Land Commission.

From 1853 to about 1860 very few had been finally passed upon by the courts, so that during that time the question for the farmer to decide was not what title is perfect, but what title is most likely to prove so by the final judgment of the Supreme Court.

Amongst the very best, in the opinion of the public, stood " Soscol."

One conclusive, unanswerable proof of that fact is this, that there was not a single settler on the grant at the time it was rejected. Not one person on it, except in subordination to the Vallejo title. Every resident on the whole tract held his land by purchase from Vallejo, or his assigns, and held just precisely the land so purchased, and not one acre more or less. This fact was not even disputed during the whole eight months of investigation through which we have just passed. It is a notorious fact that of the grants in California which have stood the test of the Supreme Court, very many have been entirely in the possession of squatters, and all with more or less of such possessions, and the final patent has alone succeeded in recovering the long-lost possession to the grantholder. There were no settlers on the " Soscol." The people had the most perfect confidence in the title. It had been twice confirmed by tribunals of high authority and great learning—first by the United States Land Commission, and then by the District Court of the United States.

It only wanted the final confirmation by the Supreme Court, and none doubted that it would follow of course. Business could not, and would not, await the nine years consumed in adjudicating this title. Farmers were obliged to have lands, and they bought them. Capital must and would seek investment, and it was lent on mortgage. When all titles required the same confirmatory decree, the citizen could not discriminate, but exercised his best judgment.

The sales of lands upon the " Soscol " were made at prices which called for perfect title ; they brought the full improved value of the land. Money was lent on mortgage in the same way.

The deeds and mortgages, which accompany the respective

cases, are the very best evidence of the opinion the public entertained of the character of the Soscol grant title. The people were amazed when it was announced that the Soscol grant had been rejected.

No fact developed by this examination has appeared so surprising to the mind of the register and receiver as that there were no pre-emption settlers on the " Soscol." This is so unusual in California that we expected to find the contrary. There was no possession on the tract adverse to the grant title.

Thus stood matters until early in the year 1862, when the intelligence reached California that the grant had been rejected by the Supreme Court. The struggle soon began. There was at that time employed upon the United States navy-yard at Mare Island, and also upon the Pacific Mail Company's works at Benicia, a large number of mechanics and laborers. There was also in the towns of Benicia and Vallejo a large floating population. Tempted by the great value of these lands in their highly improved state, many of these persons squatted upon the rancho.

The landholders in possession resisted.

The houses of the great majority of the settlers were erected in the night time, as it was necessary to enter the enclosed fields by stealth. These houses were built of rough redwood boards set up edgewise, with shed roof, and without window, fire place, or floor.

They were about eight feet square, sometimes eight by ten feet, and never over six feet high.

We have no hesitation in saying that they were utterly unfit for the habitation of human beings, and further that they were never designed for permanent residences. The mode of erecting these shanties was as follows : The planks were sawed the right length in the town of Vallejo or Benicia, in the afternoon of the day, and at nightfall were loaded upon a cart. About eleven o'clock at night the team would start for the intended settlement, reaching there about one or two o'clock in the morning. Between that hour and daylight the house would be erected and finished. Sometimes the house would be put together with nails, but when too near the residence of the landholder in possession, screws would be used to prevent the sound of the hammer attracting attention. Very few of this class of settlers remained upon their claims above a few days, but soon returned to their ordinary occupations in the towns.

Generally after they would leave the landholders would remove the shanties from the ground. In some cases they would pull them down with force immediately upon discovering them, and in the presence of the settlers.

A few of them got settlements near enough to their places of employment to enable them to work in town, or at the navy-yard, and to sleep in their shanties; some regularly, others only occasionally. These generally remained longer than the others, but none of this class remained up to the time of trial.

None of the settlers, who went on since the grant was rejected, have attempted regular improvements or cultivation. A few have harvested the grain planted by the landholders, as it grew on their $\frac{1}{4}$ [quarter-section]; they would harvest it, and offer this as evidence of good faith and cultivation.

We have no hesitation in pronouncing, from the evidence, that these are not settlers within the spirit of the pre-emption laws, but are mere speculators, desirous of getting the improvements of another to sell and to make money.

The preceding Personal Reminiscences of Early Days in California by Judge Field, with other sketches, were dictated by him to a stenographer in the summer of 1877, at San Francisco. They were afterwards printed for a few friends, but not published. The edition was small and soon exhausted, and each year since the Judge has been asked for copies. The reprint is therefore made.

The history of the attempt at his assassination by a former associate on the supreme bench of California is added. It is written by Hon. George C. Gorham, a warm personal friend of the Judge for many years, who is thoroughly informed of the events described.

THE STORY

OF THE

ATTEMPTED ASSASSINATION

OF

JUSTICE FIELD

BY A

FORMER ASSOCIATE ON THE SUPREME BENCH OF

CALIFORNIA.

———

BY HON. GEORGE C. GORHAM.

NOTE BY THE PUBLISHERS.

Mr. Gorham is a life-long friend of Justice Field. He was his clerk when the latter held the Alcalde's Court in Marysville, in 1850; and was Clerk of the U. S. Circuit Court of the District of California when it was organized, after Judge Field's appointment to the U. S. Supreme Bench. Subsequently, and for several years, he was Secretary of the U. S. Senate. Since his retirement from office he has resided in Washington. For a part of the time he edited a Republican paper in that city, but of late years he has been chiefly engaged in literary works, of which the principal one is the life and history of the late Secretary of War, Edwin M. Stanton.

INDEX.

ATTEMPTED ASSASSINATION OF JUSTICE FIELD BY A FORMER ASSOCIATE ON THE STATE SUPREME BENCH.

THE most thrilling episode in the eventful life of Justice Field was his attempted assassination at La-throp, California, on the 14th day of August, 1889, by David S. Terry, who had been Chief Justice of the State during a portion of Justice Field's service on that bench. Terry lost his own life in his desperate attempt, by the alertness and courage of David S. Neagle, a Deputy United States Marshal, who had been deputed by his principal, under an order from the Attorney-General of the United States, to protect Justice Field from the assassin, who had, for nearly a year, boldly and without concealment, proclaimed his murderous purpose. The motive of Terry was not in any manner connected with their association on the State supreme bench, for there had never been any but pleasant relations between them.

Terry resigned from the bench in 1859 to challenge Senator Broderick of California to the duel in which the latter was killed. He entered the Confederate service during the war, and some time after its close he returned to California, and entered upon the prac-tice of the law. In 1880 he was a candidate for Presi-dential elector on the Democratic ticket. His associ-ates on that ticket were all elected, while he was de-feated by the refusal of a number of the old friends of Broderick to give him their votes. It is probable that his life was much embittered by the intense hatred he had engendered among the friends of Broderick, and the severe censure of a large body of the people of the State, not especially attached to the political fortunes of the dead Senator. These facts are mentioned as furnishing a possible explanation of Judge Terry's marked descent in character and standing from the Chief-Justiceship of the State to being the counsel, partner, and finally the husband of the discarded companion of a millionaire in a raid upon the latter's property in the courts. It was during the latter stages of this litigation that Judge Terry became enraged against Justice Field, because the latter, in the discharge of his judicial duties, had been compelled to order the revival of a decree of the United States Circuit Court, in the rendering of which he had taken no part.

A proper understanding of this exciting chapter in the life of Justice Field renders necessary a narrative of the litigation referred to. It is doubtful if the annals of the courts or the pages of romance can parallel this conspiracy to compel a man of wealth to divide his estate with adventurers. Whether it is measured by the value of the prize reached for, by the character of the conspirators, or by the desperate means to which they resorted to accomplish their object, it stands in the forefront of the list of such operations.

CHAPTER I.

The victim, upon a share of whose enormous estate, commonly estimated at $15,000,000, these conspirators had set their covetous eyes, was William Sharon, then a Senator from the State of Nevada. The woman with whom he had terminated his relations, because he believed her to be dangerous to his business interests, was Sarah Althea Hill. Desirous of turning to the best advantage her previous connection with him, she sought advice from an old negress of bad repute, and the result was a determination to claim that she had a secret contract of marriage with him. This negress, who during the trial gave unwilling testimony to having furnished the sinews of war in the litigation to the extent of at least five thousand dollars, then consulted G. W. Tyler, a lawyer noted for his violent manner and reckless practices, who explained to her what kind of a paper would constitute a legal marriage contract under the laws of California. No existing contract was submitted to him, but he gave his written opinion as to what kind of a contract it would be good to have for the purpose. The pretended contract was then manufactured by Sarah Althea in accordance with this opinion, and Tyler subsequently made a written agreement with her by which he was to act as her attorney, employ all necessary assistance, and pay all expenses, and was to have one-half of all they could get out of Sharon by their joint

efforts as counsel and client. This contract was nego-
tiated by an Australian named Neilson, who was to
have one-half of the lawyer's share.

On the 7th of September, 1883, a demand was made
upon Mr. Sharon for money for Miss Hill. He drove
her emissary, Neilson, out of the hotel where he had
called upon him, and the latter appeared the next day
in the police court of San Francisco and made an affidavit charging Mr. Sharon with the crime of adultery.
A warrant was issued for the latter's arrest, and he
was held to bail in the sum of $5,000. This charge
was made for the avowed purpose of establishing the
manufactured contract of marriage already referred
to, which bore date three years before. A copy of this
alleged contract was furnished to the newspapers together with a letter having Sharon's name appended
to it, addressed at the top to " My Dear Wife," and at
the bottom to " Miss Hill." This pretended contract
and letter Mr. Sharon denounced as forgeries.

On the 3d of October, 1883, Mr. Sharon commenced
suit in the United States Circuit Court at San Francisco against Sarah Althea Hill, setting forth in his
complaint that he was a citizen of the State of Nevada,
and she a citizen of California ;

" that he was, and had been for years, an unmarried
man ; that formerly he was the husband of Maria Ann
Sharon, who died in May, 1875, and that he had never
been the husband of any other person ; that there were
two children living, the issue of that marriage, and
also grandchildren, the children of a deceased daugh-
ter of the marriage ; that he was possessed of a large
fortune in real and personal property ; was exten-
sively engaged in business enterprises and ventures,
and had a wide business and social connection ; that,
as he was informed, the defendant was an unmarried

woman of about thirty years of age, for some time a resident of San Francisco ; that within two months then past she had repeatedly and publicly claimed and represented that she was his lawful wife ; that she falsely and fraudulently pretended that she was duly married to him on the twenty-fifth day of August, 1880, at the city and county of San Francisco ; that on that day they had jointly made a declaration of marriage showing the names, ages, and residences of the parties, jointly doing the acts required by the Civil Code of California to constitute a marriage between them and that thereby they became and were husband and wife according to the law of that State.

" The complainant further alleged that these several claims, representations, and pretensions were wholly and maliciously false, and were made by her for the purpose of injuring him in his property, business, and social relations ; for the purpose of obtaining credit by the use of his name with merchants and others, and thereby compelling him to maintain her; and for the purpose of harassing him, and in case of his death, his heirs and next of kin and legatees, into payment of large sums of money to quiet her false and fraudulent claims and pretensions. He also set forth what he was informed was a copy of the declaration of marriage, and alleged that if she had any such instrument, it was 'false, forged, and counterfeited ;' that he never, on the day of its date, or at any other time, made or executed any such document or declaration, and never knew or heard of the same until within a month previous to that time, and that the same was null and void as against him, and ought, in equity and good conscience, to be so declared, and ordered to be delivered up, to be annulled and cancelled."

The complaint concluded with a prayer that it be adjudged and decreed that the said Sarah Althea Hill was not and never had been his wife ; that he did not make the said joint declaration of marriage with her, or any marriage between them ; that said contract or joint declaration of marriage be decreed and adjudged false, fraudulent, forged, and counterfeited, and ordered to be delivered up and cancelled and annulled, and that she be enjoined from setting up any claims or pretensions of marriage thereby. Sharon was a citizen of Nevada, while Miss Hill was a citizen of California.*

Before the time expired in which Miss Hill was required to answer the complaint of Mr. Sharon in the United States Circuit Court, but not until after the federal jurisdiction had attached in that court, she brought suit against him, November 1st, in a state Superior Court, in the city and county of San Francisco, to establish their alleged marriage and then obtain a decree, and a division of the property stated to have been acquired since such marriage. In her complaint she alleged that on the 25th day of August, 1880, they became, by mutual agreement, husband and wife, and thereafter commenced living together

---

* NOTE.—A court of equity having jurisdiction to lay its hands upon and control forged and fraudulent instruments, it matters not with what pretensions and claims their validity may be asserted by their possessor; whether they establish a marriage relation with another, or render him an heir to an estate, or confer a title to designated pieces of property, or create a pecuniary obligation. It is enough that, unless set aside or their use restrained, they may impose burdens upon the complaining party, or create claims upon his property by which its possession and enjoyment may be destroyed or impaired. (Sharon vs. Terry, 13 Sawyer's Rep., 406.) The Civil Code of California also declares that " a written instrument in respect to which there is a reasonable apprehension that, if left outstanding, it may cause serious injury to a person against whom it is void or voidable, may, upon his application, be so adjudged, and ordered to be delivered up or cancelled " (Sec. 3412).

as husband and wife ; that on that day they had jointly made a declaration of marriage in writing, signed by each, substantially in form as required by the Civil Code of California, and until the month of November, 1881, had lived together as husband and wife; that since then the defendant had been guilty of sundry violations of the marriage contract. The complaint also alleged that when the parties intermarried the defendant did not have in money or property more than five millions of dollars, with an income not exceeding thirty thousand dollars a month, but that since their intermarriage they had by their prudent management of mines, fortunate speculations, manipulations of the stock market, and other business enterprises, accumulated in money and property more than ten millions of dollars, and that now he had in his possession money and property of the value at least of fifteen millions of dollars, from which he received an income of over one hundred thousand dollars a month. The complaint concluded with a prayer that the alleged marriage with the defendant might be declared legal and valid, and that she might be divorced from him, and that an account be taken of the common property, and that the same be equally divided between them.

The campaign was thus fully inaugurated, which for more than six years disgraced the State with its violence and uncleanness, and finally ended in bloodshed. The leading combatants were equally resolute and determined. Mr. Sharon, who was a man of remarkable will and energy, would have expended his entire fortune in litigation before he would have paid tribute to those who thus attempted to plunder him. Sarah Althea Hill was respectably connected, but had drifted away from her relations, and pursued, without restraint, her disreputable course. She affected a reckless and daredevil character, carrying a pistol, and exhibiting it on occasions in cow-boy fashion, to convey the impression that those who antagonized her had a dangerous character with whom to deal. She was ignorant, illiterate, and superstitious. The forged document which she thought to make a passport to the enjoyment of a share of Sharon's millions was a clumsy piece of work. It was dated August 25, 1880, and contained a clause pledging secrecy for two years thereafter. But she never made it public until September, 1883, although she had, nearly two years before that, been turned out of her hotel by Sharon's orders. At this treatment she only whimpered and wrote begging letters to him, not once claiming, even in these private letters to him, to be his wife. She could then have published the alleged contract without any violation of its terms, and claimed any rights it conferred, and it is obvious to any sane man that she would have done so had any such document then been in existence.

Although Sharon's case against Sarah Althea Hill was commenced in the federal court before the commencement of Miss Hill's case against Sharon in the state court, the latter case was first brought to trial, on the 10th of March, 1884.

CHAPTER II.

Mr. Sharon defended in the state court, and prosecuted in the federal court with equal energy. In the former he made an affidavit that the pretended marriage contract was a forgery and applied to the court for the right to inspect it, and to have photographic copies of it made. Sarah Althea resisted the judge's order to produce the document in question, until he informed her that, if she did not obey, the paper would not be admitted as evidence on the trial of the action.

On the second day of the trial in the state court Miss Hill reinforced her cause by the employment of Judge David S. Terry as associate counsel. He brought to the case a large experience in the use of deadly weapons, and gave the proceedings something of the character of the ancient "wager of battle." Numerous auxiliaries and supernumeraries in the shape of lesser lawyers, fighters, and suborned witnesses were employed in the proceedings as from time to time occasion required. The woman testified in her own behalf that upon a visit to Mr. Sharon's office he had offered to pay her $1,000 per month if she would become his mistress; that she declined his offer in a business-like manner, without anger, and entered upon a conversation about getting married; she swore at a subsequent interview she drafted a marriage contract at Sharon's dictation. This document, to which she testified as having been thus drawn up, is as follows:

" In the city and county of San Francisco, State of California, on the 25th day of August, A. D. 1880, I, Sarah Althea Hill, of the city and county of San Francisco, State of California, aged twenty-seven years, do here, in the presence of Almighty God, take Senator William Sharon, of the State of Nevada, to be my lawful and wedded husband, and do here acknowledge and declare myself to be the wife of Senator William Sharon, of the State of Nevada.

"SARAH ALTHEA HILL.

" AUGUST 25, 1880, SAN FRANCISCO, CAL.

" I agree not to make known the contents of this paper or its existence for two years unless Mr. Sharon, himself, sees fit to make it known.

" SARAH ALTHEA HILL.

" In the city and county of San Francisco, State of California, on the 25th day of August, A. D. 1880, I, Senator William Sharon, of the State of Nevada, aged sixty years, do here, in the presence of Almighty God, take Sarah Althea Hill, of the city and county of San Francisco, California, to be my lawful and wedded wife, and do here acknowledge myself to be the husband of Sarah Althea Hill.

" WILLIAM SHARON,
" Nevada.

" AUGUST 25, 1880."

In his testimony Mr. Sharon contradicted every material statement made by Sarah Althea Hill. He denied every circumstance connected with the alleged drawing up of the marriage contract.

He testified that on the 7th day of November, 1881, he terminated his relations with and dismissed her, and made a full settlement with her by the payment of $3,000 in cash, and notes amounting to $4,500.

For these she gave him a receipt in full. He charged
her with subsequently stealing that receipt at one of
two or three visits made by her after her discharge.

It is unnecessary to review the voluminous testimony introduced by the parties in support of their
respective contentions. The alleged contract was
clearly proven to be a forgery. A number of witnesses testified to conversations had with Miss Hill
long after the date of the pretended marriage contract, in which she made statements entirely inconsistent with the existence of such a document. She
employed fortune-tellers to give her charms with
which she could compel Mr. Sharon to marry her,
and this, too, when she pretended to have in her possession the evidence that she was already his wife.
Not an appearance of probability attended the claim
of this bold adventuress. Every statement she made
concerning the marriage contract, and every step she
took in her endeavor to enforce it, betrayed its false
origin.

The trial of the case in the state court continued
from March 10th until May 28th, when the summer
recess intervened. It was resumed July 15th, and
occupied the court until September 17th, on which
day the argument of counsel was concluded and the
case submitted. No decision was rendered until more
than three months afterwards, namely, December 24th.
Nearly two months were then allowed to pass before
the decree was entered, February 19, 1885. The case
was tried before Judge Sullivan without a jury, by
consent of the parties. He decided for the plaintiff,
holding the marriage contract to be genuine, and to
constitute a valid marriage. It was manifest that he
made his decision solely upon the evidence given by

Sarah Althea herself, whom he nevertheless branded
in his opinion as a perjurer, suborner of perjury, and
forger. Lest this should seem an exaggeration his
own words are here quoted. She stated that she was
introduced by Sharon to certain parties as his wife.
Of her statements to this effect the Judge said:

"Plaintiff's testimony as to these occasions is directly contradicted, and in my judgment her testimony as to these matters is wilfully false."

Concerning $7,500 paid her by Sharon, which she
alleged she had placed in his hands in the early part
of her acquaintance with him, the Judge said:

"This claim, in my judgment, is utterly unfounded.
No such advance was ever made."

At another place in his opinion the Judge said:

"Plaintiff claims that defendant wrote her notes at
different times after her expulsion from the Grand
Hotel. If such notes were written, it seems strange
that they have not been preserved and produced in
evidence. I do not believe she received any such
notes."

With respect to another document which purported
to have been signed by Mr. Sharon, and which Sarah
Althea produced under compulsion, then withdrew it,
and failed to produce it afterwards, when called for,
saying she had lost it, Judge Sullivan said :

"Among the objections suggested to this paper as
appearing on its face, was one made by counsel that
the signature was evidently a forgery. The matters
recited in the paper are, in my judgment, at variance
with the facts it purports to recite. Considering the

stubborn manner in which the production of this paper was at first resisted and the mysterious manner of its disappearance, I am inclined to regard it in the light of one of the fabrications for the purpose of bolstering up plaintiff's case. I can view the paper in no other light than as a fabrication."

In another part of his opinion Judge Sullivan made a sort of a general charge of perjury against her in the following language :

" I am of the opinion that to some extent plaintiff has availed herself of the aid of false testimony for the purpose of giving her case a better appearance in the eyes of the court, but sometimes parties have been known to resort to false testimony, where in their judgment it would assist them in prosecuting a lawful claim. As I understand the facts of this case, that was done in this instance."

In another place Judge Sullivan said :

" I have discussed fully, in plain language, the numerous false devices resorted to by the plaintiff for the purpose of strengthening her case."

Miss Sarah and her attorneys had now come in sight of the promised land of Sharon's ample estate. Regular proceedings, however, under the law, seemed to them too slow ; and besides there was the peril of an adverse decision of the Supreme Court on appeal. They then decided upon a novel course. Section 137 of the Civil Code of California provides that while an action for divorce is pending, the court may, in its discretion, require the husband to pay as alimony any money necessary to enable the wife to support herself and to prosecute or defeat the action. The enterprising attorneys, sharing the bold spirit of their client, and presuming upon the compliance of a judge who had

already done so well by them, went into the court on
the 8th of January, 1885, and modestly demanded for
Sarah Althea, upon the sole authority of the provision
of law above quoted, $10,000 per month, as the money
necessary to enable her to support herself, and $150,000
for attorneys' fees to prosecute the action.   This was
to include back pay for thirty-eight months, making a
sum of $380,000, which added to the $150,000, attorneys' fees, would have made a grand total of $530,000.
This was an attempt, under the color of a beneficent
law, applicable only to actions for divorce, in which
the marriage was not denied, to extort from a man
more than one-half million dollars, for the benefit of a
woman, seeking first to establish a marriage, and then
to secure a divorce, in a case in which no decree had
as yet been entered, declaring her to be a wife.   It
was not merely seeking the money necessary to support the plaintiff and prosecute the case ; it was a
request that the inferior court should confiscate more
than half a million dollars, in anticipation of a decision of the Supreme Court on appeal.   It was as bold
an attempt at spoliation as the commencement of the
suit itself.   The Supreme Court of the State had decided that the order of a Superior Court allowing
alimony during the pendency of any action for divorce
is not appealable, but it had not decided that, under
the pretence of granting alimony, an inferior judge
could apportion a rich man's estate among champerty
lawyers, and their adventurous client, by an order
from which there could be no appeal, made prior to
any decree that there had ever been a marriage between the parties, when the fact of the marriage was
the main issue in the case.   The counsel for Sharon
insisted upon his right to have a decree entered from

which he could appeal, before being thus made to
stand and deliver, and the court entertained the motion.

Upon this motion, among other affidavits read in
opposition, was one by Mr. Sharon himself, in which
he recited the agreement between Miss Hill and her
principal attorney, George W. Tyler, in which she was
to pay him for his services, one-half of all she might
receive in any judgment obtained against Sharon, he,
Tyler, advancing all the costs of the litigation. The
original of this agreement had been filed by Tyler with
the county clerk immediately after the announcement
of the opinion in the case as an evidence of his right
to half of the proceeds of the judgment. It was conclusive evidence that Sarah Althea required no money
for the payment of counsel fees.

After the filing of a mass of affidavits, and an exhaustive argument of the motion, Judge Sullivan rendered his decision, February 16, 1885, granting to
Sarah Althea Hill an allowance of $2,500 per month,
to take effect as of the date of the motion, January 8,
1885, and further sums of $2,500 each to be paid on
the 8th day of April, and of each succeeding month
until further order of the court.

This the Judge thought reasonable allowance "in
view of the plaintiff's present circumstances and difficulties." For counsel fees he allowed the sum of
$60,000, and at the request of the victors, made in
advance, he divided the spoils among them as follows:

To Tyler and Tyler, - - - - -	$25,000
To David S. Terry, - - - - - -	10,000
To Moon and Flournoy, - - - -	10,000
To W. H. Levy, - - - - - - -	10,000
To Clement, Osmond and Clement, -	5,000

By what rule $2,500 was awarded as a proper monthly allowance to the woman whose services to Mr. Sharon had commanded but $500 per month it is difficult to conjecture. It was benevolence itself to give $60,000 to a troop of lawyers enlisted under the command of Tyler, who had agreed to conduct the proceedings wholly at his own cost, for one-half of what could be made by the buccaneering enterprise. It seemed to be the purpose of these attorneys to see how much of Mr. Sharon's money they could, with Judge Sullivan's assistance, lay their hands upon before the entry of the judgment in the case. From the judgment an appeal could be taken. By anticipating its entry they thought that they had obtained an order from which no appeal would lie.

It was not until three days after this remarkable order was made that the decree was entered by Judge Sullivan declaring plaintiff and defendant to be husband and wife ; that he had deserted her, and that she was entitled to a decree of divorce, with one-half of the common property accumulated by the parties since the date of what he decided to be a valid marriage contract. Sharon appealed from the final judgment, and also from the order for alimony. Notwithstanding this appeal, and the giving of a bond on appeal in the sum of $300,000 to secure the payment of all alimony and counsel fees, Judge Sullivan granted an order directing Mr. Sharon to show cause why he should not be punished for contempt in failing to pay alimony and counsel fees, as directed by the order.

The Supreme Court, upon application, granted an order temporarily staying proceedings in the case. This stay of proceedings was subsequently made permanent, during the pendency of the appeal.

Mr. Sharon died November 15, 1885. That very day had been set for a hearing of Sharon's motion for a new trial. The argument was actually commenced on that day and continued until the next, at which time the motion was ordered off the calendar because meantime Mr. Sharon had deceased.

CHAPTER III.

While these proceedings were being had in the state courts the case of Sharon vs. Hill in the federal court was making slow progress. Miss Hill's attorneys seemed to think that her salvation depended upon reaching a decision in her case before the determination of Sharon's suit in the United States Circuit Court. They were yet to learn, as they afterwards did, that after a United States court takes jurisdiction in a case, it cannot be ousted of that jurisdiction by the decision of a state court, in a proceeding subsequently commenced in the latter. Seldom has "the law's delay" been exemplified more thoroughly than it was by the obstacles which her attorneys were able to interpose at every step of the proceedings in the federal court.

Sharon commenced his suit in the United States Circuit Court October 3, 1883, twenty-eight days before his enemy commenced hers in the State Superior Court. By dilatory pleas her counsel succeeded in delaying her answer to Sharon's suit until after the decision in her favor in the state court. She did not enter an appearance in the federal court until the very last day allowed by the rule. A month later she filed a demurrer. Her counsel contrived to delay the argument of this demurrer for seven weeks after it was filed. It was finally argued and submitted on the 21st of January, 1884. On the 3d of March it was overruled and the defendant was ordered to answer in ten days, to wit, March 13th. Then the time for answering was extended to April 24th. When that day arrived her counsel, instead of filing an answer, filed a plea in abatement, denying the non-residence of Mr. Sharon in the State of California, on which depended his right to sue in the federal court. To this Mr. Sharon's counsel filed a replication on the 5th of May. It then devolved upon Miss Hill's counsel to produce evidence of the fact alleged in the plea, but, after a delay of five months and ten days, no evidence whatever was offered, and the court ordered the plea to be argued on the following day. It was overruled, and thirty days were given to file an answer to Sharon's suit. The case in the state court had then been tried, argued, and submitted thirty days before, but Miss Hill's counsel were not yet ready to file their answer within the thirty days given them, and the court extended the time for answer until December 30th. Six days before that day arrived Judge Sullivan rendered his decision. At last, on the 30th of December, 1884, fourteen months after the filing of Sharon's complaint, Sarah Althea's answer was filed in the federal court, in which, among other things, she set up the proceedings and decree of the state court, adjudging the alleged marriage con-tract to be genuine and legal, and the parties to be husband and wife, and three days later Sharon filed his replication. There was at no time any delay or want of diligence on the part of the plaintiff in prose-cuting this suit to final judgment. On the contrary, as is plainly shown in the record above stated, the de-lays were all on the part of the defendant. The taking of the testimony in the United States Circuit Court commenced on the 12th of February, 1885, and closed on the 12th of August following.

The struggle in the state court was going on during all the time of the taking of the testimony in the federal court, and intensified the excitement attendant thereon. Miss Hill was in constant attendance before the examiner who took the testimony, often interrupting the proceedings with her turbulent and violent conduct and language, and threatening the lives of Mr. Sharon's counsel. She constantly carried a pistol, and on occasions exhibited it during the examination of witnesses, and, pointing it at first one and then another, expressed her intention of killing them at some stage of the proceedings. She was constantly in contempt of the court, and a terror to those around her. Her conduct on one occasion, in August, 1885, became so violent that the taking of the testimony could not proceed, and Justice Field, the presiding judge of the circuit, made an order that she should be disarmed, and that a bailiff of the court should sit constantly at her side to restrain her from any murderous outbreak, such as she was constantly threatening. Her principal attorney, Tyler, was also most violent and disorderly. Judge Terry, while less explosive, was always ready to excuse and defend his client. (See Report of Proceedings in Sharon vs. Hill, 11 Sawyer's Circuit Court Reps., 122.)

Upon the request of counsel for the complainant, the examiner in one case reported to the court the language and the conduct of Miss Hill. Among other things, he reported her as saying:

"When I see this testimony [from which certain scandalous remarks of hers were omitted] I feel like taking that man Stewart* out and cowhiding him. I

* Senator Stewart, who was one of the counsel against her in the suit.

will shoot him yet ; that very man sitting there. To
think that he would put up a woman to come here and
deliberately lie about me like that. I will shoot him.
They know when I say I will do it that I will do it.
I shall shoot him as sure as you live ; that man that
is sitting right there. And I shall have that woman
Mrs. Smith arrested for this, and make her prove it."

And again :

" I can hit a four-bit piece nine times out of ten."

The examiner said that pending the examination of
one of the witnesses, on the occasion mentioned, the
respondent drew a pistol from her satchel, and held
it in her right hand ; the hand resting for a moment
upon the table, with the weapon pointed in the direction of Judge Evans. He also stated that on previous
occasions she had brought to the examiner's room
during examinations a pistol, and had sat for some
length of time holding it in her hand, to the knowledge of all persons present at the time. After the
reading of the examiner's report in open court, Justice
Field said :

" In the case of William Sharon versus Sarah Althea
Hill, the Examiner in Chancery appointed by the court
to take the testimony has reported to the court that
very disorderly proceedings took place before him on
the 3d instant ; that at that day, in his room, when
counsel of the parties and the defendant were present,
and during the examination of a witness by the name
of Piper, the defendant became very much excited,
and threatened to take the life of one of the counsel,
and that subsequently she drew a pistol and declared
her intention to carry her threat into effect. It appears also from the report of the examiner that on
repeated occasions the defendant has attended before
him, during the examination of witnesses, armed with

a pistol. Such conduct is an offense against the laws of the United States punishable by fine and imprisonment. It interferes with the due order of proceedings in the administration of justice, and is well calculated to bring them into contempt. I, myself, have not heretofore sat in this case and do not expect to participate in its decision; I intend in a few days to leave for the East, but I have been consulted by my associate, and have been requested to take part in this side proceeding, for it is of the utmost importance for the due administration of justice that such misbehavior as the examiner reports should be stopped, and measures be taken which will prevent its recurrence. My associate will comment on the laws of Congress which make the offense a misdemeanor, punishable by fine and imprisonment.

" The marshal of the court will be directed to disarm the defendant whenever she goes before the examiner or into court in any future proceeding, and to appoint an officer to keep strict surveillance over her, in order that she may not carry out her threatened purpose. This order will be entered. The Justice then said that it is to be observed that this block, embracing this building—the court-house—is under the exclusive jurisdiction of the United States. Every offense committed within it is an offense against the United States, and the State has no jurisdiction whatever. This fact seems to have been forgotten by the parties."

The following is the order then entered as directed by Justice Field:

" Whereas it appears from the report to this court of the Examiner in Chancery in this case appointed to take the depositions of witnesses, that on the 3d day of August, instant, at his office, counsel of the parties appeared, namely, William M. Stewart, Esquire, and Oliver P. Evans, Esquire, for the complainant, and W. B. Tyler, Esquire, for the defendant, and the defendant in person, and that during the examination

before said examiner of a witness named Piper, the
defendant became excited and threatened the life of
the counsel of the complainant present, and exhibited
a pistol with a declared intention to carry such threat
into effect, thereby obstructing the order of the proceedings, and endeavoring to bring the same into contempt ; and

" Whereas it further appears that said defendant
habitually attends before said examiner carrying a
pistol,

" *It is ordered*, That the marshal of this court take
such measures as may be necessary to disarm the said
defendant, and keep her disarmed, and under strict
surveillance, while she is attending the examination of
witnesses before said examiner, and whenever attending in court, and that a deputy be detailed for that
purpose."

CHAPTER IV.

The taking of the testimony being completed, the cause was set for a hearing on September 9th. After an argument of thirteen days the cause was submitted on the 29th of September, 1885. On the 26th of December, 1885, the court rendered its decision, that the alleged declaration of marriage and the letters purporting to have been addressed " My Dear Wife " were false and forged, and that the contemporaneous conduct of the parties, and particularly of the defendant, was altogether incompatible with the claim of marriage or the existence of any such declaration or letters.

A decree was ordered accordingly, and the court made the following further order :

" As the case was argued and submitted during the lifetime of the complainant, who has since deceased, the decree will be entered nunc pro tunc, as of September 29, 1885, the date of its submission and a day prior to the decease of the complainant."

The opinion of the court was delivered by Judge Deady, of the United States District Court of Oregon, who sat in the case with Judge Sawyer, the circuit judge.

Of the old negress under whose direction the fraudulent marriage contract had been manufactured, and under whose advice and direction the suit in the state court had been brought, the Judge said :

" Mary E. Pleasant, better known as Mammie Pleasant, is a conspicuous and important figure in this
affair ; without her it would probably never have been
brought before the public. She appears to be a shrewd
old negress of some means.

" In my judgment this case and the forgeries and
perjuries committed in its support had their origin
largely in the brain of this scheming, trafficking, crafty
old woman."

He found that the declaration of marriage was
forged by the defendant by writing the declaration
over a simulated signature, and that her claim to be
the wife of the plaintiff was wholly false, and had been
put forth by her and her co-conspirators for no other
purpose than to despoil the plaintiff of his property.
Judge Sawyer also filed an opinion in the case, in
which he declared that the weight of the evidence satisfactorily established the forgery and the fraudulent
character of the instrument in question.

CHAPTER V.

Sarah Althea now received a powerful recruit, who enlisted for the war. This was one of her lawyers, David S. Terry, whom she married on the 7th day of January, 1886, twelve days after the decision of the Circuit Court against her, and which he had heard announced, but before a decree had been entered in conformity with the decision. Terry seemed willing to take the chances that the decree of the Superior Court would not be reversed in the Supreme Court of the State. The decision of the federal court he affected to utterly disregard. It was estimated that not less than $5,000,000 would be Sarah Althea's share of Sharon's estate, in the event of success in her suit. She would be a rich widow if it could be established that she had ever been a wife. She had quarreled with Tyler, her principal attorney, long before, and accused him of failing in his professional duty. If she could escape from the obligations of her contract with him, she would not be compelled to divide with him the hoped-for $5,000,000.

Although Judge Terry had been Chief Justice of the Supreme Court of California, the crimes of perjury and forgery and subornation of perjury which had been loudly charged in Judge Sullivan's opinion against the woman, in whose favor he gave judgment, seemed to him but trifles. Strangely enough, neither he nor Sarah Althea ever uttered a word of resentment against him on account of these charges.

The marriage of Terry with this desperate woman in the face of an adverse decision of the Circuit Court, by which jurisdiction was first exercised upon the subject-matter, was notice to all concerned that, by all the methods known to him, he would endeavor to win her cause, which he thus made his own. He took the position that any denial of Sarah Althea's pretense to have been the wife of Sharon was an insult to her, which could only be atoned by the blood of the person who made it. This was the proclamation of a vendetta against all who should attempt to defend the heirs of Mr. Sharon in the possession of that half of their inheritance which he and Sarah Althea had marked for their own. His subsequent course showed that he relied upon the power of intimidation to secure success. He was a man of powerful frame, accustomed all his life to the use of weapons, and known to be always armed with a knife. He had the reputation of being a fighting man. He had decided that Sarah Althea had been the lawful wife of Sharon, and that therefore he had married a virtuous widow. He had not often been crossed in his purpose or been resisted when he had once taken a position. By his marriage he virtually served notice on the judges of the Supreme Court of the State, before whom the appeal was then pending, that he would not tamely submit to be by them proclaimed to be the dupe of the discarded woman of another. It was well understood that he intended to hold them personally responsible to him for any decision that would have that effect. These intentions were said to have been made known to them.

His rule in life, as once stated by himself, was to compel acquiescence in his will by threats of violence, and known readiness to carry his threats into effect. This, he said, would in most cases insure the desired result. He counted on men's reluctance to engage in personal difficulties with him. He believed in the persuasiveness of ruffianism.

Whether he thought his marriage would frighten Judges Sawyer and Deady, who had just rendered their decision in the United States Circuit Court, and cause them either to modify the terms of the decree not yet entered, or deter them from its enforcement, is a matter of uncertainty. He was of the ultra State's-rights school and had great faith in the power of the courts of a State when arrayed against those of the United States. He had always denied the jurisdiction of the latter in the case of Sarah Althea, both as to the subject-matter and as to the parties. He refused to see any difference between a suit for a divorce and a suit to cancel a forged paper, which, if allowed to pass as genuine, would entitle its holder to another's property. He persisted in denying that Sharon had been a citizen of Nevada during his lifetime, and ignored the determination of this question by the Circuit Court.

But if Judge Terry had counted on the fears of the United States judges of California he had reckoned too boldly, for on the 15th of January, 1886, eight days after his marriage, the decree of the Circuit Court was formally entered. This decree adjudged the alleged marriage contract of August 25, 1880, false, counterfeited, fabricated, and fraudulent, and ordered that it be surrendered to be cancelled and annulled, and be kept in the custody of the clerk, subject to the further order of the court; and Sarah Althea Hill and her representatives were perpetually enjoined from alleging the genuineness or the validity of the instrument, or making use of it in any way to support her claims as wife of the complainant.

The execution of this decree would, of course, put an end to Sarah Althea's claim, the hope of maintaining which was supposed to have been the motive of the marriage. To defeat its execution then became the sole object of Terry's life. This he hoped to do by antagonizing it with a favorable decision of the Supreme Court of the State, on the appeals pending therein. It has heretofore been stated that the case against Sharon in the Superior Court was removed from the calendar on the 14th day of November, 1885, because of the defendant's death on the previous day. The 11th of February following, upon proper application, the court ordered the substitution of Frederick W. Sharon as executor and sole defendant in the suit in the place of William Sharon, deceased. The motion for a new trial was argued on the 28th of the following May, and held under advisement until the 4th of the following October, when it was denied. From this order of denial an appeal was taken by the defendant.

It must be borne in mind that there were now two appeals in this case to the Supreme Court of the State from the Superior Court. One taken on the 25th of February, 1885, from the judgment of Judge Sullivan, and from his order for alimony and fees, and the other an appeal taken October 4, 1886, from the order denying the new trial in the cause.

On the 31st of January, 1888, the Supreme Court rendered its decision, affirming the judgment of the Superior Court in favor of Sarah Althea, but reversing the order made by Judge Sullivan granting counsel fees, and reducing the allowance for alimony from

$2,500 per month to $500. Four judges concurred in this decision, namely, McKinstry, Searles, Patterson, and Temple. Three judges dissented, to wit, Thornton, Sharpstein, and McFarland.

There then remained pending in the same court the appeal from the order granting a new trial. It was reasonable that Terry should expect a favorable decision on this appeal, as soon as it could be reached. This accomplished, he and Sarah Althea thought to enter upon the enjoyment of the great prize for which they had contended with such desperate energy. Terry had always regarded the decree of the Circuit Court as a mere harmless expression of opinion, which there would be no attempt to enforce, and which the state courts would wholly ignore. Whatever force it might finally be given by the Supreme Court of the United States appeared to him a question far in the future, for he supposed he had taken an appeal from the decree. This attempted appeal was found to be without effect, because when ordered the suit had abated by the death of the plaintiff, and no appeal could be taken until the case was revived by order of the court. This order was never applied for. The two years within which an appeal could have been taken expired January 15, 1888. The decree of the Circuit Court had therefore become final at that time.

CHAPTER VI.

It was at this stage of the prolonged legal controversy that Justice Field first sat in the case. The
executor of the Sharon estate, on the 12th of March,
1888, filed a bill of revivor in the United States Circuit Court. This was a suit to revive the case of
Sharon vs. Hill, that its decree might stand in the
same condition and plight in which it was at the time
of its entry, which, being *nunc pro tunc*, was of the
same effect as if the entry had preceded the death of
Mr. Sharon, the case having been argued and submitted during his lifetime. The decree directed the
surrender and cancellation of the forged marriage
certificate, and perpetually enjoined Sarah Althea
Hill, and her representatives, from alleging the genuineness or validity of that instrument, or making
any use of the same in evidence, or otherwise to support any rights claimed under it.

The necessity for this suit was the fact that the
forged paper had not been surrendered for cancellation, as ordered by the decree, and the plaintiff feared
that the defendant would claim and seek to enforce
property rights as wife of the plaintiff, by authority of
the alleged written declaration of marriage, under the
decree of another court, essentially founded thereupon, contrary to the perpetual injunction ordered by
the Circuit Court. To this suit, David S. Terry, as
husband of the defendant, was made a party. It
merely asked the Circuit Court to place its own de-

cree in a position to be executed, and thereby prevent
the spoliation of the Sharon estate, under the authority of the decree of Judge Sullivan in the suit in the
state court subsequently commenced. A demurrer
was filed by the defendant. It was argued in July
before Justice Field, Judge Sawyer, and District
Judge Sabin. It was overruled on the 3d of September, when the court ordered that the original suit of
Sharon against Hill, and the final decree therein, stand
revived in the name of Frederick W. Sharon as executor, and that the said suit and the proceedings
therein be in the same plight and condition they were
in at the death of William Sharon, so as to give the
executor, complainant as aforesaid, the full benefit,
rights, and protection of the decree, and full power
to enforce the same against the defendants, and each
of them, at all times and in all places, and in all particulars. The opinion in the case was delivered by
Justice Field. During its delivery he was interrupted
by Mrs. Terry with violent and abusive language, and
an attempt by her to take a pistol from a satchel
which she held in her hand. Her removal from the
court-room by order of Justice Field; her husband's
assault upon the marshal with a deadly weapon for
executing the order, and the imprisonment of both
the Terrys for contempt of court, will be more particularly narrated hereafter.

The commencement of the proceedings for the re-
vival of the suit was well calculated to alarm the
Terrys. They saw that the decree in the Circuit
Court was to be relied upon for something more than
its mere moral effect. Their feeling towards Judges
Sawyer and Deady was one of most intense hatred.
Judge Deady was at his home in Oregon, beyond the

reach of physical violence at their hands, but Judge Sawyer was in San Francisco attending to his official duties. Upon him they took an occasion to vent their wrath.

It was on the 14th of August, 1888, after the commencement of the revivor proceedings, but before the decision. Judge Sawyer was returning in the railway train to San Francisco from Los Angeles, where he had been to hold court. Judge Terry and his wife took the same train at Fresno. Judge Sawyer occupied a seat near the center of the sleeping-car, and Judge and Mrs. Terry took the last section of the car, behind him, and on the same side. A few minutes after leaving Fresno, Mrs. Terry walked down the aisle to a point just beyond Judge Sawyer, and turning around with an ugly glare at him, hissed out, in a spiteful and contemptuous tone: "Are you here?" to which the Judge quietly replied: "Yes, Madam," and bowed. She then resumed her seat. A few minutes after, Judge Terry walked down the aisle about the same distance, looked over into the end section at the front of the car, and finding it vacant, went back, got a small hand-bag, and returned and seated himself in the front section, with his back to the engine and facing Judge Sawyer. Mrs. Terry did not (at the moment) accompany him. A few minutes later she walked rapidly down the passage, and as she passed Judge Sawyer, seized hold of his hair at the back of his head, gave it a spiteful twitch and passed quickly on, before he could fully realize what had occurred. After passing she turned a vicious glance upon him, which was continued for some time after taking her seat by the side of her husband A passenger heard Mrs. Terry say to her husband: " I will give him a

taste of what he will get bye and bye." Judge Terry
was heard to remark: "The best thing to do with
him would be to take him down the bay and drown
him." Upon the arrival of Judge Sawyer at San
Francisco, he entered a street car, and was followed
by the Terrys. Mrs. Terry took a third seat from
him, and seeing him, said: "What, are you in this
car, too?" When the Terrys left the car Mrs. Terry
addressed some remark to Judge Sawyer in a spiteful
tone, and repeated it. He said he did not quite catch
it, but it was something like this: "We will meet
again. This is not the end of it."

Persons at all familiar with the tricks of those who
seek human life, and still contrive to keep out of the
clutches of the law, will see in the scene above recited
an attempt to provoke an altercation which would
have been fatal to Judge Sawyer, if he had resented
the indignity put upon him by Mrs. Terry, by even so
much as a word. This could easily have been made
the pretext for an altercation between the two men,
in which the result would not have been doubtful.
There could have been no proof that Judge Terry
knew of his wife's intention to insult and assault
Judge Sawyer as she passed him, nor could it have
been proven that he knew she had done so. A remonstrance from Sawyer could easily have been con-
strued by Terry, upon the statement of his wife, into
an original, unprovoked, and aggressive affront. It
is now, however, certain that the killing of Judge
Sawyer was not at that time intended. It may have
been, to use Mrs. Terry's words, " to give him a taste
of what he would get bye and bye," if he should dare
to render the decision in the revivor case adversely to
them.

This incident has been here introduced and dwelt upon for the purpose of showing the tactics resorted to by the Terrys during this litigation, and the methods by which they sought to control decisions. It is entirely probable that they had hopes of intimidating the federal judges, as many believed some state judges had been, and that thus they might " from the nettle danger, pluck the flower safety."

We have seen that they reckoned without their host. We shall now see to what extent their rage carried them on the day that the decision was rendered reviving the decree.

CHAPTER VII.

On the day after Judge Sawyer's return from Los
Angeles he called the marshal to his chambers, and
notified him of Mrs. Terry's violent conduct towards
him on the train in the presence of her husband, so
that he might take such steps as he thought proper
to keep order when they came into the court-building,
and see that there was no disturbance in the court-
room. On the morning of September 3d, the marshal
was again summoned to Judge Sawyer's room, where
Judge Field was also present. They informed him
that the decision in the revival suit would be rendered
that day, and they desired him to be present, with a
sufficient number of bailiffs to keep order in court.
They told him that judging from the action of the
Terrys on the train, and the threats they were making so publicly, and which were being constantly published in the newspapers, it was not impossible that
they might create a disturbance in the court-room.

When the court opened that day, it found Terry and
his wife already seated within the bar, and immediately
in front of the judges. As it afterward appeared, they
were both on a war-footing, he being armed with a
concealed bowie knife, and she with a 41-calibre revolver, which she carried in a small hand-bag, five of
its chambers being loaded. The judges took their
seats on the bench, and very shortly afterward Justice
Field, who presided, began reading the opinion of the
court in which both of his associates concurred. A

printed pamphlet copy of this opinion contains 61 pages, of which 18 are taken up with a statement of the case. The opinion commences at page 19 and covers the remaining 42 pages of the pamphlet.

From time to time, as the reading of the opinion progressed, Mrs. Terry, who was greatly excited, was observed to unclasp and clasp again the fastening of her satchel which contained her pistol, as if to be sure she could do so at any desired moment. At the 11th page of the opinion the following passage occurs:

" The original decree is not self-executing in all its parts ; it may be questioned whether any steps could be taken for its enforcement, until it was revived, but if this were otherwise, the surrender of the alleged marriage contract for cancellation, as ordered, requires affirmative action on the part of the defendant. The relief granted is not complete until such surrender is made. When the decree pronounced the instrument a forgery, not only had the plaintiff the right that it should thus be put out of the way of being used in the future to his embarrassment and the embarrassment of his estate, but public justice required that it should be formally cancelled, that it might constantly bear on its face the evidence of its bad character, whenever or wherever presented or appealed to."

When Mrs. Terry heard the above words concerning the surrender of the alleged marriage contract for cancellation, she first endeavored for a few seconds, but unsuccessfully, to open the satchel containing her pistol. For some reason the catch refused to yield. Then, rising to her feet, and placing the satchel before her on the table, she addressed the presiding justice, saying:

"Are you going to make me give up my marriage contract ? "

Justice Field said, " Be seated, madam."

She repeated her question :

" Are you going to take the responsibility of order-ing me to deliver up that contract ? "

She was again ordered to resume her seat. At this she commenced raving loudly and violently at the justice in coarse terms, using such phrases as these :

"Mr. Justice Field, how much have you been bought for ? Everybody knows that you have been bought ; that this is a paid decision."

" How big was the sack ? "

" How much have you been paid for the decision ? "

" You have been bought by Newland's coin ; every-body knows you were sent out here by the Newlands to make this decision."

" Every one of you there have been paid for this decision."

At the commencement of this tirade, and after her refusal to desist when twice ordered to do so, the presiding justice directed the marshal to remove her from the court-room. She said defiantly :

" I will not be removed from the court-room ; you dare not remove me from the court-room."

Judge Terry made no sign of remonstrance with her, had not endeavored to restrain her, but had, on the contrary, been seen to nod approvingly to her, as if assenting to something she had said to him just before she sprang to her feet. The instant, however, the court directed her removal from the room, of which she had thus taken temporary possession, to the total suspension of the court proceedings, his soul was " in arms and eager for the fray." As the marshal moved toward the offending woman, he rose from his seat, under great excitement, exclaiming, among other things, " No living man shall touch my wife!" or words of that import, and dealt the marshal a violent blow in the face,* breaking one of his front teeth. He then unbuttoned his coat and thrust his hand under his vest, where his bowie-knife was kept, apparently for the purpose of drawing it, when he was seized by persons present, his hands held from drawing his weapon, and he himself forced down on his back. The marshal, with the assistance of a deputy, then removed Mrs. Terry from the court-room, she struggling, screaming, kicking, striking, and scratching them as she went, and pouring out imprecations upon Judges Field and Sawyer, denouncing them as " corrupt scoundrels," and declaring she would kill them both. She was taken from the room into the main corridor, thence into the marshal's business office, and then into an inner room of his office. She did not cease struggling when she reached that room, but continued her frantic abuse.

While Mrs. Terry was being removed from the court-room Terry was held down by several strong men. He was thus, by force alone, prevented from drawing his knife on the marshal. While thus held he gave vent to coarse and denunciatory language against the officers. When Mrs. Terry was removed from the court-room he was allowed to rise. He at once made a swift rush for the door leading to the corridor on which was the marshal's office. As he was about leaving the room or immediately after stepping out of it, he succeeded in drawing his knife. As he crossed the threshold he brandished the knife above his head, saying, " I am going to my wife."

---

* One of the witnesses stated that Terry also said, " Get a written order from the court."

There was a terrified cry from the bystanders : " He
has got a knife." His arms were then seized by a
deputy marshal and others present, to prevent him
from using it, and a desperate struggle ensued. Four
persons held on to the arms and body of Terry, and
one presented a pistol to his head, threatening at the
same time to shoot him if he did not give up the knife.
To these threats Terry paid no attention, but held on
to the knife, actually passing it during the struggle
from one hand to the other. David Neagle then seized
the handle of the knife and commenced drawing it
through Terry's hand, when Terry relinquished it.

The whole scene was one of the wildest alarm and
confusion. To use the language of one of the witnesses, " Terry's conduct throughout this affair was
most violent. He acted like a demon, and all the time
while in the corridor he used loud and violent language, which could be plainly heard in the court-room,
and, in fact, throughout the building," applying to
the officers vile epithets, and threatening to cut their
hearts out if they did not let him go to his wife. The
knife which Terry drew, and which he afterwards
designated as " a small sheath knife," was, including
the handle, nine and a quarter inches long, the blade
being five inches, having a sharp point, and is commonly called a bowie-knife. He himself afterwards
represented that he drew this knife, not " because he
wanted to hurt anybody, but because he wanted to
force his way into the marshal's office."

The presiding justice had read only a small portion
of the opinion of the court when he was interrupted
by the boisterous and violent proceedings described.
On their conclusion, by the arrest of the Terrys, he
proceeded with the reading of the opinion, which oc-

cupied nearly a whole hour. The justices, without adjourning the court, then retired to the adjoining chambers of the presiding justice for deliberation. They there considered of the action which should be taken against the Terrys for their disorderly and contemptuous conduct. After determining what that should be they returned to the court-room and announced it. For their conduct and resistance to the execution of the order of the court both were adjudged guilty of contempt and ordered, as a punishment, to be imprisoned in the county jail, Terry for six months and his wife for thirty days. When Terry heard of the order, and the commitment was read to him, he said, " Judge Field " (applying to him a coarse and vituperative epithet) " thinks when I get out, when I get released from jail, that he will be in Washington, but I will meet him when he comes back next year, and it will not be a very pleasant meeting for him."

Mrs. Terry said that she would kill both Judges Field and Sawyer, and repeated the threat several times. While the prisoners were being taken to jail, Mrs. Terry said to her husband, referring to Judge Sawyer: " I wooled him good on the train coming from Los Angeles. He has never told that." To which he replied: " He will not tell that; that was too good."

She said she could have shot Judge Field and killed him from where she stood in the court-room, but that she was not ready then to kill the old villain; she wanted him to live longer. While crossing the ferry to Oakland she said, " I could have killed Judges Field and Sawyer; I could shoot either one of them, and you would not find a judge or a jury in the State would convict me." She repeated this, and Terry answered, saying: "No, you could not find a jury that would convict any one for killing the old villain," referring to Judge Field.

The jailer at Alameda testified that one day Mrs. Terry showed him the sheath of her husband's knife, saying: " That is the sheath of that big bowie-knife that the Judge drew. Don't you think it is a large knife?" Judge Terry was present, and laughed and said: " Yes; I always carry that," meaning the knife.

To J. H. O'Brien, a well-known citizen, Judge Terry said that " after he got out of jail he would horsewhip Judge Field. He said he did not think he would ever return to California, but this earth was not large enough to keep him from finding Judge Field, and horsewhipping him," and said, " if he resents it I will kill him."

To a newspaper writer, Thomas T. Williams, he said: " Judge Field would not dare to come out to the Pacific Coast, and he would have a settlement with him if he did come."

J. M. Shannon, a friend of Terry's for thirty years, testified that while the Terrys were in jail he called there with Mr. Wigginton, formerly a member of Congress from California; that during the call Mrs. Terry said something to her husband to the effect that they could not do anything at all in regard to it. He said: " Yes, we can." She asked what they could do. He said: "I can kill old Sawyer, damn him. I will kill old Sawyer, and then the President will have to appoint some one in his place." In saying this " he brought his fist down hard and seemed to be mad."

Ex-Congressman Wigginton also testified concerning this visit to Terry. It occurred soon after the commitment. He went to arrange about some case in which he and Terry were counsel on opposite sides. He told Terry of a rumor that there was some old grudge or difference between him and Judge Field. Terry said there was none he knew of. He said:

" ' When Judge Field's name was mentioned as candidate for President of the United States,'—I think he said,—' when I was a delegate to the convention, it being supposed that I had certain influence with a certain political element, that also had delegates in the convention, some friend or friends '—I will not be sure whether it was friend or friends—' of Judge Field came to me and asked for my influence with these delegates to secure the nomination for Judge Field. My answer '—I am now stating the language as near as I can of Judge Terry's—' my answer was, "No, I have no influence with that element." I understood it to be the workingmen's delegates. I could not control these delegates, and if I could would not control them for Field.' He said: ' That may have caused some alienation, but I do not know that Field knew that.' "

Mr. Wigginton said that Mrs. Terry asked her husband what he could do, and he replied, showing more feeling than he had before : " Do ? I can kill old Sawyer, and by God, if necessary, I will, and the President will then have to appoint some one else in his place."

CHAPTER VIII.

On the 12th of September Terry petitioned the Circuit Court for a revocation of the order of imprisonment in his case, and in support thereof made the
following statement under oath :

"That when petitioner's wife, the said Sarah A.
Terry, first arose from her seat, and before she uttered
a word, your petitioner used every effort in his power
to cause her to resume her seat and remain quiet, and
he did nothing to encourage her in her acts of indiscretion ; when this court made the order that petitioner's
wife be removed from the court-room your petitioner
arose from his seat with the intention and purpose of
himself removing her from the court-room quietly and
peaceably, and that he had no intention or design of
obstructing or preventing the execution of said order
of the court; that he never struck or offered to strike
the United States marshal until the said marshal had
assaulted himself, and had in his presence violently,
and as he believed unnecessarily, assaulted the petitioner's wife.

"Your petitioner most solemnly swears that he
neither drew nor attempted to draw any deadly weapon
of any kind whatever in said court-room, and that he
did not assault or attempt to assault the U. S. marshal
with any deadly weapon in said court-room or elsewhere. And in this connection he respectfully represents that after he left said court-room he heard loud
talking in one of the rooms of the U. S. marshal, and

among the voices proceeding therefrom he recognized that of his wife, and he thereupon attempted to force his way into said room through the main office of the United States marshal; the door of the room was blocked by such a crowd of men that the door could not be closed ; that your petitioner then, for the first time, drew from inside his vest a small sheath-knife, at the same time saying to those standing in his way in said door, that he did not want to hurt any one; that all he wanted was to get into the room where his wife was. The crowd then parted and your petitioner entered the doorway, and there saw a United States deputy marshal with a revolver in his hand pointed to the ceiling of the room. Some one then said : ' Let him in if he will give up his knife,' and your petitioner immediately released hold of the knife to some one standing by.

" In none of these transactions did your petitioner have the slightest idea of showing any disrespect to this honorable court or any of the judges thereof.

" That he lost his temper, he respectfully submits was a natural consequence of himself being assaulted when he was making an honest effort to peaceably and quietly enforce the order of the court, so as to avoid a scandalous scene, and of his seeing his wife so unnecessarily assaulted in his presence."

It will be observed that Terry, in his petition, contradicts the facts recited in the orders for the commitment of himself and his wife. These orders were made by Justice Field, Circuit Judge Sawyer, and District Judge Sabin from the district of Nevada, who did not depend upon the testimony of others for information as to the facts in the case, but were, themselves, eye-witnesses and spoke from personal observation and absolute knowledge.

In passing upon Terry's petition, these judges, speaking through Justice Field, who delivered the

opinion of the court, bore testimony to a more particular account of the conduct of Terry and his wife than
had been given in the order for the commitment. As
the scene has already been described at length, this
portion of the opinion of the court would be a mere
repetition, and is therefore omitted. After reciting
the facts, Justice Field referred to the gravity of
Terry's offense in the following terms :

" The misbehavior of the defendant, David S. Terry,
in the presence of the court, in the court-room, and in
the corridor, which was near thereto, and in one of
which (and it matters not which) he drew his bowie-
knife, and brandished it with threats against the
deputy of the marshal and others aiding him, is sufficient of itself to justify the punishment imposed.
But, great as this offense was, the forcible resistance
offered to the marshal in his attempt to execute the
order of the court, and beating him, was a far greater
and more serious affair. The resistance and beating
was the highest possible indignity to the Government.
When the flag of the country is fired upon and in-
sulted, it is not the injury to the bunting, the linen,
or silk on which the stars and stripes are stamped
which startles and arouses the country. It is the
indignity and insult to the emblem of the nation's
majesty which stirs every heart, and makes every pa-
triot eager to resent them. So, the forcible resistance
to an officer of the United States in the execution of
the process, orders, and judgments of their courts is
in like manner an indignity and insult to the power
and authority of the Government which can neither
be overlooked nor extenuated."

After reviewing Terry's statement, Justice Field
said :

" We have read this petition with great surprise at
its omissions and misstatements. As to what occurred

under our immediate observation, its statements do not accord with the facts as we saw them ; as to what occurred at the further end of the room and in the corridor, its statements are directly opposed to the concurring accounts of the officers of the court and parties present, whose position was such as to preclude error in their observations. According to the sworn statement of the marshal, which accords with our own observations, so far from having struck or assaulted Terry, he had not even laid his hands upon him when the violent blow in the face was received. And it is clearly beyond controversy that Terry never voluntarily surrendered his bowie-knife, and that it was wrenched from him only after a violent struggle.

" We can only account for his misstatement of facts as they were seen by several witnesses, by supposing that he was in such a rage at the time that he lost command of himself, and does not well remember what he then did, or what he then said. Some judgment as to the weight this statement should receive, independently of the incontrovertible facts at variance with it, may be formed from his speaking of the deadly bowie-knife he drew as ' a small sheath-knife,' and of the shameless language and conduct of his wife as ' her acts of indiscretion.'

" No one can believe that he thrust his hand under his vest where his bowie-knife was carried without intending to draw it. To believe that he placed his right hand there for any other purpose—such as to rest it after the violent fatigue of the blow in the marshal's face or to smooth down his ruffled linen— would be childish credulity.

" But even his own statement admits the assaulting of the marshal, who was endeavoring to enforce the order of the court, and his subsequently drawing a knife to force his way into the room where the marshal had removed his wife. Yet he offers no apology for his conduct ; expresses no regret for what he did, and makes no reference to his violent and vituperative language against the judges and officers of the court, while under arrest, which is detailed in the affidavits filed."

In refusing to grant the petition the court said :

" There is nothing in his petition which would justify
any remission of the imprisonment. The law imputes
an attempt to accomplish the natural result of one's
acts, and when these acts are of a criminal nature it
will not accept, against such implication, the denial of
the transgressor. No one would be safe if the denial
of a wrongful or criminal act would suffice to release
the violator of the law from the punishment due his
offenses."

On September 17, 1888, after the announcement of
the opinion of the court by Mr. Justice Field denying
the petition of D. S. Terry for a revocation of the
order committing him for contempt, Mr. Terry made
public a correspondence between himself and Judge
Solomon Heydenfeldt, which explains itself, and is as
follows :

" MY DEAR TERRY:

" The papers which our friend Stanley sends you
will explain what we are trying to do. I wish to see
Field to-morrow and sound his disposition, and if it
seems advisable I will present our petition. But in
order to be effective, and perhaps successful, I wish
to feel assured and be able to give the assurance that
failure to agree will not be followed by any attempt
on your part to break the peace either by action or
demonstration. I know that you would never com-
promise me in any such manner, but it will give me
the power to make an emphatic assertion to that effect
and that ought to help.

" Please answer promptly.
" S. HEYDENFELDT."

The reply of Judge Terry is as follows :

" DEAR HEYDENFELDT :

" Your letter was handed me last evening. I do not
expect a favorable result from any application to the

Circuit Court, and I have very reluctantly consented
that an application be made to Judge Field, who will
probably wish to pay me for my refusal to aid his
presidential aspirations four years ago. I had a conversation with Garber on Saturday last in which I told
him if I was released I would seek no personal satisfaction for what had passed. You may say as emphat-
ically as you wish that I do not contemplate breaking
the peace, and that, so far from seeking, I will avoid
meeting any of the parties concerned. I will not
promise that I will refrain from denouncing the decision or its authors. I believe that the decision was
purchased and paid for with coin from the Sharon estate, and I would stay here for ten years before I would
say that I did not so believe. If the judges of the
Circuit Court would do what is right they would re-
voke the order imprisoning my wife. She certainly
was in contempt of court, but that great provocation
was given by going outside the record to smirch her
character ought to be taken into consideration in
mitigation of the sentence. Field, when a legislator,
thought that no court should be allowed to punish
for contempt by imprisonment for a longer period
than five days. My wife has already been in prison
double that time for words spoken under very great
provocation. No matter what the result, I propose
to stay here until my wife is dismissed.

       " Yours truly,

              " D. S. TERRY."

In the opinion of the court, referred to in the foregoing letter as "smirching the character" of Mrs.
Terry, there was nothing said reflecting upon her,
except what was contained in quotations from the
opinion of Judge Sullivan of the State court in the
divorce case of Sharon vs. Hill in her favor. These
quotations commenced at page 58 of the pamphlet
copy of Justice Field's opinion, when less than three
pages remained to be read. It was at page 29 of

the pamphlet that Justice Field was reading when Mrs. Terry interrupted him and was removed from the court-room. After her removal he resumed the reading of the opinion, and only after reading 29 pages, occupying nearly an hour, did he reach the quotations in which Judge Sullivan expressed his own opinion that Mrs. Terry had committed perjury several times in his court. The reading of them could not possibly have furnished her any provocation for her conduct. She had then been removed from the court-room more than an hour. Besides, if they "smirched" her character, why did she submit to them complacently when they were originally uttered from the bench by Judge Sullivan in his opinion rendered in her favor?

Justice Field, in what he was reading that so incensed Mrs. Terry, was simply stating the effect of a decree previously rendered in a case, in the trial of which he had taken no part. He was stating the law as to the rights established by that decree. The efforts then made by Terry, and subsequently by his friends and counsel, to make it appear that his assault upon the marshal and defiance of the court were caused by his righteous indignation at assaults made by Judge Field upon his wife's character were puerile, because based on a falsehood. The best proof of this is the opinion itself.

Judge Terry next applied to the Supreme Court of the United States for a writ of habeas corpus. In that application he declared that on the 12th day of September, 1888, he addressed to the Circuit Court a petition duly verified by his oath, and then stated the petition for release above quoted. Yet in a communication published in the *San Francisco Examiner* of

October 22d he solemnly declared that this very petition was not filed by any one on his behalf. After
full argument by the Supreme Court the writ was
denied, November 12, 1888, by an unanimous court,
Justice Field, of course, not sitting in the case. Justice Harlan delivered the opinion of the Court.

CHAPTER IX.

Before the petition for habeas corpus was presented to the Supreme Court of the United States, Judge Terry's friends made a strenuous effort to secure his pardon from President Cleveland. The President declined to interfere. In his efforts in that direction Judge Terry made gross misrepresentations as to Judge Field's relations with himself, which were fully refuted by Judge Heydenfeldt, the very witness he had invoked. Judge Heydenfeldt had been an associate of Judge Terry on the State supreme bench. These representations and their refutation are here given as a necessary element in this narrative.

Five days after he had been imprisoned, to wit, September 8, Terry wrote a letter to his friend Zachariah Montgomery at Washington, then Assistant Attorney-General for the Interior Department under the Cleveland Administration, in which he asked his aid to obtain a pardon from the President. Knowing that it would be useless to ask this upon the record of his conduct as shown by the order for his commitment, he resorted to the desperate expedient of endeavoring to overcome that record by putting his own oath to a false statement of the facts, against the statement of the three judges, made on their own knowledge, as eye-witnesses, and supported by the affidavits of court officers, lawyers, and spectators.

To Montgomery he wrote:

"I have made a plain statement of the facts which occurred in the court, and upon that propose to ask the intervention of the President, and I request you to see the President; tell him all you know of me, and what degree of credit should be given to a statement by me upon my own knowledge of the facts. When you read the statement I have made you will be satisfied that the statement in the order of the court is false."

He then proceeded to tell his story as he told it in his petition to the Circuit Court. His false representations as to the assault he made upon the marshal, and as to his alleged provocation therefor, were puerile in the extreme. He stood alone in his declaration that the marshal first assaulted him, while the three judges and a dozen witnesses declared the very opposite. His denial that he had assaulted the marshal with a deadly weapon was contradicted by the judges and others, who said that they saw him attempt to draw a knife in the court-room, which attempt, followed up as it was continually until successful, constituted an assault with that weapon. To call his bowie-knife "a small sheath-knife," and the outrageous conduct of his wife "acts of indiscretion;" to pretend that he lost his temper because he was assaulted "while making an honest effort to peaceably and quietly enforce the order of the court," and finally to pretend that his wife had been "unnecessarily assaulted" in his presence, was all not only false, but simply absurd and ridiculous.

He said: "I don't want to stay in prison six months for an offense of which I am not guilty. There is no way left except to appeal to the President. The record of a court imports absolute verity, so I am not allowed to show that the record of the Circuit Court is absolutely false. If you can help me in this matter you will confer on me the greatest possible favor."

He told Montgomery that it had been suggested to him that one reason for Field's conduct was his refusal to support the latter's aspirations for the Presidency. In this connection he made the following statement:

" In March, 1884, I received a note from my friend Judge Heydenfeldt, saying that he wished to see me on important business, and asking me to call at his office. I did so, and he informed me that he had received a letter from Judge Field, who was confident that if he could get the vote of California in the Democratic National Convention, which would assemble that year, he would be nominated for President and would be elected as, with the influence of his family and their connection, that he would certainly carry New York; that Judge Field further said that a Congressman from California and other of his friends had said that if I would aid him, I could give him the California delegation; that he understood I wanted official recognition as, because of my duel years ago, I was under a cloud; that if I would aid him, I should have anything I desired."

It will be observed that he here positively states that Judge Heydenfeldt told him he had received a letter from Judge Field, asking Terry's aid and promising, for it, a reward. Judge Heydenfeldt, in a letter dated August 21, 1889, to the *San Francisco Examiner*, branded Terry's assertion as false. The letter to the *Examiner* is as follows:

" The statement made in to-day's *Examiner* in reference to the alleged letter from Justice Field to me, derived, as is stated by Mr. Ashe, from a conversation with Judge Terry, is utterly devoid of truth.

" I had at one time, many years ago, a letter from Justice Field, in which he stated that he was going to devote his leisure to preparing for circulation among his friends his reminiscences, and, referring to those of early California times, he requested me to obtain from Judge Terry his, Terry's, version of the Terry-Broderick duel, in order that his account of it might be accurate. As soon as I received this letter, I wrote to Judge Terry, informing him of Judge Field's wishes, and recommending him to comply, as coming, as the account would, from friendly hands, it would put him correct upon the record, and would be in a form which would endure as long as necessary for his reputation on that subject.

" I received no answer from Judge Terry, but meeting him, some weeks after, on the street in this city, he excused himself, saying that he had been very busy, and adding that it was unnecessary for him to furnish a version of the duel, as the published and accepted version was correct.

" The letter to me from Justice Field above referred to is the only letter from Justice Field to me in which Judge Terry's name was ever mentioned, and, with the exception of the above-mentioned street conversation, Judge Field was never the subject of conversation between Judge Terry and myself, from the time I left the bench, on the 1st of January, 1857, up to the time of Terry's death.

" As to the statement that during Terry's trouble with the Sharon case, I offered Terry the use of Field's letter, it results from what I have above stated—that it is a vile falsehood, whoever may be responsible for it.

" I had no such letter, and consequently could have made no such offer.

" San Francisco, August 21, 1889.

" S. HEYDENFELDT."

Judge Heydenfeldt subsequently addressed the following letter to Judge Field :

" San Francisco, *August* 31, 1889.

" My Dear Judge : I received yours of yesterday
with the extract from the Washington *Post* of the
22d inst., containing a copy of a letter from the late
Judge Terry to the Hon. Zack Montgomery.

" The statement in that letter of a conversation between Terry and myself in reference to you is untrue.
The only conversation Terry and I ever had in relation
to you was, as heretofore stated, in regard to a request
from you to me to get from Terry his version of the
Terry-Broderick duel, to be used in your intended
reminiscences.

" I do not see how Terry could have made such an
erroneous statement, unless, possibly, he deemed that
application as an advance made by you towards obtaining his political friendship, and upon that built
up a theory, which he moulded into the fancy written
by him in the Montgomery letter.

" In all of our correspondence, kept up from time
to time since your first removal to Washington down
to the present, no letter of yours contained a request
to obtain the political support of any one.

" I remain, dear Judge, very truly yours,

" S. HEYDENFELDT.

" Hon. Stephen J. Field,
    " Palace Hotel, San Francisco."

At the hearing of the Neagle case, Justice Field was
asked if he had been informed of any statements made
by Judge Terry of ill feeling existing between them
before the latter's imprisonment for contempt. He
relpied :

" Yes, sir. Since that time I have seen a letter purporting to come from Terry to Zack Montgomery,
published in Washington, in which he ascribed my
action to personal hostility, because he had not supported me in some political aspiration. There is not
one particle of truth in that statement. It is a pure

invention. In support of his statement he referred to a letter received or an interview had with Judge Heydenfeldt. There is not the slightest foundation for it, and I cannot understand it, except that the man seems to me to have been all changed in the last few years, and he did not hesitate to assert that the official actions of others were governed by improper considerations. I saw charges made by him against judges of the State courts; that they had been corrupt in their decisions against him; that they had been bought. That was the common assertion made by him when decisions were rendered against him."

He then referred to the above letters of Judge Heydenfeldt, declaring Terry's assertion to be false.

It should be borne in mind that Terry's letter to Montgomery was written September 8th. It directly contradicts what he had said to ex-Congressman Wigginton on the 5th or 6th of the same month. To that gentleman he declared that he knew of no "old grudge or little difference" between himself and Judge Field. He said he had declined to support the latter for the Presidency, and added : " That may have caused some alienation, but I do not know that Judge Field knew that."

In his insane rage Terry did not realize how absurd it was to expect people to believe that Judge Sawyer and Judge Sabin, both Republicans, had participated in putting him in jail, to punish him for not having supported Justice Field for the Presidency in a National Democratic Convention years before.

Perhaps Terry thought his reference to the fact that Judge Field's name had been previously used in Democratic Conventions, in connection with the Presidency, might have some effect upon President Cleveland's mind.

This letter was not forwarded to Zachariah Montgomery until a week after it was written. He then stated in a postscript that he had delayed sending it upon the advice of his attorneys pending the application to the Circuit Court for his release. Again he charged that the judges had made a false record against him, and that evidence would be presented to the President to show it.

Terry and his friends brought all the pressure to bear that they could command, but the President refused his petition for a pardon, and, as already shown, the Supreme Court unanimously decided that his imprisonment for contempt had been lawfully ordered. He was therefore obliged to serve out his time.

Mrs. Terry served her thirty days in jail, and was released on the 3d of October.

There is a federal statute that provides for the reduction of a term of imprisonment of criminals for good behavior. Judge Terry sought to have this statute applied in his case, but without success. The Circuit Court held that the law relates to state penitentiaries, and not to jails, and that the system of credits could not be applied to prisoners in jail. Besides this, the credits in any case are counted by the year, and not by days or months. The law specifies that prisoners in state prisons are entitled to so many months' time for the first year, and so many for each subsequent year. As Terry's sentence ran for six months, the court said the law could not apply. He consequently remained in jail until the 3d of March, 1889.

CHAPTER X.

Justice Field left California for Washington in September, 1888, a few days after the denial of Terry's petition to the Circuit Court for a release. The threats against his life and that of Judge Sawyer so boldly made by the Terrys were as well known as the newspaper press could make them. In addition to this source of information, reports came from many other directions, telling of the rage of the Terrys and their murderous intentions. From October, 1888, till his departure for California, in June following, 1889, his mail almost every day contained reports of what they were saying, and the warnings and entreaties of his friends against his return to that State. These threats came to the knowledge of the Attorney-General of the United States, who gave directions to the marshal of the northern district of California to see to it that Justice Field and Judge Sawyer should be protected from personal violence at the hands of these parties.

Justice Field made but one answer to all who advised against his going to hold court in California in 1889, and that was, "I cannot and will not allow threats of personal violence to deter me from the regular performance of my judicial duties at the times and places fixed by law. As a judge of the highest court of the country, I should be ashamed to look any man in the face if I allowed a ruffian, by threats against my person, to keep me from holding the regular courts in my circuit."

Terry's murderous intentions became a matter of

public notoriety, and members of Congress and Senators from the Pacific Coast, in interviews with the Attorney-General, confirmed the information derived by him from other sources of the peril to which the United States judges in California were subjected. He, in consequence, addressed the following letter on the subject to Marshal Franks:

> "DEPARTMENT OF JUSTICE,
> "WASHINGTON, *April* 27, 1889.

"JOHN C. FRANKS,
> "*United States Marshal,*
> > *San Francisco, Cal.*

"SIR: The proceedings which have heretofore been had in the case of Mr. and Mrs. Terry in your United States Circuit Court have become matter of public notoriety, and I deem it my duty to call your attention to the propriety of exercising unusual precaution, in case further proceedings shall be had in that case, for the protection of His Honor Justice Field, or whoever may be called upon to hear and determine the matter. Of course, I do not know what may be the feelings or purpose of Mr. and Mrs. Terry in the premises, but many things which have happened indicate that violence on their part is not impossible. It is due to the dignity and independence of the court and the character of its judges that no effort on the part of the Government shall be spared to make them feel entirely safe and free from anxiety in the discharge of their high duties.

"You will understand, of course, that this letter is not for the public, but to put you upon your guard. It will be proper for you to show it to the District Attorney if deemed best.

> "Yours truly,
> > "W. H. H. MILLER,
> > > "*Attorney-General.*"

A month later the Attorney-General authorized the employment of special deputies for the purpose named in the foregoing letter.

CHAPTER XI.

Mrs. Terry did not wait for the release of her husband from jail before renewing the battle. On the 22d
of January, 1889, she gave notice of a motion in the
Superior Court for the appointment of a receiver who
should take charge of the Sharon estate, which she
alleged was being squandered to the injury of her interest therein acquired under the judgment of Judge
Sullivan. On the 29th of January an injunction was
issued by the United States Circuit Court commanding her and all others to desist from this proceeding.
The Terrys seemed to feel confident that this would
bring on a final trial of strength between the federal
and state courts, and that the state court would prevail in enforcing its judgment and orders.

The motion for a receiver was submitted after full
argument, and on the 3d of June following Judge Sullivan rendered a decision asserting the jurisdiction of
his court to entertain the motion for a receiver, and
declaring the decree of the United States Circuit Court
inoperative. In his opinion Judge Sullivan reviewed
the opinion of Justice Field in the revivor suit, taking
issue therewith. As that decision had been affirmed
by the Supreme Court of the United States nearly a
month before, to wit, on the 13th of May, 1889, it was
rather late for such a discussion. Having thus decided, however, that the motion for a receiver could
be made, he set the hearing of the same for July 15,
1889.

On the 27th of May, one week before the rendering of this decision by Judge Sullivan, the mandate of the United States Supreme Court had been filed in the Circuit Court at San Francisco, by which the decree of that court was affirmed. Whether a receiver would be appointed by Judge Sullivan, in the face of the decision of the Supreme Court of the United States, became now an interesting question. Terry and his lawyers affected to hold in contempt the Supreme Court decree, and seemed to think no serious attempt would be made to enforce it.

Meantime, both of the Terrys had been indicted in the United States Circuit Court for the several offenses committed by them in assaulting the marshal in the court-room as hereinbefore described. These indictments were filed on the 20th of September. Dilatory motions were granted from time to time, and it was not until the 4th of June that demurrers to the indictments were filed. The summer vacation followed without any argument of these demurrers. It was during this vacation that Justice Field arrived in California, on the 20th of June. The situation then existing was as follows:

The criminal proceedings against the Terrys were at a standstill, having been allowed to drag along for nine months, with no further progress than the filing of demurrers to the indictments.

The appeal to the Supreme Court of the State from Judge Sullivan's order denying a new trial had been argued and submitted on the 4th of May, but no decision had been rendered.

Despite the pendency of that appeal, by reason of which the judgment of the Supreme Court of the State had not yet become final, and despite the mandate of the United States Supreme Court affirming the decree in the revivor case, Judge Sullivan had, as we have already seen, set the 15th of July for the hearing of the motion of the Terrys for the appointment of a receiver to take charge of the Sharon estate. For them to proceed with this motion would be a contempt of the United States Circuit Court.

The arrival of Justice Field should have instructed Judge Terry that the decree of that court could not be defied with impunity, and that the injunction issued in it against further proceedings upon the judgment in the state court would be enforced with all the power authorized by the Constitution and laws of the United States for the enforcement of judicial process.

As the 15th of July approached, the lawyers who had been associated with Terry commenced discussing among themselves what would be the probable consequence to them of disobeying an injunction of the United States Circuit Court. The attorneys for the Sharon estate made known their determination to apply to that court for the enforcement of its writ in their behalf. The Terrys' experience in resisting the authority of that court served as a warning for their attorneys.

On the morning of the 15th of July Judge Terry and his wife appeared, as usual, in the Superior Court room. Two of their lawyers came in, remained a few minutes and retired. Judge Terry himself remained silent. His wife arose and addressed the court, saying that her lawyers were afraid to appear for her. She said they feared if they should make a motion in her behalf, for the appointment of a receiver, Judge Field would put them in jail; therefore, she said, she appeared for herself. She said if she got in jail she would rather have her husband outside, and this was why she made the motion herself, while he remained a spectator.

The hearing was postponed for several days. Before the appointed day therefor, the Supreme Court of the State, on the 17th of July, rendered its decision, reversing the order of Judge Sullivan refusing a new trial, thereby obliterating the judgment in favor of Sarah Althea, and the previous decision of the appellate court affirming it. The court held that this previous judgment had not become the law of the case pending the appeal from the order denying a new trial. It held that where two appeals are taken in the same case, one from the judgment and the other from the order denying a new trial, the whole case must be held to be under the control of the Supreme Court until the whole is disposed of, and the case remanded for further proceedings in the court below. The court reversed its previous decision, and declared that if the statements made by Sarah Althea and by her witnesses had been true, she never had been the wife of William Sharon, for the reason that, after the date of the alleged contract of marriage, the parties held themselves out to the public as single and unmarried people, and that even according to the findings of fact by Judge Sullivan the parties had not assumed marital rights, duties, and obligations. The case was therefore remanded to the Superior Court for a new trial.

On the 2d of August the demurrers to the several indictments against the Terrys came up to be heard in the United States District Court. The argument upon them concluded on the 5th. On the 7th the demurrer to one of the indictments against Sarah

Althea was overruled and she entered a plea of not guilty. No decision was rendered at that time upon either of the five other indictments.

On the following day, August 8th, Justice Field left San Francisco and went to Los Angeles for the purpose of holding court.

CHAPTER XII.

ATTEMPTED ASSASSINATION OF JUSTICE FIELD, RESULTING IN TERRY'S OWN DEATH AT THE HANDS OF A DEPUTY UNITED STATES MARSHAL.

In view of what was so soon to occur, it is important to understand the condition of mind into which Judge Terry and his wife had now wrought themselves. They had been married about two years and a half. In their desperate struggle for a share of a rich man's estate they had made themselves the terror of the community. Armed at all times and ready for mortal combat with whoever opposed their claims, they seemed, up to the 17th of July, to have won their way in the State courts by intimidation. The decision of the United States Circuit Court was rendered before they were married. It proclaimed the pretended marriage agreement a forgery, and ordered it to be delivered to the clerk of the court for cancellation. Terry's marriage with Sarah Althea, twelve days after this, was a declaration of intention to resist its authority.

The conduct of the pair in the Circuit Court on the 3d of September must have had some object. They may have thought to break up the session of the court for that day, and to so intimidate the judges that they would not carry out their purpose of rendering the decision; or they may have hoped that, if rendered, it would be allowed to slumber without any attempt to enforce it; or even that a rehearing might be granted, and a favorable decision forced from the court. It takes a brave man on the bench to stand

firmly for his convictions in the face of such tactics as
were adopted by the Terrys. The scene was expected
also to have its effect upon the minds of the judges
of the Supreme Court of the State, who then were yet
to pass finally upon Sullivan's judgment on the appeal from the order denying a new trial.

But the Terrys had not looked sufficiently at the
possible consequence of their actions. They had thus
far gone unresisted. As District Attorney Carey
wrote to the Attorney-General:

"They were unable to appreciate that an officer
should perform his official duty when that duty in any
way requires that his efforts be directed against them."

When, therefore, Justice Field directed the removal
of Mrs. Terry from the court, and when her doughty
defendant and champion, confident of being able to
defeat the order, found himself vanquished in the encounter, disarmed, arrested, and finally imprisoned,
his rage was boundless. He had found a tribunal
which cared nothing for his threats, and was able to
overcome his violence. A court that would put him
in the Alameda jail for six months for resisting its
order would enforce all its decrees with equal certainty.

From the time of the Terrys' incarceration in the
Alameda county jail their threats against Justice Field
became a matter of such notoriety that the drift of
discussion was not so much whether they would murder the Justice, as to when and under what circumstances they would be likely to do so.

There is little doubt that Terry made many threats
for the express purpose of having them reach the
knowledge of Judge Field at Washington, in the hope

and belief that they would deter him from going to California. He probably thought that the Judge would prefer to avoid a violent conflict, and that if his absence could be assured it might result in allowing the decree of the United States Circuit Court to remain a dead letter.

He told many people that Justice Field would not dare come out to the Pacific Coast. He got the idea into his mind, or pretended to, that Justice Field had put him in jail in order to be able to leave for Washington before a meeting could be had with him. Terry would of course have preferred Field's absence and a successful execution of Sullivan's judgment to his presence in the State and the enforcement of the federal decree.

When the announcement was made that Justice Field had left Washington for San Francisco, public and private discussions were actively engaged in, as to where he would be likely to encounter danger. A special deputy was sent by the marshal to meet the overland train on which he was travelling, at Rena, in Nevada. The methods of Mrs. Terry defied all calculations. She was as likely to make her appearance, with her burly husband as an escort, at the State line, as she finally did at the breakfast table at Lathrop. Justice Field reached his quarters in San Francisco on the 20th of June. From that day until the 14th of August public discussion of what the Terrys would do continued. Some of the newspapers seemed bent upon provoking a conflict, and inquired with devilish mischief when Terry was going to carry out his threatened purpose.

The threats of the Terrys and the rumors of their intended assault upon Justice Field were reported to him and he was advised to go armed against such assault, which would be aimed against his life. He answered : " No, sir ! I will not carry arms, for when it is known that the judges of our courts are compelled to arm themselves against assaults in consequence of their judicial action it will be time to dissolve the courts, consider government a failure, and let society lapse into barbarism."

As the time approached for the hearing of the motion for a receiver before Judge Sullivan, July 15th, grave apprehensions were entertained of serious trouble. Great impatience was expressed with the Supreme Court of the State for not rendering its decision upon the appeal from the order denying a new trial. It was hoped that the previous decision might be reversed, and a conflict between the two jurisdictions thus avoided. When the decision came, on the 17th of July, there seemed to be some relaxation of the great tension in the public mind. With the Supreme Court of the State, as well as the Supreme Court of the United States, squarely on the record against Mrs. Terry's pretensions to have been the wife of William Sharon, it was hoped that the long war had ended.

When Justice Field left San Francisco for Los Angeles he had no apprehensions of danger, and strenuously objected to being accompanied by the deputy marshal. Some of his friends were less confident. They realized better than he did the bitterness that dwelt in the hearts of Terry and his wife, intensified as it was by the realization of the dismal fact that their last hope had expired with the decision of the Supreme Court of the State. The marshal was impressed with the danger that would attend Justice Field's journey to and from the court at Los Angeles.

He went from San Francisco on the 8th of August. After holding court in Los Angeles he took the train for San Francisco August 13th, the deputy marshal occupying a section in the sleeping car directly opposite to his. Judge Terry and his wife left San Francisco for their home in Fresno the day following Justice Field's departure for Los Angeles. Fresno is a station on the Southern Pacific between Los Angeles and San Francisco. His train left Los Angeles for San Francisco at 1.30 Tuesday afternoon, August 13th. The deputy marshal got out at all the stations at which any stop was made for any length of time, to observe who got on board. Before retiring he asked the porter of the car to be sure and wake him in time for him to get dressed before they reached Fresno. At Fresno, where they arrived during the night, he got off the train and went out on the platform. Among the passengers who took the train at that station were Judge Terry and wife. He immediately returned to the sleeper and informed Justice Field, who had been awakened by the stopping of the train, that Terry and his wife had got on the train. He replied: "Very well. I hope that they will have a good sleep."

Neagle slept no more that night. The train reached Merced, an intervening station between Fresno and Lathrop, at 5.30 that morning. Neagle there conferred with the conductor, on the platform, and referred to the threats so often made by the Terrys. He told him that Justice Field was on the train, and that he was accompanying him. He requested him to telegraph to Lathrop, to the constable usually in attendance there, to be at hand, and that if any trouble occurred he would assist in preventing violence.

Justice Field got up before the train reached Lathrop, and told the deputy marshal that he was going to take his breakfast in the dining-room at that place. The following is his statement of what took place :

" He said to me, ' Judge, you can get a good breakfast at the buffet on board.' I did not think at the time what he was driving at, though I am now satisfied that he wanted me to take breakfast on the car and not get off. I said I prefer to have my breakfast at this station. I think I said I had come down from the Yosemite Valley a few days before, and got a good breakfast there, and was going there for that purpose.

" He replied : ' I will go with you.' We were among the first to get off from the train."

As soon as the train arrived, Justice Field, leaning on the arm of Neagle, because of his lameness, proceeded to the dining-room, where they took seats for breakfast.

There were in this dining-room fifteen tables, each one of which was ten feet long and four feet wide. They were arranged in three rows of five each, the tables running lengthwise with each other, with spaces between them of four feet. The aisles between the two rows were about seven feet apart, the rows running north and south.

Justice Field and Neagle were seated on the west side of the middle table in the middle row, the Justice being nearer the lower corner of the table, and Neagle at his left. Very soon after—Justice Field says " a few minutes," while Neagle says " it may be a minute or so "—Judge Terry and his wife entered the dining-room from the east. They walked up the aisle, between the east and middle rows of tables, so that Justice Field and Neagle were faced towards them.

Judge Terry preceded his wife. Justice Field saw them and called Neagle's attention to them. He had already seen them.

As soon as Mrs. Terry had reached a point nearly in front of Justice Field, she turned suddenly around, and scowling viciously, went in great haste out of the door at which she had come in. This was for the purpose, as it afterwards appeared, of getting her satchel with the pistol in it, which she had left in the car. Judge Terry apparently paid no attention to this movement, but proceeded to the next table above and seated himself at the upper end of it, facing the table at which Justice Field was seated. Thus there were between the two men as they sat at the tables a distance equal to two table-lengths and one space of four feet, making about twenty-four feet. Terry had been seated but a very short time—Justice Field thought it a moment or two, Neagle thought it three or four minutes—when he arose and moved down towards the door, this time walking through the aisle *behind* Justice Field, instead of the one in front of him as before. Justice Field supposed, when he arose, that he was going out to meet his wife, as she had not returned, and went on with his breakfast; but when Terry had reached a point behind him, and a little to the right, within two or three feet of him, he halted. Justice Field was not aware of this, nor did he know that Terry had stopped, until he was struck by him a violent blow in the face from behind, followed instantaneously by another blow at the back of his head. Neagle had seen Terry stop and turn. Between this and Terry's assault there was a pause of four or five seconds. Instantaneously upon Terry's dealing a blow, Neagle leaped from his chair and interposed

his diminutive form between Justice Field and the enraged and powerful man, who now sought to execute
his long-announced and murderous purpose. Terry
gave Justice Field no warning of his presence except
a blow from behind with his right hand.

As Neagle rose, he shouted: "Stop, stop, I am an
officer." Judge Terry had drawn back his right arm
for a third blow at Justice Field, and with clinched
fist was about to strike, when his attention was thus
arrested by Neagle, and looking at him he evidently
recognized in him the man who had drawn the knife
from his hand in the corridor before the marshal's
office on the third of September of the preceding
year, while he was attempting to cut his way into the
marshal's office. Neagle put his right hand up as he
ordered Terry to stop, when Terry carried his right
hand at once to his breast, evidently to seize the
knife which he had told the Alameda county jailer he
" always carried." Says Neagle:

"This hand came right to his breast. It went a
good deal quicker than I can explain it. He continued looking at me in a desperate manner and his hand
got there."

The expression of Terry's face at that time was described by Neagle in these words:

" The most desperate expression that I ever saw on
a man's face, and I have seen a good many in my time.
It meant life or death to me or him."

Having thus for a moment diverted the blow aimed
at Justice Field and engaged Terry himself, Neagle did
not wait to be butchered with the latter's ready knife,
which he was now attempting to draw, but raised his

six-shooter with his left hand (he is left-handed) and holding the barrel of it with his right hand, to prevent the pistol from being knocked out of his hands, he shot twice; the first shot into Terry's body and the second at his head. Terry immediately commenced sinking very slowly. Knowing by experience that men mortally wounded have been often known to kill those with whom they were engaged in such an encounter, Neagle fired the second shot to defend himself and Justice Field against such a possibility.

The following is an extract from Justice Field's testimony, commencing at the point where Judge Terry rose from his seat at the breakfast table:

"I supposed, at the time, he was going out to meet his wife, as she had not returned, so I went on with my breakfast. It seems, however, that he came around back of me. I did not see him, and he struck me a violent blow in the face, followed instantaneously by another blow. Coming so immediately together, the two blows seemed like one assault. I heard 'Stop, stop,' cried by Neagle. Of course I was for a moment dazed by the blows. I turned my head around and saw that great form of Terry's with his arm raised and fist clinched to strike me. I felt that a terrific blow was coming, and his arm was descending in a curved way as though to strike the side of my temple, when I heard Neagle cry out: 'Stop, stop, I am an officer.' Instantly two shots followed. I can only explain the second shot from the fact that he did not fall instantly. I did not get up from my seat, although it is proper for me to say that a friend of mine thinks I did, but I did not. I looked around and saw Terry on the floor. I looked at him and saw that particular movement of the eyes that indicates the presence of death. Of course it was a great shock to me. It is impossible for any one to see a man in the full vigor of life, with all those faculties that constitute life instantly extinguished without being affected, and I was. I looked at him for a moment, then went around and looked at him again, and passed on. Great excitement followed. A gentleman came to me, whom I did not know, but I think it was Mr. Lidgerwood, who has been examined as a witness in this case, and said: 'What is this?' I said: 'I am a Justice of the Supreme Court of the United States. My name is Judge Field. Judge Terry threatened my life and attacked me, and the deputy marshal has shot him.' The deputy marshal was perfectly cool and collected, and stated: 'I am a deputy marshal, and I have shot him to protect the life of Judge Field.' I cannot give you the exact words, but I give them to you as near as I can remember them. A few moments afterwards the deputy marshal said to me: 'Judge, I think you had better go to the car.' I said, 'Very well.' Then this gentleman, Mr. Lidgerwood, said: 'I think you had better.' And with the two I went to the car. I asked Mr. Lidgerwood to go back and get my hat and cane, which he did. The marshal went with me, remained some time, and then left his seat in the car, and, as I thought, went back to the dining-room. (This is, however, I am told, a mistake, and that he only went to the end of the car.) He returned, and either he or some one else stated that there was great excitement; that Mrs. Terry was calling for some violent proceedings. I must say here that, dreadful as it is to take life, it was only a question of seconds whether my life or Judge Terry's life should be taken. I am firmly convinced that had the marshal delayed two seconds both he and myself would have been the victims of Terry.

"In answer to a question whether he had a pistol or other weapon on the occasion of the homicide, Justice Field replied: 'No, sir. I have never had on my person or used a weapon since I went on the bench of the Supreme Court of this State, on the 13th of October, 1857, except once, when, years ago, I rode over the Sierra Nevada mountains in a buggy with

General Hutchinson, and at that time I took a pistol with me for protection in the mountains. With that exception, I have not had on my person, or used, any pistol or other deadly weapon.'"

Judge Terry had fallen very near the place where he first stopped, near the seat occupied by Justice Field at the table.

Neagle testified that if Justice Field had had a weapon, and been active in using it, he was at such a disadvantage, seated as he was, with Terry standing over him, that he would have been unable to raise his hand in his own defense.

A large number of witnesses were examined, all of whom agreed upon the main facts as above stated. Some of them distinctly heard the blows administered by Terry upon Justice Field's face and head. All testified to the loud warning given Terry by Neagle that he was an officer of the law, accompanied by his command that Terry should desist. It was all the work of a few seconds. Terry's sudden attack, the quick progress of which, from the first blow, was neither arrested nor slackened until he was disabled by the bullet from Neagle's pistol, could have been dealt with in no other way. It was evidently a question of the instant whether Terry's knife or Neagle's pistol should prevail. Says Neagle :

"He never took his eyes off me after he looked at me, or I mine off him. I did not hear him say anything. The only thing was he looked like an infuriated giant to me. I believed if I waited two seconds I should have been cut to pieces. I was within four feet of him."

Q. "What did the motion that Judge Terry made with his right hand indicate to you?"

A. "That he would have had that knife out there

within another second and a half, and trying to cut my head off."

Terry, in action at such a time, from all accounts, was more like an enraged wild animal than a human being. The supreme moment had arrived to which he had been looking forward for nearly a year, when the life of the man he hated was in his hands. He had repeatedly sworn to take it. Not privately had he made these threats. With an insolence and an audacity born of lawlessness and of a belief that he could hew his way with a bowie-knife in courts as well as on the streets, he had publicly sentenced Judge Field to death as a penalty for vindicating the majesty of the law in his imprisonment for contempt.

It would have been the wildest folly that can be conceived of for the murderous assault of such a man to have been met with mild persuasion, or an attempt to arrest him. As well order a hungry tiger to desist from springing at his prey, to sheathe his outstretched claws and suffer himself to be bound, as to have met Terry with anything less than the force to which he was himself appealing. Every man who knows anything of the mode of life and of quarrelling and fighting among the men of Terry's class knows full well that when they strike a blow they mean to follow it up to the death, and they mean to take no chances. The only way to prevent the execution of Terry's revengeful and openly avowed purpose was by killing him on the spot. Only a lunatic or an imbecile or an accomplice would have pursued any other course in Neagle's place than the one he pursued, always supposing he had Neagle's nerve and cool self-possession to guide him in such a crisis.

While this tragedy was being enacted Mrs. Terry was absent, having returned to the car for the satchel containing her pistol. Before she returned, the shot had been fired that defeated the conspiracy between her and her husband against the life of a judge for the performance of his official duties. She returned to the hotel with her satchel in her hand just as her husband met his death. The manager of the hotel stopped her at the door she was entering, and seized her satchel. She did not relinquish it, but both struggled for its possession. A witness testified that she screamed out while so struggling: "Let me get at it; I will fix him." Many witnesses testified to her frantic endeavor to get the pistol. She called upon the crowd to hang the man that killed Judge Terry, and cried out, "Lynch Judge Field." Again and again she made frantic appeals to those present to lynch Judge Field. She tried to enter the car where he was, but was not permitted to do so. She cried out, "If I had my pistol I would fix him."

The testimony subsequently taken left no room to doubt that Terry had his deadly knife in its place in his breast at the time he made the attack on Justice Field. As the crowd were all engaged in breakfasting, his movements attracted little attention, and his motion toward his breast for the knife escaped the notice of all but Neagle and one other witness. Neagle rushed between Terry and Justice Field, and the latter had not a complete view of his assailant at the moment when the blow intended for him was changed into a movement for the knife with which Judge Terry intended to dispose of the alert little man, with whom he had had a former experience, and who now stood between him and the object of his greater wrath.

But the conduct of Mrs. Terry immediately after the homicide was proof enough that her husband's knife had been in readiness. The conductor of the train swore that he saw her lying over the body of her husband about a minute, and when she rose up she unbuttoned his vest and said : "You may search him; he has got no weapon on him." Not a word had been said about his having had a weapon. No one had made a movement towards searching him, as ought to have been done ; but this woman, who had been to the car for her pistol and returned with it to join, if necessary, in the murderous work, had all the time and opportunity necessary for taking the knife from its resting-place under his vest, smearing one of her hands with his blood, which plainly showed where it had been and what she had been doing. Neagle could not search the body, for his whole attention was directed to the protection of Justice Field. Mrs. Terry repeated the challenge to search the body for the knife after it had been removed. This showed clearly that the idea uppermost in her mind was to then and there manufacture testimony that he had not been armed at all. Her eagerness on this subject betrayed her. Had she herself then been searched, after rising from Terry's body, the knife would doubtless have been found concealed upon her person. A number of witnesses testified to her conduct as above described. She said also : "You will find that he has no arms, for I took them from him in the car, and I said to him that I did not want him to shoot Justice Field, but I did not object to a fist bout."

This reference to a fist bout was, of course, an admission that they had premeditated the assault. It was Judge Terry's knife and not a pistol that Judge

Field had to fear. Terry's threats had always pointed to some gross indignity that he would put upon Justice Field, and then kill him if he resented or resisted it. One of his threats was that he would horsewhip Judge Field, and that if he resented it he would kill him. In short, his intentions seem to have been to commit an assassination in alleged self-defense.

The train soon left the station for San Francisco. A constable of Lathrop had taken the train, and addressing Neagle told him that he would have to arrest him. This officer had no warrant and did not himself witness the homicide. Justice Field told him that he ought to have a warrant before making the arrest, remarking, if a man should shoot another when he was about to commit a felony, such as setting fire to your house, you would not arrest him for a murder; or if a highwayman got on the train to plunder. The officer replied very courteously by the suggestion that there would have to be an inquest. Neagle at once said, "I am ready to go," thinking it better to avoid all controversy, and being perfectly willing to answer anywhere for what he had done. Arriving at the next station (Tracy), Neagle and the officer took a buggy and went to the county jail at Stockton. Thus was a deputy marshal of the United States withdrawn from the service of his Government while engaged in a most important and as yet unfinished duty because he had with rigid faithfulness performed that duty. He was arrested by an officer who had no warrant and had not witnessed the homicide, and lodged in jail.

Meanwhile a detective in San Francisco received a telegram from the sheriff of San Joaquin county to arrest Judge Field. Supposing it to be his duty to comply with this command, the detective crossed the bay to meet the train for that purpose. Marshal Franks said to him: "You shall not arrest him. You have no right to do so. It would be an outrage, and if you attempt it I will arrest you."

The news of these exciting events produced an intense excitement in San Francisco. Upon his arrival at this place, under the escort of the marshal and many friends, Justice Field repaired to his quarters in the Palace Hotel.

CHAPTER XIII.

The body of Judge Terry was taken from Lathrop
to Stockton, accompanied by his wife, soon after his
death. On that very evening Sarah Althea Terry
swore to a complaint before a justice of the peace
named Swain, charging Justice Field and Deputy
Marshal Neagle with murder. After the investigation before the coroner Assistant District Attorney
Gibson stated that the charge against Justice Field
would be dismissed, as there was no evidence whatever to connect him with the killing.

Mrs. Terry did not see the shooting and was not in
the hotel at the time of the homicide. Having, therefore, no knowledge upon which to base her statement,
her affidavit was entitled to no greater consideration
than if it had stated that it was made solely upon her
belief without any positive information on the subject.

Only the most violent of Terry's friends favored the
wanton indignity upon Justice Field, and his arrest,
but they had sufficient influence with the district attorney, Mr. White, a young and inexperienced lawyer, to
carry him along with them. The justice of the peace
before whom Sarah Althea had laid the information
issued a warrant on the following day for the arrest
both of Justice Field and Neagle. From this time
this magistrate and the district attorney appeared to
act under orders from Mrs. Terry.

The preliminary examination was set for Wednesday of the following week, during which time the district attorney stated for publication that Justice Field would have to go to jail and stay there during the six intervening days. It was obvious to all rational minds that Mrs. Terry's purpose was to use the machinery of the magistrate's court for the purpose of taking Judge Field to Stockton, where she could execute her threats of killing him or having him killed; and if she should fail to do so, or postpone it, then to have the satisfaction of placing a justice of the Supreme Court of the United States in a prisoner's cell, and hold him there for six days awaiting an examination, that being the extreme length of time that he could be so held under the statute. The district attorney was asked if he had realized the danger of bringing Justice Field to Stockton, where he might come in contact with Mrs. Terry. The officer replied:

"We had intended that if Justice Field were brought here, Mrs. Terry would be placed under the care of *her friends*, and that all precautions to prevent any difficulty that was in the power of the district attorney would be taken." That was to say, Mrs. Terry would do no violence to Justice Field unless "her friends" permitted her to do so. As some of them were possessed of the same murderous feelings towards Justice Field as those named here, the whole transaction had the appearance of a conspiracy to murder him.

No magistrate can lawfully issue a warrant without sufficient evidence before him to show probable cause. It was a gross abuse of power and an arbitrary and lawless act to heed the oath of this frenzied woman, who notoriously had not witnessed the shooting, and had, but a few hours before, angrily insisted upon having her own pistol returned to her that she, her-

self, might kill Justice Field. It was beyond belief
that the magistrate believed that there was probable
cause, or the slightest appearance of a cause, upon
which to base the issue of the warrant.

Neagle was brought into court at Stockton at 10
o'clock on the morning after the shooting, to wit, on
Thursday, the 15th, and his preliminary examination
set for Wednesday, the 21st. Bail could not be given
prior to that examination. This examination could
have proceeded at once, and a delay of six days can
only be accounted for by attributing it to the malice
and vindictiveness of the woman who seemed to be in
charge of the proceedings.

The keen disappointment of Mrs. Terry, and those
who were under her influence, at Judge Terry's failure
to murder Justice Field, must have been greatly
soothed by the prospect of having yet another chance
at the latter's life, and, in any event, of seeing him in
a cell in the jail during the six days for which the examination could be delayed for that express purpose.
The sheriff of San Joaquin county proceeded to San
Francisco with the warrant for his arrest on Thursday
evening. In company with the chief of police and
Marshal Franks, he called upon Justice Field, and
after a few moments' conversation it was arranged
that he should present the warrant at one o'clock on
the following day, at the building in which the federal
courts are held.

CHAPTER XIV.

At the appointed hour Justice Field awaited the
sheriff in his chambers, surrounded by friends, including judges, ex-judges, and members of the bar.
As the sheriff entered Justice Field arose and pleasantly greeted him. The sheriff bore himself with
dignity, and with a due sense of the extraordinary
proceeding in which his duty as an officer required
him to be a participant. With some agitation he said:
" Justice Field, I presume you are aware of the nature
of my errand." " Yes," replied the Justice, " proceed
with your duty; I am ready. An officer should always do his duty." The sheriff stated to him that he
had a warrant, duly executed and authenticated, and
asked him if he should read it. " I will waive that,
Mr. Sheriff," replied the Justice. The sheriff then
handed him the warrant, which he read, folded it up
and handed it back, saying pleasantly: " I recognize
your authority, sir, and submit to the arrest; I am,
sir, in your custody."

Meanwhile a petition had been prepared to be presented to Judge Sawyer for a writ of *habeas corpus*,
returnable at once before the United States court.
As soon as the arrest was made the petition was
signed and presented to Judge Sawyer, who ordered
the writ to issue returnable forthwith. In a very few
minutes U. S. Marshal Franks served the writ on the
sheriff.

While the proceedings looking to the issue of the writ were going on, Justice Field had seated himself, and invited the sheriff to be seated. The latter complied with the invitation, and began to say something in regard to the unpleasant duty which had devolved upon him, but Justice Field promptly replied : " Not so, not so ; you are but doing your plain duty, and I mine in submitting to arrest. It is the first duty of judges to obey the law."

As soon as the *habeas corpus* writ had been served, the sheriff said he was ready to go into the court. " Let me walk with you," said Justice Field, as they arose, and took the sheriff's arm. In that way they entered the court-room. Justice Field seated himself in one of the chairs usually occupied by jurors. Time was given to the sheriff to make a formal return to the writ, and in a few minutes he formally presented it. The petition of Judge Field for the writ set forth his official character, and the duties imposed upon him by law, and alleged that he had been illegally arrested, while he was in the discharge of those duties, and that his illegal detention interfered with and prevented him from discharging them.

Then followed a statement of the facts, showing the arrest and detention to be illegal. This statement embraced the principal facts connected with the contempt proceedings in 1888, and the threats then and thereafter made by the Terrys of violence upon Justice Field; the precautions taken in consequence thereof by the Department of Justice for his protection from violence at their hands, and the murderous assault made upon him, and his defense by Deputy Marshal Neagle, resulting in the death of Terry, and that he, the petitioner, in no manner defended or protected himself, and gave no directions to the deputy marshal, and that he was not armed with any weapon. The petition then states : " That under the circumstances detailed, the said Sarah Althea Terry, as your petitioner is informed and believes, and upon such information and belief alleges, falsely and maliciously swore out the warrant of arrest hereinbefore set out against your petitioner, without any further basis for the charge of murder than the facts hereinbefore detailed, and that the warrant aforesaid was issued by such justice of the peace, without any just or probable cause therefor. * * * And your petitioner further represents that the charge against him, and the warrant of arrest in the hands of said sheriff, are founded upon the sole affidavit of Mrs. Sarah Althea Terry, who was not present and did not see the shooting which caused the death of said David S. Terry."

In order to show the little reliance to be placed in the oath of Mrs. Terry, the petition stated : " That in a suit brought by William Sharon, now deceased, against her before her marriage to the said Terry, it was proved and held by the Circuit Court of the United States that she had committed the forgery of the document produced in that case, and had attempted to support it by perjury and subornation of perjury, and had also been guilty of acts and conduct showing herself to be an abandoned woman, without veracity. * * *

" Your petitioner further represents that the abandoned character of the said Sarah Althea Terry, and the fact that she was found guilty of perjury and forgery in the case above mentioned by the said Circuit Court, and the fact of the revengeful malice entertained toward your petitioner by said Sarah Althea Terry, are notorious in the State of California, and are notorious in the city of Stockton, and as your petitioner believes are well known to the district attorney of the said county of San Joaquin, and also to the said justice of the peace who issued the said warrant; and your petitioner further alleges that had either of the said officers taken any pains whatever to ascertain the truth in the case, he would have ascertained and known that there was not the slightest pretext or foundation for any such charge as was made, and also that the affidavit of the said Sarah Althea Terry was not entitled to the slightest consideration whatever.

" Your petitioner further states that it is to him incomprehensible how any man, acting in a consideration of duty, could have listened one moment to charges from such a source, and without having sought some confirmation from disinterested witnesses; and your petitioner believes and charges that the whole object of the proceeding is to subject your petitioner to the humiliation of arrest and confinement at Stockton, where the said Sarah Althea Terry may be able, by the aid of partisans of hers, to carry out her long-continued and repeated threats of personal violence upon your petitioner, and to prevent your petitioner from discharging the duties of his office in cases pending against her in the federal court at San Francisco."

The sheriff's return was as follows :

" Return of sheriff of San Joaquin county, Cala., County of San Joaquin, State of California :

" Sheriff's Office.

" *To the Honorable Circuit Court of the United States for the Northern District of California :*

"I hereby certify and return that before the coming to me of the hereto-annexed writ of *habeas corpus*, the said Stephen J. Field was committed to my custody, and is detained by me by virtue of a warrant issued out of the justice's court of Stockton township, State of California, county of San Joaquin, and by the endorsement made upon said warrant. Copy of said warrant and endorsement is annexed hereto, and made a part of this return. Nevertheless, I have the body of the said Stephen J. Field before the honorable court, as I am in the said writ commanded.

" August 16, 1889.

" THOMAS CUNNINGHAM,
" *Sheriff, San Joaquin Co., California.*"

In order to give the petitioner time to traverse the return if he thought it expedient to do so, and to give him and the State time to produce witnesses, the further hearing upon the return was adjourned until the following Thursday morning, the 22d, and the petitioner was released on his recognizance with a bond fixed at $5,000.

On the same day a petition on the part of Neagle was presented to Judge Sawyer asking that a writ of *habeas corpus* issue in his behalf to Sheriff Cunningham. The petition was granted at once, and served upon the sheriff immediately after the service of the writ issued on behalf of Justice Field. Early on the morning of Saturday, August 17, Neagle was brought from Stockton by the sheriff at 4.30 A. M. District Attorney White and Mrs. Terry's lawyer, Maguire, were duly notified of this movement and were passengers on the same train. At 10.30 Sheriff Cunningham

appeared in the Circuit Court with Neagle to respond
to the writ. He returned that he held Neagle in custody under a warrant issued by a justice of the peace
of that county, a copy of which he produced; and
also a copy of the affidavit of Sarah Althea Terry
upon which the warrant was issued. A traverse to
that return was then filed, presenting various grounds
why the petitioner should not be held, the most important of which were that an officer of the United
States, specially charged with a particular duty, that
of protecting one of the justices of the Supreme
Court of the United States whilst engaged in the
performance of his duty, could not, for an act constituting the very performance of that duty, be taken
from the further discharge of his duty and imprisoned by the State authorities, and that when an officer
of the United States in the discharge of his duties
is charged with an offense consisting in the performance of those duties, and is sought to be arrested, and
taken from the further performance of them, he
can be brought before the tribunals of the nation of
which he is an officer, and the fact then inquired into.
The attorney-general of the State appeared with the
district attorney of San Joaquin county, and contended that the offense of which the petitioner was
charged could only be inquired into before the
tribunals of the State.

CHAPTER XV.

The funeral of Judge Terry occurred on Friday, the 16th. An unsuccessful attempt was made for a public demonstration. The fear entertained by some that eulogies of an incendiary character would be delivered was not realized. The funeral passed off without excitement. The rector being absent, the funeral service was read by a vestryman of the church.

On the day after Judge Terry's death the following proceedings occurred in the Supreme Court of the State:

Late in the afternoon, just after the counsel in a certain action had concluded their argument, and before the next cause on the calendar was called, James L. Crittenden, Esq., who was accompanied by W. T. Baggett, Esq., arose to address the court. He said:

"Your honors, it has become my painful and sad duty to formally announce to the court the death of a former chief justice "——

Chief Justice Beatty: "Mr. Crittenden, I think that is a matter which should be postponed until the court has had a consultation about it."

The court then, without leaving the bench, held a whispered consultation. Mr. Crittenden then went on to say: "I was doing this at the request of several friends of the deceased. It has been customary for the court to take formal action prior to the funeral. In this instance, I understand the funeral is to take place to-morrow."

Chief Justice Beatty : " Mr. Crittenden, the members of the court wish to consult with each other on this matter, and you had better postpone your motion of formal announcement until to-morrow morning."

Mr. Crittenden and Mr. Baggett then withdrew from the court-room.

On the following day, in the presence of a large assembly, including an unusually large attendance of attorneys, Mr. Crittenden renewed his motion. He said :

" If the court please, I desire to renew the matter which I began to present last evening. As a friend— a personal friend—of the late Judge Terry, I should deem myself very cold, indeed, and very far from discharging the duty which is imposed upon that relation, if I did not present the matter which I propose to present to this bench this morning. I have known the gentleman to whom I have reference for over thirty years, and I desire simply now, in stating that I make this motion, to say that the friendship of so many years, and the acquaintance and intimacy existing between that gentleman and his family and myself for so long a period, require that I should at this time move this court, as a court, out of recollection for the memory of the man who presided in the Supreme Court of this State for so many years with honor, ability, character, and integrity, and, therefore, I ask this court, out of respect for his memory, to adjourn during the day on which he is to be buried, which is to-day."

Chief Justice Beatty said :

" I regret very much that counsel should have persisted in making this formal announcement, after the intimation from the court. Upon full consultation we thought it would be better that it should not be done. The circumstances of Judge Terry's death are notorious, and under these circumstances this court had determined that it would be better to pass this matter in silence, and not to take any action upon it ; and that is the order of the court."

The deceased had been a chief justice of the tribunal which, by its silence, thus emphasized its condemnation of the conduct by which he had placed himself without the pale of its respect.

CHAPTER XVI.

On Thursday, August 22d, the hearing of the *habeas corpus* case of Justice Field commenced in the United States Circuit Court, under orders from the Attorney-General, to whom a report of the whole matter had been telegraphed. The United States district attorney appeared on behalf of Justice Field. In addition to him there also appeared as counsel for Justice Field, Hon. Richard T. Mesick, Saml. M. Wilson, Esq., and W. F. Herrin, Esq. The formal return of the writ of *habeas corpus* had been made by the sheriff of San Joaquin county on the 16th. To that return Justice Field presented a traverse, which was in the following language, and was signed and sworn to by him :

" The petitioner, Stephen J. Field, traverses the return of the sheriff of San Joaquin county, State of California, made by him to the writ of *habeas corpus* by the circuit judge on the ninth circuit, and made returnable before the Circuit Court of said circuit, and avers:

" That he is a justice of the Supreme Court of the United States, allotted to the ninth judicial circuit, and is now and has been for several weeks in California, in attendance upon the Circuit Court of said circuit in the discharge of his judicial duties ; and, further, that the said warrant of the justice of the peace, H. V. J. Swain, in Stockton, California, issued on the 14th day of August, 1889, under which the petitioner is held, was issued by said justice of the peace without reasonable or probable cause, upon the sole affidavit of one Sarah Althea Terry, who did not see the commission of the act which she charges to have been a murder, and who is herself a woman of abandoned character, and utterly unworthy of belief respecting any matter whatever ; and, further, that the said warrant was issued in the execution of a conspiracy, as your petitioner is informed, believes, and charges, between the said Sarah Althea Terry and the district attorney, White, and the said justice of the peace, H. V. J. Swain, and one E. L. Colnon, of said Stockton, to prevent by force and intimidation your petitioner from discharging the duties of his office hereafter, and to injure him in his person on account of the lawful discharge of the duties of his office heretofore, by taking him to Stockton, where he could be subjected to indignities and humiliation, and where they might compass his death.

" That the said conspiracy is a crime against the United States, under the laws thereof, and was to be executed by an abuse of the process of the State court, two of said conspirators being officers of the said county of San Joaquin, one the district attorney and the other a justice of the peace, the one to direct and the other to issue the warrant upon which your petitioner could be arrested.

" And the petitioner further avers that the issue of said writ of *habeas corpus* and the discharge of your petitioner thereunder were and are essential to defeat the execution of the said conspiracy.

" And your petitioner further avers that the accusation of crime against him, upon which said warrant was issued, is a malicious and malignant falsehood, for which there is not even a pretext ; that he neither advised nor had any knowledge of the intention of any one to commit the act which resulted in the death of David S. Terry, and that he has not carried or used any arm or weapon of any kind for nearly thirty years.

" All of which your petitioner is ready to establish by full and competent proof.

" Wherefore your petitioner prays that he may be discharged from said arrest and set at liberty.

" STEPHEN J. FIELD."

The facts alleged in this document were beyond

dispute, and constituted an outrageous crime, and one for which the conspirators were liable to imprisonment for a term of six years, under section 5518 of the Revised Statutes of the United States. To this traverse the counsel for the sheriff filed a demurrer, on the ground that it did not appear by it that Justice Field was in custody for an act done or omitted in pursuance of any law of the United States, or of any order or process or decree of any court or judge thereof, and it did not appear that he was in custody in violation of the Constitution or any law or treaty of the United States. The case was thereupon submitted with leave to counsel to file briefs at any time before the 27th of August, to which time the further hearing was adjourned.

Before that hearing the Governor of the State addressed the following communication to the attorney-general:

"EXECUTIVE DEPARTMENT,
"STATE OF CALIFORNIA,
"SACRAMENTO, *August* 21, 1889.
" Hon. A. G. JOHNSTON,
"*Attorney-General, Sacramento.*

" DEAR SIR : The arrest of Hon. Stephen J. Field, a justice of the Supreme Court of the United States, on the unsupported oath of a woman who, on the very day the oath was taken, and often before, threatened his life, will be a burning disgrace to the State unless disavowed. I therefore urge upon you the propriety of at once instructing the district attorney of San Joaquin county to dismiss the unwarranted proceedings against him.

" The question of the jurisdiction of the state courts in the case of the deputy United States marshal, Neagle, is one for argument. The unprecedented indignity on Justice Field does not admit of argument.

" Yours truly,
"R. W. WATERMAN,
"*Governor.*"

This letter of Governor Waterman rang out like an alarm bell, warning the chief law officer of the State that a subordinate of his was prostituting its judicial machinery to enable a base woman to put a gross indignity upon a justice of the Supreme Court of the United States, whom she had just publicly threatened to kill, and also to aid her in accomplishing that purpose. The wretched proceeding had already brought upon its authors indignant denunciation and merciless ridicule from every part of the Union. The attorney-general responded to the call thus made upon him by instructing the district attorney to dismiss the charge against Justice Field, because no evidence existed to sustain it.

The rash young district attorney lost no time in extricating himself from the position in which the arrest of Justice Field had placed him. On the 26th of August, upon his motion, and the filing of the attorney-general's letter, the charge against Justice Field was dismissed by the justice of the peace who had issued the warrant against him.

The dismissal of this charge released him from the sheriff's claim to his custody, and the *habeas corpus* proceedings in his behalf fell to the ground. On the 27th, the day appointed for the further hearing, the sheriff announced that in compliance with the order of the magistrate he released Justice Field from custody, whereupon the case of *habeas corpus* was dismissed.

In making the order, Circuit Judge Sawyer severely animadverted on what he deemed the shameless proceeding at Stockton. He said :

" We are glad that the prosecution of Mr. Justice

Field has been dismissed, founded, as it was, upon the sole, reckless, and as to him manifestly false affidavit of one whose relation to the matters leading to the tragedy, and whose animosity towards the courts and judges who have found it their duty to decide against her, and especially towards Mr. Justice Field, is a part of the judicial and notorious public history of the country.

"It was, under the circumstances, and upon the sole affidavit produced, especially after the coroner's inquest, so far as Mr. Justice Field is concerned, a shameless proceeding, and, as intimated by the Governor of the Commonwealth, if it had been further persevered in, would have been a lasting disgrace to the State.

"While a justice of the Supreme Court of the United States, like every other citizen, is amenable to the laws, he is not likely to commit so grave an offense as murder, and should he be so unfortunate as to be unavoidably involved in any way in a homicide, he could not afford to escape, if it were in his power to do so; and when the act is so publicly performed by another, as in this instance, and is observed by so many witnesses, the officers of the law should certainly have taken some little pains to ascertain the facts before proceeding to arrest so distinguished a dignitary, and to attempt to incarcerate him in prisons with felons, or to put him in a position to be further disgraced, and perhaps assaulted by one so violent as to be publicly reported, not only then but on numerous previous occasions, to have threatened his life.

"We are extremely gratified to find that, through the action of the chief magistrate, and the attorney-general, a higher officer of the law, we shall be spared the necessity of further inquiring as to the extent of the remedy afforded the distinguished petitioner, by the Constitution and laws of the United States, or of enforcing such remedies as exist, and that the stigma cast upon the State of California by this hasty and, to call it by no harsher term, ill-advised arrest, will not be intensified by further prosecution."

Thus ended this most remarkable attempt upon the liberty of a United States Supreme Court Justice, under color of State authority, the execution of which would again have placed his life in great peril.

The grotesque feature of the performance was aptly presented by the following imaginary dialogue which appeared in an Eastern paper:

Newsboy: " Man tried to kill a judge in California!"
Customer: "What was done about it?"
Newsboy: " Oh! They arrested the judge."

The illegality of Justice Field's arrest will be perfectly evident to whoever will read sections 811, 812, and 813 of the Penal Code of California. These sections provide that no warrant can be issued by a magistrate until he has examined, on oath, the informant, taken depositions setting forth the facts tending to establish the commission of the offense and the guilt of the accused, and himself been satisfied by these depositions that there is reasonable ground that the person accused has committed the offense. None of these requirements had been met in Justice Field's case.

It needs no lawyer to understand that a magistrate violates the plain letter as well as the spirit of these provisions of law when he issues a warrant without first having before him some evidence of the probable, or at least the possible, guilt of the accused. If this were otherwise, private malice could temporarily sit in judgment upon the object of its hatred, however blameless, and be rewarded for perjury by being allowed the use of our jails as places in which to satisfy its vengeance. Such a view of the law made Sarah Althea the magistrate at Stockton on the 14th of

August, and Justice Swain her obsequious amanuensis. Such a view of the law would enable any convict who had just served a term in the penitentiary to treat himself to the luxury of dragging to jail the judge who sentenced him, and keeping him there without bail as long as the magistrate acting for him could be induced to delay the examination.

The arrest of Justice Field was an attempt to kidnap him for a foul purpose, and if the United States circuit judge had not released him he would have been the victim of as arbitrary and tyrannical treatment as is ever meted out in Russia to the most dangerous of nihilists, to punish him for having narrowly escaped assassination by no act or effort of his own.

CHAPTER XVII

This narrative would not be complete without a statement of the proceedings in the United States Circuit Court, and in the United States Supreme Court on appeal, in the *habeas corpus* proceedings in the case of Neagle, the deputy marshal, whose courageous devotion to his official duties had saved the life of Justice Field at the expense of that of his would-be assassin. We have already seen that Neagle, being in the custody of the sheriff of San Joaquin county, upon a charge of murder in the shooting of Judge Terry, had presented a petition to the United States Circuit Court for a writ of *habeas corpus* to the end that he might thereby be restored to his liberty.

A writ was issued, and upon its return, August 17th, the sheriff of San Joaquin county produced Neagle and a copy of the warrant under which he held him in custody, issued by the justice of the peace of that county, and also of the affidavit of Sarah Althea Terry, upon which the warrant was granted. Neagle being desirous of traversing the return of the sheriff, further proceedings were adjourned until the 22d of the month, and in the meantime he was placed in the custody of the United States marshal for the district. On the 22d a traverse of the return was filed by him stating the particulars of the homicide with which he was charged as narrated above, and averring that he was at the time of its commission a deputy marshal of the United States for the district, acting under the orders of his

superior, and under the directions of the Attorney-
General of the United States in protecting the Associate Justice, whilst in the discharge of his duties,
from the threatened assault and violence of Terry,
who had declared that on meeting the Justice he
would insult, assault, and kill him, and that the homicide with which the petitioner is charged was committed in resisting the attempted execution of these
threats in the belief that Terry intended at the time
to kill the Justice, and that but for such homicide he
would have succeeded in his attempt. These particulars are stated with great fulness of detail. To this
traverse, which was afterwards amended, but not in
any material respect, a demurrer was interposed for
the sheriff by the district attorney of San Joaquin
county. Its material point was that it did not appear
from the traverse that Neagle was in the custody of
the sheriff for an act done or omitted in pursuance of
any law of the United States, or any order, process,
or decree of any court or judge thereof, or in violation of the Constitution or a treaty of the United
States. The court then considered whether it should
hear testimony as to the facts of the case, or proceed
with the argument of the demurrer to the traverse.
It decided to take the testimony, and to hear counsel
when the whole case was before it, on the merits as
well as on the question of jurisdiction. The testimony was then taken. It occupied several days, and
brought out strongly the facts which have been
already narrated, and need not here be repeated.
When completed, the question of the jurisdiction of
the Circuit Court of the United States to interfere in
the matter was elaborately argued by the attorney-
general of the State, and special counsel who ap-

peared with the district attorney of San Joaquin county on behalf of the State, they contending that the offense, with which the petitioner was charged, could only be inquired into before a tribunal of the State. Mr. Carey, United States district attorney, and Messrs. Herrin, Mesick, and Wilson, special counsel, appeared on behalf of the petitioner, and contended for the jurisdiction, and for the discharge of the petitioner upon the facts of the case. They did not pretend that any person in the State, be he high or low, might not be tried by the local authorities for a crime committed against the State, but they did contend that when the alleged crime consisted in an act which was claimed to have been done in the performance of a duty devolving upon him by a law of the United States, it was within the competency of their courts to inquire, in the first instance, whether that act thus done was in the performance of a duty devolving upon him ; and if it was, that the alleged offender had not committed a crime against the State, and was entitled to be discharged. Their arguments were marked by great ability and learning, and their perusal would be interesting and instructive, but space will not allow me to give even a synopsis of them.

The court, in deciding the case, went into a full and elaborate consideration, not only of its jurisdiction, but of every objection on the merits presented by counsel on behalf of the State. Only a brief outline can be given.

The court held that it was within the competency of the President, and of the Attorney-General as the head of the Department of Justice, representing him, to direct that measures be taken for the protection of officers of the Government whilst in the discharge of their duties, and that it was specially appropriate that such protection should be given to the justices of the Supreme Court of the United States, whilst thus engaged in their respective circuits, and in passing to and from them; that the Attorney-General, representing the President, was fully justified in giving orders to the marshal of the California district to appoint a deputy to look specially to the protection of Justices Field and Sawyer from assault and violence threatened by Terry and his wife; and that the deputy marshal, acting under instructions for their protection, was justified in any measures that were necessary for that purpose, even to taking the life of the assailant.

The court recognized that the Government of the United States exercised full jurisdiction, within the sphere of its powers, over the whole territory of the country, and that when any conflict arose between the State and the General Government in the administration of their respective powers, the authority of the United States must prevail, for the Constitution declares that it and the laws of the United States in pursuance thereof " shall be the supreme law of the land, and that the judges in every State shall be bound thereby, anything in the Constitution and laws of any State to the contrary notwithstanding." The court quoted the language of the Supreme Court in Tennessee v. Davis (100 U. S. 257, 263), that "It [the General Government] can act only through its officers and agents, and they must act within the States. If, when thus acting and within the scope of their authority, those officers can be arrested and brought to trial in a State court, for an alleged offense against the law of the State, yet warranted by the Federal authority they possess, and if the General Government is powerless to interfere at once for their protection—if their protection must be left to the action of the State court—the operations of the General Government may, at any time, be arrested at the will of one of its members. The legislation of a State may be unfriendly. It may affix penalties to acts done under the immediate direction of the National Government and in obedience to its laws. It may deny the authority conferred by those laws. The State court may administer not only the laws of the State, but equally Federal law, in such a manner as to paralyze the operations of the Government. And even if, after trial and final judgment in the State court, a case can be brought into the United States court for review, the officer is withdrawn from the discharge of his duty during the pendency of the prosecution, and the exercise of acknowledged Federal power arrested. We do not think such an element of weakness is to be found in the Constitution. The United States is a government with authority extending over the whole territory of the Union, acting upon the States and upon the people of the States. While it is limited in the number of its powers, so far as its sovereignty extends, it is supreme. No State government can exclude it from the exercise of any authority conferred upon it by the Constitution, obstruct its authorized officers against its will, or withhold from it, for a moment, the cognizance of any subject which that instrument has committed to it." To this strong language the Circuit Court added:

" The very idea of a government composed of executive, legislative, and judicial departments necessarily comprehends the power to do all things, through its appropriate officers and agents, within the scope of its

general governmental purposes and powers, requisite
to preserve its existence, protect it and its ministers,
and give it complete efficiency in all its parts. It
necessarily and inherently includes power in its executive department to enforce the laws, keep the national
peace with regard to its officers while in the line of
their duty, and protect by its all-powerful arm all the
other departments and the officers and instrumentali-
ties necessary to their efficiency while engaged in the
discharge of their duties."

In language attributed to Mr. ex-Secretary Bayard,
used with reference to this very case, which we quote,
not as a controlling judicial authority, but for its in-
trinsic, sound, common sense, " The robust and essential principle must be recognized and proclaimed,
that the inherent powers of every government which
is sufficient to authorize and enforce the judgment of
its courts are, equally, and at all times, and in all
places, sufficient to protect the individual judge who,
fearlessly and conscientiously in the discharge of his
duty, pronounces those judgments."

In reference to the duties of the President and the
powers of the Attorney-General under him, and of the
latter's control of the marshals of the United States,
the court observed that the duties of the President are
prescribed in terse and comprehensive language in
section 3 of article II of the Constitution, which declares that " he shall take care that the laws be faithfully executed; " that this gives him all the authority
necessary to accomplish the purposes intended—all
the authority necessarily inherent in the office, not
otherwise limited, and that Congress, added the court,
in pursuance of powers vested in it, has provided for
seven departments, as subordinate to the President, to
aid him in performing his executive functions. Sec-

tion 346, R. S., provides that "there shall be at the seat of government an executive department to be known as the Department of Justice, and an Attorney-General, who shall be the head thereof." He thus has the general supervision of the executive branch of the national judiciary, and section 362 provides, as a portion of his powers and duties, that he "shall exercise general superintendence and direction over the attorneys and marshals of all the districts in the United States and the Territories as to the manner of discharging their respective duties; and the several district attorneys and marshals are required to report to the Attorney-General an account of their official proceedings, and of the state and condition of their respective offices, in such time and manner as the Attorney-General may direct." Section 788, R. S., provides that "the marshals and their deputies shall have, in each State, the same powers in executing the laws of the United States as the sheriffs and their deputies in such State may have, by law, in executing the laws thereof." By section 817 of the penal code of California the sheriff is a "peace officer," and by section 4176 of the political code he is "to preserve the peace" and "prevent and suppress breaches of the peace." The marshal is, therefore, under the provisions of the statute cited, "a peace officer," so far as keeping the peace in any matter wherein the powers of the United States are concerned, and as to such matters he has all the powers of the sheriff, as peace officer under the laws of the State. He is, in such matters, "to preserve the peace" and "prevent and suppress breaches of the peace." An assault upon or an assassination of a judge of a United States court while engaged in any matter pertaining to his official duties, on account or by reason of his judicial decisions, or action in performing his official duties, is a breach of the peace, affecting the authority and interests of the United States, and within the jurisdiction and power of the marshal or his deputies to prevent as a peace officer of the National Government. Such an assault is not merely an assault upon the person of the judge as a man; it is an assault upon the national judiciary, which he represents, and through it an assault upon the authority of the nation itself. It is, necessarily, a breach of the national peace. As a national peace officer, under the conditions indicated, it is the duty of the marshal and his deputies to prevent a breach of the national peace by an assault upon the authority of the United States, in the person of a judge of its highest court, while in the discharge of his duty. If this be not so, in the language of the Supreme Court, "Why do we have marshals at all?" What useful functions can they perform in the economy of the National Government?

Section 787 of the Revised Statutes also declares that "It shall be the duty of the marshal of each district to attend the District and Circuit Courts when sitting therein, and to execute throughout the district all lawful precepts directed to him and issued under the authority of the United States, and he shall have power to command all necessary assistance in the execution of his duty." There is no more authority specifically conferred upon the marshal by this section to protect the judge from assassination in open court, without a specific order or command, than there is to protect him out of court, when on the way from one court to another in the discharge of his official duties. The marshals are in daily attendance upon the judges, and performing official duties in their chambers. Yet no statute specifically points out those duties or requires their performance. Indeed, no such places as chambers for the circuit judges or circuit justices are mentioned at all in the statutes. Yet the marshal is as clearly authorized to protect the judges there as in the court-room. All business done out of court by the judge is called chamber business. But it is not necessary to be done in what is usually called chambers. Chamber business may be done, and often is done, on the street, in the judge's own house, at the hotel where he stops, when absent from home, or it may be done in transitu, on the cars in going from one place to another within the proper jurisdiction to hold court. Mr. Justice Field could, as well, and as authoritatively, issue a temporary injunction, grant a writ of *habeas corpus*, an order to show cause, or do any other chamber business for the district in the dining-room at Lathrop, as at his chambers in San Francisco, or in the court-room. The chambers of the judge, where chambers are provided, are not an element of jurisdiction, but are a convenience to the judge, and to suitors—places where the judge at proper times can be readily found, and the business conveniently transacted.

But inasmuch as the Revised Statutes of the United States (sec. 753) declare that the writ of *habeas corpus* shall not extend to "a prisoner in jail unless where he is in custody—for an act done or omitted in pursuance of a *law* of the United States, or of an order, process, or decree of a court or judge thereof, or in custody in violation of the Constitution or of a law or treaty of the United States," it was urged in the argument by counsel for the State that there is no statute which specifically makes it the duty of a marshal or deputy marshal to protect the judges of the United States whilst out of the court-room, travelling from one point to another in their circuits, on official business, from the violence of litigants who have become offended at the adverse decisions made by them in the performance of their judicial duties, and that such officers are not within the provisions of that section. To this the court replied that the language of the section is, "an act done in pursuance of a *law* of the United States"—not in pursuance of a statute of the United States; and that the statutes do not present in express terms all the law of the United States; that their incidents and implications are as much a part of the law as their express provisions; and that when they prescribe duties providing for the accomplishment of certain designated objects, or confer authority in general terms, they carry with them all the powers essential to effect the ends designed. As said by Chief Justice Marshall in Osborn v. Bank of the United States (9 Wheaton, 865–866), "It is not unusual for a legislative act to involve consequences which are not expressed. An officer, for example, is ordered to arrest an individual. It is not necessary, nor is it usual, to say that he shall not be punished for obeying this order. His security is implied in the order itself. It is no unusual thing for an act of Congress to imply, without expressing, this very exemption from State control, which is said to be so objectionable in this instance. The collectors of the revenue, the carriers of the mail, the mint establishment, and all those institutions which are public in their nature, are examples in point. It has never been doubted that all who are employed in them are protected while in the line of duty; and yet this protection is not expressed in any act of Congress. It is incidental to, and is implied in, the several acts by which these institutions are created; and is secured to the individuals employed in them by the judicial power alone—that is, the judicial power is the instrument employed by the Government in administering this security."

Upon this the Circuit Court observed:

"If the officers referred to in the preceding passage are to be protected while in the line of their duty, without any special law or statute requiring such protection, the judges of the courts, the principal officers in a department of the Government second to no other, are also to be protected, and their executive subordinates — the marshals and their deputies — shielded from harm by the national laws while honestly engaged in protecting the heads of the courts from assassination."

NOTE.—I find the following apt illustrations of this doctrine in a journal of the day:

If a military or naval officer of the United States, in the necessary suppression of a mutiny or enforcement of obedience, should wound or take the life of a subordinate, would it be contended that, if arrested for that act by the State authority, he could not be released on *habeas corpus*, because no statute expressly authorized the performance of the act? If the commander of a revenue cutter should be directed to pursue and retake a vessel which, after seizure, had escaped from the custody of the law, and the officer in the performance of that duty, and when necessary to overcome resistance, should injure or kill a member of the crew of the vessel he was ordered to recapture, and if for that act he should be arrested and accused of crime under the State authority, will any sensible person maintain that the provisions of the *habeas corpus* act could not be invoked for his release, notwithstanding that no statute could be shown which directly authorized the act for which he

To the position that the preservation of the peace of the State is devolved solely upon the officers of the State, and not in any respect upon the marshals of the UnitedStates, the court replied: This position is already answered by what has been said. But it is undoubtedly true that it was the imperative duty of the State to preserve the public peace and amply protect the life of Justice Field, *but it did not do it*, and had the United States relied upon the State to keep the peace as to him—one of the justices of the highest court—in relation to matters concerning the performance of his official duties, they would have leaned upon a broken reed. The result of the efforts to obtain an officer from the State to assist in preserving the peace

---

was arrested? If by command of the President a company of troops were marched into this city to protect the subtreasury from threatened pillage, and in so doing life were taken, would not the act of the officer who commanded the troops be an act done in pursuance of the laws of the United States, and in the lawful exercise of its authority? Could he be imprisoned and tried before a State jury on the charge of murder, and the courts of the United States be powerless to inquire into the facts on *habeas corpus* and to discharge him if found to have acted in the performance of his duty? Can the authority of the United States for the protection of their officers be less than their authority to protect their property?

There appears to be but one rational answer to these questions.

In all these cases the authority vested in the officer to suppress a mutiny, or to overtake and capture an escaped vessel, or to protect the subtreasury from threatened pillage, carries with it power to do all things necessary to accomplish the object desired, even the killing of the offending party. The law conferring the authority thus extended to the officer in these cases, is in the sense of the *habeas corpus* act, a law of the United States to do all things necessary for the execution of that authority.

and protecting him at Lathrop was anything but successful. The officer of the State at Lathrop, instead of arresting the conspirator of the contemplated murderer, the wife of the deceased, arrested the officer of the United States, assigned by the Government to the special duty of protecting the justice against the very parties, while in the actual prosecution of duties assigned to him, without warrant, thereby leaving his charge without the protection provided by the Government he was serving, at a time when such protection seemed most needed. And, besides, the use of the State police force beyond the limits of a county for the protection of Justice Field would have been impracticable, as the powers of the sheriff would have ended at its borders, and of other township and city peace officers at the boundaries of their respective townships and cities. Only a United States marshal or his deputy could have exercised these official functions throughout the judicial district, which embraces many counties. The only remedy suggested on the part of the State was to arrest the deceased and hold him to bail to keep the peace under section 706 of the Penal Code, the highest limit of the amount of bail being $5,000. But although the threats are conceded to have been publicly known in the State, no State officer took any means to provide this flimsy safeguard. And the execution of a bond in this amount to keep the peace would have had no effect in deterring the intended assailants from the commission of the offense contemplated, when the penalties of the law would not deter them.

As to the deliberation and wisdom of Neagle's conduct under the circumstances, the court, after stating the established facts, concludes as follows:

"When the deceased left his seat, some thirty feet distant, walked stealthily down the passage in the rear of Justice Field and dealt the unsuspecting jurist two preliminary blows, doubtless by way of reminding him that the time for vengeance had at last come, Justice Field was already at the traditional 'wall' of the law. He was sitting quietly at a table, back to the assailant, eating his breakfast, the side opposite being occupied by other passengers, some of whom were women, similarly engaged. When, in a dazed condition, he awoke to the reality of the situation and saw the stalwart form of the deceased with arm drawn back for a final mortal blow, there was no time to get under or over the table, had the law, under any circumstances, required such an act for his justification. Neagle could not seek a 'wall' to justify his action without abandoning his charge to certain death. When, therefore, he sprang to his feet and cried, 'Stop! I am an officer,' and saw the powerful arm of the deceased drawn back for the final deadly stroke instantly change its direction to his left breast, apparently seeking his favorite weapon, the knife, and at the same time heard the half-suppressed, disappointed growl of recognition of the man who, with the aid of half a dozen others, had finally succeeded in disarming him of his knife at the court-room a year before, the supreme moment had come, or, at least, with abundant reason he thought so, and fired the fatal shot. The testimony all concurs in showing this to be the state of facts, and the almost universal consensus of public opinion of the United States seems to justify the act. On that occasion a second, or two seconds, signified, at least, two valuable lives, and a reasonable degree of prudence would justify a shot one or two seconds too soon rather than a fraction of a second too late. Upon our minds the evidence leaves no doubt whatever that the homicide was fully justified by the circumstances. Neagle on the scene of action, facing the party making a murderous assault, knowing by personal experience his physical powers and his desperate character, and by general reputation his life-long habit of carrying arms, his readiness to use them, and his angry, murderous threats, and seeing his demoniac looks, his stealthy assault upon Justice Field from behind, and, remembering the sacred trust committed to his charge— Neagle, in these trying circumstances, was the party to determine when the supreme moment for action had come, and if he, honestly, acted with reasonable judgment and discretion, the law justifies him, even if he erred. But who will have the courage to stand up in the presence of the facts developed by the testimony in this case, and say that he fired the smallest fraction of a second too soon ?

"In our judgment he acted, under the trying circumstances surrounding him, in good faith and with consummate courage, judgment, and discretion. The homicide was, in our opinion, clearly justifiable in law, and in the forum of sound, practical common sense commendable. This being so, and the act having been 'done * * * in pursuance of a law of the United States,' as we have already seen, it cannot be an offense against, and he is not amenable to, the laws of the State."

The petitioner was accordingly discharged from arrest.

CHAPTER XVIII.

EXPRESSIONS OF PUBLIC OPINION.

This case and all the attendant circumstances—the attempted assassination of Justice Field by his former associate, Terry; the defeat of this murderous attempt by Deputy Marshal Neagle; the arrest of Justice Field and the deputy marshal upon the charge of murder, and their discharge—created very great interest throughout the United States. They were the subject of articles in all the leading journals of the country; and numerous telegrams and letters of congratulation were sent to the Justice on his escape from the murderous attempt. Satisfaction was very generally expressed at the fate which Terry met, and much praise was given to the courageous conduct of Neagle and at the bearing of Justice Field under the trying circumstances.

A few of the letters received by him are here given, and citations are made from some of the periodicals, which indicated the general sentiment of the country.

Letter from Hon. T. F. Bayard, ex-Secretary of State:

WILMINGTON, DELAWARE, *August* 18, 1889.

MY DEAR BROTHER FIELD:

I was absent from home when I first saw in the newspapers an account of the infamous assault of the Terrys—husband and wife—upon you, and the prompt and courageous action of Deputy Marshal Neagle that happily frustrated the iniquitous plot against your life.

Accept, my dear friend, my fervent congratulations on your escape from the designs of this madman and of the shameless creature who was his wife and accomplice.

For the sake of our country and its reputation in the eyes of Christendom, I am indeed grateful that this vile stab at its judicial power, as vested in your personality, miscarried, and that by good fortune the insane malice of a disappointed suitor should have been thwarted.

Your dignified courage in this tragical episode is most impressive, and, while it endears you the more to those who love you, will wring even from your foes a tribute of respect and admiration.

Passing over the arguments that may be wrought out of the verbiage of our dual constitution of government, the robust and essential principle *must* be recognized and proclaimed—that the *inherent powers* of every government which are sufficient to authorize and enforce the judgments of its courts are equally and at all times and in all places sufficient to protect the individual judge who fearlessly and conscientiously, in the discharge of his duty, pronounces those judgments.

The case, my dear friend, is not yours alone; it is equally mine and that of every other American. A principle so vital to society, to the body politic, was never more dangerously and wickedly assailed than by the assault of Terry and his wife upon you for your just and honorable performance of your duty as a magistrate.

I can well comprehend the shock to which this occurrence has subjected you, and I wish I could be by your side to give you assurance orally (if any were needed) of that absolute sympathy and support to which you are so fully entitled. But these lines will perhaps suffice to make you feel the affectionate and steadfast regard I entertain for you, and which this terrible event has but increased.

I cannot forbear an expression of the hope that the arguments of jurisdictional and other points which must attend the litigation and settlement of this tragedy may not be abated or warped to meet any temporary local or partisan demand.

The voice of Justice can never speak in clearer or more divine accents than when heard in vindication and honor of her own faithful ministers.

Ever, my dear Judge Field,
Sincerely yours,
T. F. BAYARD.

The Hon. STEPHEN J. FIELD,
San Francisco Cal.

Letter from Hon. E. J. Phelps, former Minister to England:

BURLINGTON, VERMONT, *August* 17, 1889.

MY DEAR JUDGE FIELD:

Pray let me congratulate you most heartily on the Terry transaction. Nothing that has ever occurred in the administration of justice has given me more satisfaction than this prompt, righteous, and effectual vindication through an officer of the court of the sanctity of the judiciary when in the discharge of its duty. What your marshal did was exactly the right thing, at the right time, and in the right way. I shall be most happy to join in a suitable testimonial to him, if our profession will, as they ought, concur in presenting it. * * *

Your own coolness and carriage in confronting this danger in the discharge of your duty must be universally admired, and will shed an additional lustre on a judicial career which was distinguished enough without it.

You have escaped a great peril—acquired a fresh distinction—and vindicated most properly the dignity of your high station.

I am glad to perceive that this is the general opinion.

Anticipating the pleasure of seeing you in Washington next term,

I am always, dear sir,
Most sincerely yours,
E. J. PHELPS.

Letter from Hon. George F. Hoar, Senator from Massachusetts:

WORCESTER, *August* 16, 1889.

MY DEAR JUDGE FIELD:

I think I ought to tell you, at this time, how high you stand in the confidence and reverence of all good men here, how deeply they were shocked by this outrage attempted not so much on you as on the judicial office itself, and how entirely the prompt action of the officer is approved. I hope you may long be spared to the public service.

I am faithfully yours,
GEO. F. HOAR.

Letter from Hon. J. Proctor Knott, for many years a Member of Congress from Kentucky and Chairman of the Judiciary Committee of the House of Representatives, and afterwards Governor of Kentucky:

LEBANON, KENTUCKY, *September* 5, 1889.

MY DEAR JUDGE: * * *

I have had it in mind to write you from the moment I first heard of your fortunate escape from the fiendish assassination with which you were so imminently threatened, but I have, since the latter part of May, been suffering from a most distressing affection of the eyes which has rendered it extremely difficult, and frequently, for days together, quite impossible to do so. Even now, though much improved, I write in great pain, but I cannot get my consent to delay it longer on any account. You are to be congratulated, my dear friend, and you know that no one could possibly do so with more genuine, heartfelt sincerity than I do myself. * * *

I had been troubled, ever since I saw you had gone to your circuit, with apprehensions that you would be assassinated, or at least subjected to some gross outrage, and cannot express my admiration of the serene heroism with which you went to your post of duty, determined not to debase the dignity of your exalted position by wearing arms for your defense, notwithstanding you were fully conscious of the danger which menaced you. It didn't surprise me, however, for I knew the stuff you were made of had been tested before. But I *was* surprised and disgusted, too, that *you* should have been charged or even suspected of anything wrong in the matter. The magistrate who issued the warrant for your arrest may possibly have thought it his duty to do so, without looking beyond the "railing accusation" of a baffled and infuriated murderess, which all the world instinctively knew to be false, yet I suppose there is not an intelligent man, woman, or child on the continent who does not consider in an infamous and unmitigated outrage, or who is not thoroughly satisfied that the brave fellow who defended you so opportunely was legally and morally justifiable in what he did. I have not been in a condition to *think* very coherently, much less to read anything in relation to the question of jurisdiction raised by the State authorities in the *habeas corpus* issued in your behalf by the U. S. Circuit Court, and it may be that, from the mere newspaper's reports that have reached me, I have been unable to fully apprehend the objections which are made to the courts hearing all the facts on the trial of the writ; but it occurs to me as a plain principle of common sense that the federal government should not only have the power, but that it is necessary to its own preservation, to protect its officers from being wantonly or maliciously interfered with, hindered or obstructed in the lawful exercises of their official duties, not arbitrarily of course, but through its regularly constituted agencies, and according to the established principles of law; and where such obstruction consists in the forcible restraint of the officer's liberty, I see no reason why the federal judiciary should not inquire into it on *habeas corpus*, when it is alleged to be not only illegal but contrived for the very purpose of hindering the officer in the discharge of his official duties, and impairing the efficiency of the public service. It is true that in such an investigation a real or apparent conflict between State and federal authority may be presented, which a due regard to the respective rights of the two governments would require to be considered with the utmost caution, such caution, at least, as it is fair to presume an intelligent court would always be careful to exercise, in view of the absolute importance of maintaining as far as possible the strictest harmony between the two jurisdictions. Yet those rights are determined and by fixed legal principles, which it would be impossible for a court to apply in any case without a competent knowledge of the *facts* upon which their application in the particular case might depend. For instance, if your court should issue a writ of *habeas corpus* for the relief of a federal officer upon the averments in his petition that he was forcibly and illegally restrained of his liberty for the purpose of preventing him from performing his official duties, and it should appear in the return to the writ that the person detaining the prisoner was a ministerial officer of the State government authorized by its laws to execute its process, and that he held the petitioner in custody by virtue of a warrant of arrest in due form, issued by a competent magistrate, to answer for an offense against the State laws, I presume the court, in the absence of any further showing, would instantly remand the petitioner to the custody of the State authorities without regard to his official position or the nature of his public duties. But, on the other hand, suppose there should be a traverse of the return, averring that the warrant of the arrest, though apparently regular in all respects, was in truth but a fraudulent contrivance designed and employed for the sole purpose of hindering and obstructing the petitioner in the performance of his duties as an officer of the government of the United States; that the magistrate who issued it, knowingly and maliciously abused his authority for that purpose in pursuance of a conspiracy between himself and others, and not in good faith, and upon probable cause to bring the prisoner to justice for a crime against the State. How then? Here is an

apparent conflict—not a *real* one—between the rights
of the government of the United States and the government of the State. The one has a right to the service of its officer, and the right to prevent his being
unlawfully interfered with or obstructed in the performance of his official duties; the other has the right
to administer its laws for the punishment of crime
through its own tribunals; but it must be observed that
the former has no right to shield one of its officers from
a valid prosecution for a violation of the laws of the
latter not in conflict with the Constitution and laws of
the United States, nor can it be claimed that the latter
has any right to suffer its laws to be prostituted, and its
authority fraudulently abused, in aid of a conspiracy
to defeat or obstruct the functions of the former.
Such an abuse of authority is not, and cannot be in
any sense, a *bona fide* administration of State laws,
but is itself a crime against them. What, then, would
your court do? You would probably say: If it is
true that this man is held without probable cause under a fraudulent warrant, issued in pursuance of a
conspiracy to which the magistrate who issued it was
a party, to give legal color to a malicious interference
with his functions as a federal official, he is the victim
of a double crime—a crime against the United States
and a crime against the State—and it is not only our
duty to vindicate his right to the free exercise of his
official duties, but the right of the federal government
to his services, and its right to protect him in the legal
performance of the same. But if, on the other hand,
he has raised a mere " false clamor "—if he is held in
good faith upon a valid warrant to answer for a crime
committed against the State, it is equally as obligatory
upon us to uphold its authority, and maintain its right
to vindicate its own laws through its own machinery.
To determine between these two hypotheses we must
know the *facts.* * * * The same simple reasoning, it occurs to me, applies to Mr. Neagle's case.
Whether he acted in the line of his duty under the
laws of the United States, as an officer of that government, is clearly a question within the jurisdiction of

the federal judiciary. If he *did*, he cannot be held responsible to the State authority; if he did *not*, he should answer, if required, before its tribunals of justice. I presume no court of ordinary intelligence, State or federal, would question these obvious principles; but how *any* court could determine whether he did or did not act in the line of his official duty under the laws of his government without a judicial inquiry into the *facts* connected with the transaction I am unable to imagine.   *   *   *

I am, as always,
Your faithful friend,
J. PROCTOR KNOTT.

Hon. S. J. FIELD,
    Associate Justice Supreme Court U. S.

Letter from Hon. William D. Shipman, formerly U. S. District Judge for the District of Connecticut:

NEW YORK, *October* 20, 1889.

DEAR JUDGE:

*   *   *   *   *   *   *   *   *

I have attentively read Judge Sawyer's opinion in the Neagle *habeas corpus* case, and I agree with his main conclusions. It seems to me that the whole question of jurisdiction turns on the fact whether you were, at the time the assault was made on you, engaged in the performance of your official duty.

You had been to Los Angeles to hold court there and had finished that business. In going there you were performing an official duty as much as you were when you had held court there. It was then your official duty to go from Los Angeles to San Francisco and hold court there. You could not hold court at the latter place without going, and you were engaged in the line of your official duty in performing that journey for that purpose, as you were in holding the court after you got there. The idea that a judge is not performing official duty when he goes from court-house to court-house or from court-room to court-room in his own circuit seems to me to be absurd. The distance from one court-house or court-room to another is not material, and does not change or modify the act or duty of the judge.

Now, Neagle was an officer of your court, charged with the duty of protecting your person while you were engaged in the performance of your official duty. *His* duty was to see to it that you were not unlawfully prevented from performing *your* official duty—not hindered or obstructed therein. For the State authorities to indict him for repelling the assault on you in the only way which he could do so effectually seems to me to be as unwarranted by law as it would be for them to indict him for an assault on Terry when he assisted in disarming the latter in the court-room last year.

When, therefore, it was conceded on the argument that if the affair at Lathrop had taken place in the court-room during the sitting of the court, the jurisdiction of the Circuit Court would be unquestionable, it is difficult for me to see why the whole question of federal jurisdiction was not embraced in that concession. Assassinating a judge *on* the bench would no more obstruct and defeat public justice than assassinating him on his way to the bench. In each case he is *proceeding in the line of official duty imposed on him by law and* his official oath. The law requires him to go to court wherever the latter is held, and he is as much engaged in performing the duty thus imposed on him while he is proceeding to the place of his judicial labors as he is in performing the latter after he gets there.

It would, therefore, seem to go without saying that any acts done in defense and protection of the judge in the performance of the duties of his office must pertain to the exclusive jurisdiction of the court of which he forms a part.

The fact that the assault on you was avowedly made in revenge for your judicial action in a case heard by you gives a darker tinge to the deed, but, perhaps, does not change the legal character of the assault itself.

That Neagle did his whole duty, and in no way exceeded it, is too plain for argument.

Yours faithfully,

W. D. SHIPMAN.

Mr. Justice FIELD.

Letter from James C. Welling, president of Columbian University, Washington:

HARTFORD, *August* 15, 1889.

MY DEAR JUDGE:

It is a relief to know that Justice, as well as the honored justice of our Supreme Judiciary, has been avenged by the pistol-shot of Neagle. The life of Terry has long since been forfeited to law, to decency, and to morals. He has already exceeded the limit assigned by holy scripture to men of his ilk. "The bloody-minded man shall not live out half his days." The mode of his death was in keeping with his life. Men who break all the laws of nature should not expect to die by the laws of nature.

In all this episode you have simply worn the judicial ermine without spot or stain. You defeated a bold, bad man in his machinations, and the enmity you thereby incurred was a crown of honor. I am glad that you are to be no longer harassed by the menace of this man's violence, for such a menace is especially trying to a minister of the law. We all know that Judge Field the *man* would not flinch from a thousand Terrys, but Judge Field the *Justice* could hardly take in his own hands the protection of his ·person, where the threatened outrage sprang *entirely* from his official acts.

I wish, therefore, to congratulate you on your escape alike from the violence of Terry and from the necessity of killing him with your own hands. It was meet that you should have been defended by an executive officer of the court assailed in your person. For doubtless Terry, and the hag who was on the hunt with him, were minded to murder you.

366

Convey my cordial felicitations to Mrs. Field, and
believe me ever, my dear Mr. Justice,

Your faithful friend,

JAMES C. WELLING.

Mr. Justice FIELD.

Letter from Right Rev. B. Wistar Morris, Episcopal
Bishop of Oregon:

BISHOPCROFT, PORTLAND, OREGON,
August 22, 1889.

MY DEAR JUDGE FIELD:

I hope a word of congratulation from your Oregon
friends for your escape in the recent tragedy will not
be considered an intrusion. Of course we have all
been deeply interested in its history, and proud that
you were found as you were, without the defenses of
a bully.

I will not trespass further on your time than to
subscribe myself,

Very truly your friend,

B. WISTAR MORRIS.

Mr. Justice FIELD.

A copy of the following card was enclosed in this
letter:

AN UNARMED JUSTICE.

PORTLAND OREGON, *August* 19.

To the Editor of the Oregonian:

There is one circumstance in the history of the
Field and Terry tragedy that seems to me is worthy
of more emphatic comment than it has yet received.
I mean the fact that Judge Field had about his person
no weapon of defense whatever, though he knew that
this miserable villain was dogging his steps for the
purpose of assaulting him, perhaps of taking his life.
His brother, Mr. Cyrus W. Field, says:

"It was common talk in the East here, among my
brother's friends, that Terry's threats to do him

bodily harm were made with the full intent to follow them up. Terry threatened openly to shoot the Justice, and we, who knew him, were convinced he would certainly do it if he ever got a chance.

"I endeavored to dissuade my brother from making the trip west this year, but to no purpose, and he said, 'I have a duty to perform there, and this sort of thing can't frighten me away. I know Terry will do me harm if he gets a chance, and as I shall be in California some time, he will have chances enough. Let him take them.'

"When urged to arm himself he made the same reply. He said that when it came to such a pass in this country that judges find it necessary to go armed, it will be time to close the courts themselves."

This was a manly and noble reply and must recall to many minds that familiar sentiment: "He is thrice armed who has his quarrel just." With the daily and hourly knowledge that this assassin was ever upon his track, this brave judge goes about his duty and scorns to take to himself the defenses of a bully or a brigand; and in doing so, how immeasurably has he placed himself above the vile creature that sought his life, and all others who resort to deeds of violence. "They that take the sword shall perish with the sword," is a saying of wide application, and had it been so in this case; had this brave and self-possessed man been moved from his high purpose by the importunity of friends, and when slain by his enemy, had been found armed in like manner with the murderer himself, what a stain would it have been upon his name and honor? And how would our whole country have been disgraced in the eyes of the civilized world, that her highest ministers of justice must be armed as highwaymen as they go about their daily duties!

Well said this undaunted servant of the state: "Then will it be time to close the courts themselves." May we not hope, Mr. Editor, that this example of one occupying this high place in our country may have some influence in staying the spirit and deeds of violence now so rife, and that they who are so ready to resort to the rifle and revolver may learn to regard them only as the instruments of the coward or the scoundrel?

B. WISTAR MORRIS.

The citations given below from different journals, published at the time, indicated the general opinion of the country. With rare exceptions it approved of the action of the Government, the conduct of Neagle, and the bearing of Justice Field.

The *Alta California*, a leading paper in California, had, on August 15, 1889, the day following the tragedy, the following article:

THE TERRY TRAGEDY.

The killing of David S. Terry by the United States Marshal David Neagle yesterday was an unfortunate affair, regretted, we believe, by no one more than by Justice Field, in whose defense the fatal shot was fired. There seems, however, to be an almost undivided sentiment that the killing was justifiable. Every circumstance attending the tragedy points to the irresistible conclusion that there was a premeditated determination on the part of Terry and his wife to provoke Justice Field to an encounter, in which Terry might either find an excuse for killing the man against whom he had threatened vengeance, or in which his wife might use the pistol which she always carries, in the pretended defense of her husband. For some time past it has been feared that a meeting between Terry and Justice Field would result in bloodshed. There is now indisputable proof that Terry had made repeated threats that he would assault Justice Field the first time he met him off the bench, and that if the Judge resisted he would kill him. Viewed in the light of these threats, Terry's presence on the same train with Justice Field will hardly be regarded as accidental, and his actions in the breakfast-room at Lathrop were directly in line with the intentions he had previously expressed. Neagle's prompt and deadly use of his revolver is to be judged with due reference to the character and known disposition of the man with whom he had to deal and to his previous actions and threats. He was attending Justice Field, against the will of the latter and in spite of his protest, in obedience to an order from the Attorney-General of the United States to Marshal Franks to detail a deputy to protect the person of Justice Field from Terry's threatened violence. A slap in the face may not, under ordinary circumstances, be sufficient provocation to justify the taking of human life; but it must be remembered that there were no ordinary circumstances and that Terry was no ordinary man. Terry was a noted pistol-shot; it was known that he invariably carried arms and that he boasted of his ability to use them. If on this occasion he was unarmed, as Mrs. Terry asserts,* Neagle had no means of knowing that fact; on the contrary, to his mind every presumption was in favor of the belief that he carried both pistol and knife, in accordance with his usual habit. As a peace officer, even apart from the special duty which had been assigned to him, he was justified in taking the means necessary to prevent Terry from continuing his assault; but the means necessary in the case of one man may be wholly inadequate with a man bearing the reputation of David S. Terry, a man who only a few months previously had drawn a knife while resisting the lawful authority of another United States officer. It is true that if Terry was unarmed, the deputy marshal might have arrested him without taking his life or seriously endangering his own; but Terry was a man of gigantic stature, and, though aged, in possession of a giant's strength; and there is no one who was acquainted with him, or has had opportunity to learn his past history, who does not know that he was a desperate

---

* It has been conclusively established since that he was armed with his usual bowie-knife at the time.

man, willing to take desperate chances and to resort to desperate means when giving way to his impulses of passion, and that any person who should at such a moment attempt to stay his hand would do so at the risk of his life. Whether he had a pistol with him at that moment or not, there was every reason to believe that he was armed, and that the blow with his hand was intended only as the precursor to a more deadly blow with a weapon. At such moments little time is allowed for reflection. The officer of the law was called upon to act and to act promptly. He did so, and the life of David S. Terry was the forfeit. He fell, a victim to his own ungovernable passions, urged on to his fate by the woman who was at once his wife and his client, and perhaps further incited by sensational newspaper articles which stirred up the memory of his resentment for fancied wrongs, and taunted him with the humiliation of threats unfulfilled.

The close of Judge Terry's life ends a career and an era. He had the misfortune to carry into a ripened state of society the conditions which are tolerable only where social order is not fully established. Restless under authority, and putting violence above law, he lived by the sword and has perished by it.

That example which refused submission to judicial finalities was becoming offensive to California, but the incubus of physical fear was upon many who realized that the survival of frontier ways into non-frontier period was a damage to the State. But, be this as it may, the stubborn spirit that defied the law has fallen by the law.

When Justice Field showed the highest judicial courage in the opening incidents of the tragedy that has now closed, the manhood of California received a distinct impetus. When the Justice,. with threats made against his life, returned to the State unarmed, and resentful of protection against assault, declaring that when judges must arm to defend themselves from assault offered in reprisal of their judicial actions society must be considered dissolved, he was rendering to our institutions the final and highest possible service. The event that followed, the killing of Terry in the act of striking him the second time from behind, while he sat at table in a crowded public dining-room, was the act of the law. The Federal Department of Justice, by its chief, the Attorny-General of the United States, had ordered its officer, the United States marshal for the northern district of California, to take such means and such measures as might be necessary to protect the persons of the judges against assault by Judge Terry, in carrying out the threats that he had made. This order was from the executive arm of the Government, and it was carried out to the letter. Judge Terry took the law into his own hands and fell. Nothing can add to the lesson his fate teaches. It is established now that in California no man is above the law ; that no man can affect the even poise of justice by fear. Confiding in his own strength as superior to the law, David S. Terry fell wretchedly.

No more need be said. New California inscribes upon her shield, " Obedience to the law the first condition of good citizenship," and the past is closed.

The Record-Union of Sacramento, one of the leading papers of California, on August 15, 1889, the day following the tragedy, had the following article under the head—

KILLING OF JUDGE TERRY.

In the news columns of the *Record-Union* will be found all the essential details of the circumstances of the killing of D. S. Terry. It will be evident to the reader that they readily sap the whole case, and that there is no substantial dispute possible concerning the facts. These truths we assert, without fear of successful condradiction, establish the justifiableness of the act of the United States marshal who fired upon and killed Terry. We think there will be no dispute among sensible men that a federal circuit judge or a justice of the supreme bench, passing from one portion of the circuit to another in which either is required to open a court and hear causes, and for the purpose of fully discharging his official duties, is while en route in the discharge of an official function, and constructively his court is open to the extent that an assault upon him, because of matters pending in his court, or because of judgments he has rendered or is to render, is an assault upon the court, and his bailiff or marshal detailed to attend the court or to aid in preserving the order and dignity of the court has the same right to protect him from assault then that he would have, had the judge actually reached his court-room.

But further than this, we hold that in view of the undeniable fact that the Justice had knowledge of the fact that the Terrys, man and wife, had sworn to punish him; that they had indulged in threats against him of the most pronounced character; that they had boarded a train on which it is probable they knew he had taken passage from one part of his circuit to another in his capacity as a magistrate; in view of the fact that Terry sought the first opportunity to approach and strike him, and that, too, when seated; and in view of the notorious fact that Terry always went armed—the man who shot Terry would have been justified in doing so had he not even been commissioned as an officer of the court. He warned the assailant to desist, and knowing his custom to go armed, and that he had threatened the Justice, and Terry refusing to restrain his blows, it was Neagle's duty to save life, to strike down the assailant in the most effectual manner. Men who, having the ability to prevent murder, stand by and see it committed, may well be held to accountability for criminal negligence.

But in this case it is clear that murder was intended on the part of the Terrys. One of them ran for her pistol and brought it, and would have reached the other's side with it in time, had she not been detained by strong men at the door. Neagle saw this woman depart, and coupling it with the advance of Terry,

knew, as a matter of course, what it meant. He had
been deputed by the chief law officer of the Government—in view of previous assaults by the Terrys and
their threats and display of weapons in court—to
stand guard over the judges and protect them. He
acted, therefore, precisely as it was proper he should
do. Had he been less prompt and vigorous, all the
world knows that not he but Terry would to-day be
in custody, and not Terry but the venerable justice of
the Supreme Court of the United States would to-day
be in the coffin.

These remarks have grown too extended for any
elaboration of the moral of the tragedy that culminated in the killing of David S. Terry yesterday. But
we cannot allow the subject to be even temporarily
dismissed without calling the thought of the reader
to contemplation of the essential truth that society is
bound to protect the judges of the courts of the land
from violence and the threats of violence ; otherwise
the decisions of our courts must conform to the violence threatened, and there will be an end of our judicial system, the third and most valuable factor in the
scheme of representative government. Society cannot, therefore, punish, but must applaud the man who
defends the courts of the people and the judges of
those courts from such violence and threats of violence.
For it must be apparent to even the dullest intellect
that all such violence is an outrage upon the judicial
conscience, and therefore involves and puts in peril
the liberties of the people.

The New Orleans *Times-Democrat*, in one of its
issues at this period, used the following language :

The judge in America who keeps his official ermine
spotless, who faithfully attends to the heavy and responsible duties of his station, deserves that the people should guard the sanctity of his person with a
strength stronger than armour of steel and readier
than the stroke of lance or sword. Though the
judges be called to pass on tens of thousands of

cases, to sentence to imprisonment or to death thousands of criminals, they should be held by the people safe from the hate and vengeance of those criminals as if they were guarded by an invulnerable shield.

If Judge Field, of the Supreme Court, one of the nine highest judges under our republican government, in travelling recently over his circuit in California, had been left to the mercy of the violent man who had repeatedly threatened his life, who had proved himself ready with the deadly knife or revolver, it would have been a disgrace to American civilization; it would have been a stigma and stain upon American manhood; it would have shown that the spirit of American liberty, which exalts and pays reverence to our judiciary, had been replaced by public apathy that marked the beginning of the decline of patriotism.

Judge Field recognized this when, in being advised to arm himself in case his life was endangered, he uttered the noble words: "No, sir; I do not and will not carry arms, for when it is known that the judges of the court are compelled to arm themselves against assaults offered in consequence of their judicial action it will be time to dissolve the courts, consider the government a failure, and let society lapse into barbarism." That ringing sentence has gone to the remotest corner of the land, and everywhere it has gone it should fire the American heart with a proud resolve to protect forever the sanctity of our judiciary.

Had not Neagle protected the person of Judge Field from the assault of a dangerous and violent ruffian, apparently intent on murder, by his prompt and decisive action, shooting the assailant down to his death, it is certain that other brave men would have rushed quickly to his rescue; but Neagle's marvelous quickness forestalled the need of any other's action. The person of one of the very highest American judges was preserved unharmed, while death palsied the murderous hand that had sworn to take his life.

That act of Neagle's was no crime. It was a deed that any and every American should feel proud of having done. It was an act that should be applauded over the length and breadth of this great land. It should not have consigned him for one minute to prison walls. It should have lifted him high in the esteem of all the American people. When criminals turn executioners, and judges are the victims, we might as well close our courts and hoist the red flag of anarchy over their silent halls and darkened chambers.

The New York *Herald,* in its issue of August 19, 1889, said:

The sensation of the past week is a lesson in republicanism and a eulogium on the majesty of the law.

It was not a personal controversy between Stephen J. Field and David S. Terry. It was a conflict between law and lawlessness—between a judicial officer who represented the law and a man who sought to take it into his own hands. One embodied the peaceful power of the nation, the will of the people; the other defied that power and appealed to the dagger.

Justice Field's whole course shows a conception of judicial duty that lends grandeur to a republican judiciary. It is an inspiring example to the citizens and especially to the judges of the country. He was reminded of the danger of returning to California while Judge Terry and his wife were at large. His firm answer was that it was his duty to go and he would go. He was then advised to arm himself for self-defense. His reply embodies a nobility that should make it historic: "When it comes to such a pass in this country that judges of the courts find it necessary to go armed it will be time to close the courts themselves."

This sentiment was not born of any insensibility to danger; Justice Field fully realized the peril himself. But above all feeling of personal concern arose a lofty sense of the duty imposed upon a justice of the nation's highest court. The officer is a representative of the

law—a minister of peace. He should show by his
example that the law is supreme ; that all must bow
to its authority; that all lawlessness must yield to it.
When judges who represent the law resort to violence
even in self-defense, the pistol instead of the court
becomes the arbiter of controversies, and the authority
of the government gives way to the power of the mob.

Rather than set a precedent that might tend to such
a result, that would shake popular confidence in the
judiciary, that would lend any encouragement to violence, a judge, as Justice Field evidently felt, may well
risk his own life for the welfare of the commonwealth.
He did not even favor the proposition that a marshal
be detailed to guard him.

The course of the venerable Justice is an example
to all who would have the law respected. It is also
a lesson to all who would take the law into their own
hands.

Not less exemplary was his recognition of the supremacy of the law when the sheriff of San Joaquin
appeared before him with a warrant of arrest on the
grave charge of murder. The warrant was an outrage, but it was the duty of the officer to serve it,
even on a justice of the United States Supreme Court.
When the sheriff hesitated and began to apologize
before discharging his painful duty, Justice Field
promptly spoke out: "Officer, proceed with your
duty. I am ready, and an officer should always do
his duty." These are traits of judicial heroism worthy
the admiration of the world.

The *Albany Evening Union*, in one of its issues at
this time, has the following :

JUSTICE FIELD RELIES UPON THE LAW FOR HIS DEFENSE.

The courage of Justice Stephen J. Field in declin-
ing to carry weapons and declaring that it is time to
close the courts when judges have to arm themselves,
and at the same time proceeding to do his duty on the

bench when his life was threatened by a desperate man, is without parallel in the history of our judiciary. We do not mean by this that he is the only judge on the bench that would be as brave as he was under the circumstances, but every phase of the affair points to the heroism of the man. He upheld the majesty of the law in a fearless manner and at the peril of his life. He would not permit the judiciary to be lowered by any fear of the personal harm that might follow a straight-forward performance of his duty. His arrest for com-plicity in a murder was borne by the same tranquil bravery—a supreme reliance upon a due process of law. He did not want the officer to apologize to him for doing his duty. He had imprisoned Judge Terry and his wife Sarah Althea for contempt of court. * * * The threats by Judge Terry did not even frighten him to carry weapons of self-defense. This illustration of upholding the majesty of the law is without precedent, and is worth more to the cause of justice than the en-tire United States army could be if called out to sup-press a riotous band of law-breakers. Justice Field did what any justice should do under the circumstances, but how many judges would have displayed a like courage had they been in his place?

The New York *World*, in its issue of Monday even-ing, August 26th, has the following article:

A NEW LEAF TURNED.

When Judge Field, knowing that his life was threat-ened, went back unarmed into the State of California and about his business there, he gave wholesome re-buke to the cowardice that prompts men to carry a pistol—a cowardice that has been too long popular on the coast. He did a priceless service to the cause of progress in his State, and added grace to his er-mine when he disdained so take arms in answer to the threats of assassins.

The men who have conspired to take Judge Field's life ought to need only one warning that a new day has dawned in California, and to find that warning in the doom of the bully Terry. The law will protect the ermine of its judges.

The New York *World* of August 18th treats of the arrest of Justice Field as an outrage, and speaks of it as follows:

THE ARREST OF FIELD AN OUTRAGE AND AN ABSURDITY.

The California magistrate who issued a warrant for Justice Field's arrest is obviously a donkey of the most precious quality. The Justice had been brutally assailed by a notorious ruffian who had publicly declared his intention to kill his enemy. Before Justice Field could even rise from his chair a neat-handed deputy United States marshal shot the ruffian. Justice Field had no more to do with the shooting than any other bystander, and even if there had been doubt on that point it was certain that a justice of the United States Supreme Court was not going to run away beyond the jurisdiction. His arrest was, therefore, as absurd as it was outrageous. It was asked for by the demented widow of the dead desperado simply as a means of subjecting the Justice to an indignity, and no magistrate possessed of even a protoplasmic possibility of common sense and character would have lent himself in that way to such a service.

The Kansas City *Times*, in its issue at this period, uses the following language:

NO ONE WILL CENSURE.

Gratitude for Judge Field's Escape the Chief Sentiment.

Deputy Marshal Neagle acted with terrible promptitude in protecting the venerable member of the Supreme Court with whose safety he was specially charged, but few will be inclined to censure him. He had to deal with a man of fierce temper, whose readiness to use firearms was part of the best known history of California.

It is a subject for general congratulation that Justice Field escaped the violence of his assailant. The American nation would be shocked to learn that a judge of its highest tribunal could not travel without danger of assault from those whom he had been compelled to offend by administering the laws. Justice Field has the respect due his office and that deeper and more significant reverence produced by his character and abilities. Since most of the present generation were old enough to observe public affairs he has been a jurist of national reputation and a sitting member of the Supreme Court. In that capacity he has earned the gratitude of his countrymen by bold and unanswerable defense of sound constitutional interpretation on more than one occasion. In all the sad affair the most prominent feeling will be that of gratitude at his escape.

The Army and Navy Journal, in its issue of August 24, 1889, had the following article under the head of—

MARSHAL NEAGLE'S CRIME.

The public mind appears to be somewhat unsettled upon the question of the right of Neagle to kill Terry while assaulting Judge Field. His justification is as clear as is the benefit of his act to a long-suffering community. Judge Field was assaulted unexpectedly from behind, while seated at a dining-table, by a notorious assassin and ruffian, who had sworn to kill him, and who, according to the testimony of at least one witness, was armed with a long knife, had sent his wife for a pistol, and was intending to use it as soon as obtained. * * *

The rule is that the danger which justifies homicide in self-defense must be actual and urgent. And was it not so in this case? No one who reflects upon the features of the case—an old man without means of defense, fastened in a sitting posture by the table at which he sat and the chair he occupied, already smitten with one severe blow and about to receive another more severe from a notorious ruffian who had publicly avowed his intention to slay him—no one surely can deny that the peril threatening Judge Field was both actual and urgent in the very highest degree.

"A man may repel force by force in the defense of his person, habitation, or property, against one or many who manifestly intend and endeavor by violence or surprise to commit a known felony on either." "In such a case he is not obliged to retreat, but may pursue his adversary till he find himself out of danger; and if in a conflict between them he happens to kill, such killing is justifiable. The right of self-defense in case of this kind is founded on the law of nature, and is not, nor can be, superseded by any law of society. Where a known felony is attempted upon the person, be it to rob or murder, the party assaulted may repel force by force; and even his servant attendant on him, or any person present, may interpose for preventing mischief, and, if death ensue, the party interposing will be justified." (Wharton Amer. Crim. Law, Vol. 2, Sec. 1019.)

This is the law, as recognized at the present day and established by centuries of precedent, and it completely exonerates Neagle—of course Judge Field needs no exoneration—from any, the least, criminality in what he did. He is acquitted of wrong-doing, not only in his character of attendant servant, but in that of bystander simply. He was as much bound to kill Terry under the circumstances as every bystander in the room was bound to kill him; and in his capacity of guard, especially appointed to defend an invaluable life against a known and imminent felony, he was so bound in a much greater degree.

"A sincere and apparently well-grounded belief that a felony is about to be perpetrated will extenuate a homicide committed in prevention of it, though the defendant be but a private citizen" (25 Ala., 15.)

See Wharton, above quoted, who embodies the doctrine in his text (Vol. 2, Sec. 1039).

* * * * * * * * *

Let us be grateful from our hearts that the old Mosaic law, "Whoso sheddeth man's blood by man shall his blood be shed," is shown by this memorable event to have not yet fallen altogether into innocuous desuetude; and let us give thanks to God that he has seen fit on this occasion to preserve from death at the hands of an intolerable ruffian the life of that high-minded, pure-handed, and excellent jurist and magistrate, Stephen J. Field.

The Philadelphia *Times* of August 15th has the following:

ONLY ONE OPINION.

Marshal Neagle Could Not Stand Idly By.

The killing of Judge Terry of California is a homicide that will occasion no regret wherever the story of his stormy and wicked life is known. At the same time, the circumstances that surrounded it will be deeply lamented. This violent man, more than once a murderer, met his death while in the act of assaulting Justice Field of the Supreme Court of the United States. Had he not been killed when he was, Judge Field would probably have been another of his victims. Terry had declared his purpose of killing the Justice, and this was their first meeting since his release from deserved imprisonment.

In regard to the act of United States Marshal Neagle, there can be only one opinion. He could not stand idly by and see a judge of the Supreme Court murdered before his eyes. The contumely that Terry sought to put upon the judge was only the insult that was to go before premeditated murder. The case has no moral except the certainty that a violent life will end in a violent death.

The *Philadelphia Inquirer* of the same date says
as follows:

A PREMEDITATED INSULT.

Followed Quickly by a Deserved Retribution.

Ex-Judge Terry's violent death was a fitting termi-
nation to a stormy life, and the incidents of his last
encounter were characteristic of the man and his
methods. He was one of the few lingering representatives of the old-time population of California.
He was prominent there when society was organizing
itself, and succeeded in holding on to life and position when many a better man succumbed to the rude
justice of the period. Most of his early associates
died with their boots on, a generation ago. Terry
lived, assailed on all sides, despised by the better element and opposed by the law, in trouble often, but
never punished as he deserved. His last act was to
offer a gross, premeditated insult to the venerable
Justice Field, and the retribution he had long defied
followed it quickly. California will have little reason
to mourn his loss.

The *Cleveland Leader,* in its issue of August 18th,
speaks of the conduct of Neagle as follows:

THE KILLING OF TERRY.

We have already expressed the opinion in these columns that the killing of David S. Terry by Deputy
Marshal Neagle at Lathrop, California, Wednesday,
was entirely justifiable. In that opinion it is a pleasure to note that the press of the country concur
almost unanimously. The judgment of eminent members of the legal profession, as published in our telegraph columns and elsewhere, support and bear out
that view of the case. The full account of the trouble
makes the necessity of some such action on the part
of the deputy marshal clear. The judgment of the

country is that Neagle only did his duty in defending the person of Justice Field, and in that judgment the California jury will doubtless concur when the case is brought before it.

The *Argonaut*, a leading paper of San Francisco, not a political, but a literary paper, and edited with great ability, in its issue of August 26, 1889, used the following language:

The course of Judge Field throughout this troublesome business has been in the highest degree creditable to him. He has acted with dignity and courage, and his conduct has been characterized by most excellent taste. His answer, when requested to go armed against the assault of Terry, is worthy of preservation. And now that his assailant has been arrested in his career by death, all honest men who respect the law will breathe more freely. Judge Terry had gained a most questionable reputation, not for courage in the right direction; not for generosity which overlooked or forgave, or forgot offenses against himself or his interests. He never conceded the right to any man to hold an opinion in opposition to his prejudices, or cross the path of his passion with impunity. He could with vulgar whisper insult the judge who rendered an opinion adverse to his client, and with profane language insult the attorney who had the misfortune to be retained by a man whose cause he did not champion. He had become a terror to society and a walking menace to the social circle in which he revolved. His death was a necessity, and, except here and there a friend of blunted moral instincts, there will be found but few to mourn his death or criticise the manner of his taking off. To say that Marshal Neagle should have acted in any other manner than he did means that he was to have left Justice Field in the claws of a tiger, and at the mercy of an infuriated, angry monster, who had never shown mercy or generosity to an enemy in his power.   *   *   *

Judge Field has survived the unhappy conflict which carried Judge Terry to his grave. He is more highly honored now than when this quarrel was thrust upon him ; he has lost no friends ; he has made thousands of new ones who honor him for protecting with his life the honor of the American bench, the dignity of the American law, and the credit of the American name. In the home where Judge Terry lived he went to the grave almost unattended by the friends of his social surroundings, no clergyman consenting to read the service at his burial. The Supreme Court over which he had presided as chief justice refused to adjourn in honor of his death, the press and public opinion, for a wonder, in accord over the manner of his taking off.

Indeed, the public opinion of the country, as shown by the press and declarations of prominent individuals, was substantially one in its approval of the action of the Government, the conduct of Neagle, and the bearing of Justice Field.*

---

* NOTE.—Whilst there was a general concurrence of opinion as to the threats of Terry and of the fate he met at the hands of Neagle and of the bearing of Justice Field through all the proceedings, there were exceptions to this judgment. There were persons who sympathized with Terry and his associates and grieved at his fate, although he had openly avowed his intention not merely to insult judicial officers for their judicial conduct, but to kill them in case they resented the insult offered. He married Sarah Althea Hill after the United States Circuit Court had delivered its opinion, in open court, announcing its decision that she had committed forgery, perjury, and subornation of perjury, and was a woman of abandoned character. And yet a writer in the *Overland Monthly* in October, 1889, attributes his assault upon the marshal—striking him violently in the face for the execution of the order of the court to remove her from the court-room because of her gross imputation upon the judges—chiefly to his chivalric spirit to protect his wife, and declares that "the universal verdict"

The *Daily Report*, a paper of influence in San Francisco at the time, published the following article on " The Lesson of the Hour," from the pen of an eminent lawyer of California, who was in no way connected with the controversy which resulted in Judge Terry's death :

The universal acquiescence of public opinion in the justifiable character of the act which terminated the life of the late David S. Terry is to be accounted for by the peculiar nature of the offense which he had committed. It was not for a mere assault, though perpetrated under circumstances which rendered it peculiarly reprehensible, that he met his death without eliciting from the community one word of condemnation for the slayer or of sympathy with the slain.

Mr. Justice Field is an officer of high rank in the most important department of the Government of the United States, namely, that which is charged with the administration of legal justice. When David S Terry publicly and ostentatiously slapped the face of this high official—this representative of public justice—the blow being in all probability the intended prelude to a still more atrocious offense, he committed a gross violation of the peace and dignity of the United States. The echo of the blow made the blood tingle in the veins of every true American, and from every quarter,

---

upon him " will be that he was possessed of *sterling integrity of purpose*, and stood out from the rest of his race as a strongly individualized character, which has been well called an anachronism in our civilization." And Gov. Pennoyer, of Oregon, in his message to the legislature of that State, pronounced the officer appointed by the marshal under the direction of the Attorney-General to protect Justices Field and Sawyer from threatened violence and murder as a "*secret armed assassin*," who accompanied a Federal judge in California, and who shot down in cold blood an unarmed citizen of that State.

far and near, thick and fast, came denunciations of the outrage. That any man under a government created "by the people, for the people" shall assume to be a law unto himself, the sole despot in a community based on the idea of the equality of all before the law, and the willing submission and obedience of all to established rule, is simply intolerable.

In his audacious assault on "the powers that be" Terry took his life in his hand, and no lover of peace and good order can regret that, of the two lives in peril, his was extinguished. He threw down the gage of battle to the whole community, and it is well that he was vanquished in the strife.

In the early part of the war of the rebellion General Dix, of New York, was placed in charge of one of the disaffected districts. We had then hardly begun to see that war was a very stern condition of things, and that it actually involved the necessity of killing. Those familiar with the incidents of that time will remember how the General's celebrated order, "If any one attempts to haul down the American flag, shoot him on the spot," thrilled the slow pulses of the Northern heart like the blast of a bugle. Yet some adverse obstructionist might object that the punishment pronounced far exceeded the offense, which was merely the effort to detach from its position a piece of colored bunting. But it is the *animus* that characterizes the act. An insult offered to a mere symbol of authority becomes, under critical circumstances, an unpardonable crime. If the symbol, instead of being an inanimate object, be a human being—a high officer of the Government—does not such an outrage as that committed by Terry exceed in enormity the offense denounced by General Dix? And if so, why should the punishment be less?

In every civilized community, society, acting with a keen instinct of self-preservation, has always punished with just severity those capital offenders against peace and good order who strike at the very foundation on which all government must rest.

CHAPTER XIX.

With the discharge from arrest of the brave deputy marshal, Neagle, who had stood between Justice Field and the would-be assassin's assault, and the vindication by the Circuit Court of the right of the general government to protect its officers from personal violence, for the discharge of their duties, at the hands of disappointed litigants, the public mind, which had been greatly excited by the proceedings narrated, became quieted. No apprehension was felt that there would be any reversal of the decision of the Circuit Court on the appeal which was taken to the Supreme Court. General and absolute confidence was expressed in the determination of the highest tribunal of the nation. The appeal was argued on the part of Neagle by the Attorney-General of the United States and Joseph H. Choate, Esq., of the New York bar; and the briefs of counsel in the Circuit Court were also filed. The attorney-general of California and Mr. Zachariah Montgomery appeared upon behalf of the State, and briefs of Messrs. Shellabarger and Wilson were also filed in its behalf.

The argument of the Attorney-General of the United States was exceedingly able. He had watched all the proceedings of the case from the outset. He had directed that protection should be extended by the marshal to Justice Field and Judge Sawyer against any threatened violence, and he believed strongly in the doctrine that the officers of the general government were entitled to receive everywhere throughout the country full protection against all violence whilst in the discharge of their duties. He believed that such protection was necessary to the efficiency and permanency of the government ; and its necessity in both respects was never more ably presented.

The argument of Mr. Choate covered all the questions of law and fact in the case and was marked by that great ability and invincible logic and by that clearness and precision of statement which have rendered him one of the ablest of advocates and jurists in the country, one who all acknowledge has few peers and no superiors at the bar of the nation.*

The argument of the attorney-general of the State consisted chiefly of a repetition of the doctrine that,

---

* NOTE.—Mr. Choate took great interest in the question involved—the right of the Government of the United States to protect its officers from violence whilst engaged in the discharge of their duties,—deeming its maintenance essential to the efficiency of the Government itself ; and he declined to make any charge or take any fee for his professional services in the case. The privilege of supporting this great principle before the highest tribunal of the country, where his powers would be most effectively engaged in securing its recognition, was considered by him as sufficient reward. Certainly he has that reward in the full establishment of that principle—for which, also, both he and Attorney-General Miller will receive the thanks of all who love and revere our national government and trust that its existence may be perpetuated.

Mr. James C. Carter, the distinguished advocate of New York, also took a deep interest in the questions involved, and had several consultations with Mr. Choate upon them ; and his professional services were given with the same generous and noble spirit that characterized the course of Mr. Choate.

for offenses committed within its limits, the State alone has jurisdiction to try the offenders—a position which within its proper limits, and when not carried to the protection of resistance to the authority of the United States, has never been questioned.

The most striking feature of the argument on behalf of the State was presented by Zachariah Montgomery. It may interest the reader to observe the true Terry flavor introduced into his argument, and the manifest perversion of the facts into which it led him. He deeply sympathized with Terry in the grief and mortification which he suffered in being charged with having assaulted the marshal with a deadly weapon in the presence of the Circuit Court in September, 1888. He attempted to convince the Supreme Court that one of its members had deliberately made a misrecital, in the order committing Terry for contempt, and treated this as a mitigation of that individual's subsequent attack on Justice Field. He did not, however, attempt to gainsay the testimony of the numerous witnesses who swore that Terry did try to draw his knife while yet in the court-room on that occasion, and that, being temporarily prevented from doing so by force, he completed the act as soon as this force was withdrawn, and pursued the marshal with knife in hand, loudly declaring in the hearing of the court, in language too coarse and vulgar to be repeated, that he would do sundry terrible things to those who should obstruct him on his way to his wife. As she was then in the custody of the marshal and in his office, under an order of the court; and as Terry had resisted her arrest and removal from the court-room until overpowered by several strong men, and as he had instantly on being released rushed madly from the court-room, drawing and brandishing his knife as he went, the conclusion is irresistible that he was determined upon her rescue from the marshal, if, with the aid of his knife, he could accomplish it. That Mr. Montgomery allowed these facts, which constitute the offense of an assault with a deadly weapon, to go unchallenged, compels us to the charitable presumption that he did not know the law.

A reading of the decisions on this subject would have taught him that in order to constitute that offense it is not necessary that the assailant should actually stab with his knife or shoot with his pistol. The assault by Terry was commenced in the court-room, under the eyes of the judges, and was a continuing act, ending only with the wrenching of the knife from his hands. It was all committed "in the presence of the court," for the Supreme Court has decided in the Savin case that "the jury-room and hallway were parts of the place in which the court was required by law to hold its sessions, and that the court, at least when in session, is present in every part of the place set apart for its own use and for the use of its officers, jurors, and witnesses, and that misbehavior in such a place is misbehavior in the presence of the court. (See Vol. 131, U. S. Reports, page 277, where the case is reported.)

Mr. Montgomery was reckless enough to contradict the record when he stated that Justice Field in his opinion in the revivor case "took occasion to discuss at considerable length the question of the genuineness of the aforesaid marriage document, maintaining very strenuously that it was a forgery, and that this it was that so aroused the indignation of Mrs. Terry that she sprang to her feet and charged Justice Field with having been bought."

There is not a word of truth in this statement. Justice Field, in overruling the demurrer, never discussed at all the genuineness of the marriage agreement. How, then, could it be true that words, nowhere to be found in Judge Field's opinion, " so aroused the indignation of Mrs. Terry that she sprang to her feet and charged Justice Field with having been bought"? Justice Field discussed only the legal effect of the decree already rendered by the United States Circuit Court. He said nothing to excite the woman's ire, except to state the necessary steps to be taken to enforce the decree. He had not participated in the trial of the original case, and had never been called upon to express any opinion concerning the agreement. Mr. Montgomery said in his brief that the opinion read by Justice Field, " while overruling a demurrer, assails this contract, in effect pronouncing it a forgery." This statement is totally unfounded. From it the casual reader would suppose that the demurrer was to the complaint in the original case, and that the court was forestalling evidence, whereas it was a demurrer in a proceeding to revive the suit, which had abated by the death of the party, and to give effect to the decree already rendered therein, after a full hearing of the testimony.

Mr. Montgomery said:

" The opinion also charges Mrs. Terry with perjury, after she has sworn that it was genuine."

The judgment of a court may be referred to by one of its judges, even though the rendering of the judgment convicted a party or a witness, of perjury, without furnishing the perjurer with a justification for denouncing the judge. Mr. Montgomery furthermore said that the "opinion charged her not only with forgery and perjury, but with unchastity as well; for if she had not been Sharon's wife, she had unquestionably been his kept mistress." He says:

"At the announcement of this decision from the bench in the presence of a crowded court-room; a decision which she well knew, before the going down of another sun, would be telegraphed to the remotest corners of the civilized world, to be printed and re-printed with sensational head-lines in every news-paper, and talked over by every scandal-monger on the face of the earth; was it any wonder—not that it was right—but was it any wonder that this high-spirited, educated woman, sprung from as respectable a family as any in the great State of Missouri, proud of her ancestry, and prizing her good name above everything on this earth, when she heard herself thus adjudged in one breath to be guilty of forgery, per-jury, and unchastity, and thus degraded from the exalted position of wife—to which the Supreme Court of her State had said she was entitled—down to that of a paid harlot; was it any wonder, I say, that like an enraged tigress she sprang to her feet, and in words of indignation sought to defend her wounded honor?"

Mr. Montgomery did not speak truly when he said that on this occasion such a decision was announced from the bench. The decision was announced on the 24th of December, 1885, nearly three years before. The only decision announced on this occasion was that the case did not die with the plaintiff therein—William Sharon—but that the executor of his estate had the right to act—had a right to be substituted for the deceased, and to have the decree executed just as it would have been if Mr. Sharon had lived. It was amazing effrontery and disregard of the truth on the part of Mr. Montgomery to make such a statement as he did to the Supreme Court, when the record, lying open before them, virtually contradicted what he was saying.

Towards the close of the decision Justice Field did make reference to Mrs. Terry's testimony in the Superior Court. He said that in the argument some stress had been laid upon the fact that in a State court, where the judge had decided in Mrs. Terry's favor, the witnesses had been examined in open court, where their bearing could be observed by the judge; while in the federal court the testimony had been taken before an examiner, and the court had not the advantage of hearing and seeing the witnesses. In reply to this Justice Field called attention to the fact that Judge Sullivan, while rendering his decision in favor of Mrs. Terry, had accused her of having wilfully perjured herself in several instances while testifying in her own case, and of having suborned perjury, and of having knowingly offered in evidence a forged document. But this reference to Judge Sullivan's accusations against Mrs. Terry was not reached in the reading of Justice Field's opinion until nearly an hour after Mrs. Terry had been forcibly removed from the court-room for contempt, and therefore she did not hear it. This fact appears on record in the contempt proceedings.

But the most extraordinary feature of Mr. Montgomery's brief is yet to be noticed. He says that "If the assault so made by Judge Terry was not for the purpose of then and there killing or seriously injuring the party assaulted, but for the purpose of provoking him into a duel, then the killing of the assailant for such an assault was a crime."

And again he says:

"I have said that if the purpose of Judge Terry's assault upon Field was for the purpose of killing him then and there, Neagle, and not Neagle only, but anybody else, would have been justifiable in killing Terry to save the life of Field; but that if Terry's object in assaulting Field was not then and there to kill or otherwise greatly injure him, but to draw him into a duel, then such an assault was not sufficient to justify the killing."

He then proceeds to speak of Judge Terry's duel with Senator Broderick, in which the latter was killed. He refers to many eminent citizens who have fought duels, although he admits that dueling is a sin. He then explains that "as a rule the duelist who considers himself wronged by another, having the position and standing of a gentleman, tenders him an insult, either by a slap in the face or otherwise, in order to attract a challenge. Such undoubtedly was Terry's purpose in this case. All of Terry's threats point precisely to that."

Here Mr. Montgomery seems to be in accord with Sarah Althea Terry, who, as we have seen, stated that "Judge Terry intended to take out his satisfaction in slaps." In the same direction is the declaration of Porter Ashe, when he said:

"Instant death is a severe punishment for slapping a man on the face. I have no suspicion that Terry meant to kill Field or to do him further harm than to humiliate him."

And also that of Mr. Baggett, one of Terry's counsel, who said:

"I have had frequent conversations with Terry about Field, and he has often told me that Field has used his court and his power as a judge to humiliate him, and that he intended to humiliate him in return to the extent of his power. 'I will slap his face,' said Terry to me, 'if I run across him, but I shall not put myself out of the way to meet him. I do not intend to kill him, but I will insult him by slapping his face, knowing that he will not resent it.'"

What knightly courage was here. If ever a new edition of the dueling code is printed, it should have for a frontispiece a cut representing the stalwart Terry dealing stealthy blows from behind upon a justice of the United States Supreme Court, 72 years of age, after having previously informed a trusted friend that he believed himself safe from any resistance by the object of his attack. It may be here also said that Justice Field, as was well known to every one, had for many years suffered from great lameness in consequence of an injury received by him in early life, and with difficulty could walk without assistance.

Mr. Montgomery, with freezing candor, informs the Supreme Court that, in strict accordance with the chivalrous code of honor, Judge Terry administered blows upon a member of that court, to force him into a duel, because of a judicial act with which he was displeased.

He says:

"The most conclusive proof that Terry had no intention, for the time being, of seriously hurting Field, but that his sole purpose was to tender him an insult, is found in the fact that he only used his open hand, and that, too, in a mild manner."

We often hear of the "mild-mannered men" who "scuttle ships" and "cut throats," but this is the very first one whose "very mild manner " of beating a justice of the Supreme Court of the United States with his hand was ever certified to by an attorney and counsellor of that court in the argument of a case before it.

It would be difficult to conceive of anything more puerile or absurd than this pretense that Terry had the slightest expectation of provoking a man of Justice Field's age, official position, and physical condition, to fight a duel with him in vindication of the right of the court over which he presided to imprison a man for contempt for beating the marshal in the face with his fist, and afterwards pursuing him with a knife, in the presence of the court, for obeying an order of the court.

Mr. Montgomery appears to have been imported into the case mainly for the purpose of reviewing the facts and giving them the Terry stamp. His ambition seems to have been to insult Justice Field and his associates in the Circuit Court by charging them with misrepresenting the facts of the occurrence, thus repeating Terry's reckless accusations to that effect. For Terry he had only words of eulogy and admiration, and said he was "straightforward, candid, and incapable of concealment or treachery himself, and therefore never suspected treachery, even in an enemy."

These noble qualities Terry had illustrated by assaulting Justice Field from behind while the latter was in a position which placed him entirely at the mercy of his assailant.

Montgomery thought that not only Neagle, but the President, Attorney-General, district attorney, and Marshal Franks should be arraigned for Terry's murder.

Although Justice Field had expressly advised the

marshal that it was unnecessary for anybody to accompany him to Los Angeles, and although Neagle
went contrary to his wish, and only because the marshal considered himself instructed by the Attorney-
General to send him, yet Mr. Montgomery especially
demanded that he (Justice Field) should be tried for
Terry's homicide. This, too, in the face of the fact
that under instructions from the attorney-general of
the State of California, aroused to his duty by the
Governor, the false, malicious, and infamous charge
made against Justice Field by Sarah Althea Terry
was dismissed by the magistrate who had entertained
it, on the ground that it was manifestly destitute of
the shadow of a foundation, and that any further proceedings against him would be " a burning disgrace
to the State."

The decision of the Circuit Court discharging Neagle
from the custody of the sheriff of San Joaquin county
was affirmed by the Supreme Court of the United
States on the 14th of April, 1890. Justice Field did
not sit at the hearing of the case, and took no part in
its decision, nor did he remain in the conference room
with his associate justices at any time while it was
being considered or on the bench when it was delivered. The opinion of the Court was delivered by
Justice Miller. Dissenting opinions were filed by
Chief Justice Fuller and Justice Lamar. Justice Miller's opinion concludes as follows :

" We have thus given, in this case, a most attentive
consideration to all the questions of law and fact which
we have thought to be properly involved in it. We
have felt it to be our duty to examine into the facts
with a completeness justified by the importance of the
case, as well as from the duty imposed upon us by the

statute, which we think requires of us to place ourselves, as far as possible, in the place of the Circuit
Court and to examine the testimony and the arguments
in it, and to dispose of the party as law and justice
require.

" The result at which we have arrived upon this
examination is, that in the protection of the person
and the life of Mr. Justice Field, while in the discharge
of his official duties, Neagle was authorized to resist
the attack of Terry upon him; that Neagle was correct in the belief that without prompt action on his
part the assault of Terry upon the Judge would have
ended in the death of the latter; that such being his
well-founded belief, he was justified in taking the life
of Terry, as the only means of preventing the death
of the man who was intended to be his victim; that
in taking the life of Terry, under the circumstances,
he was acting under the authority of the law of the
United States, and was justified in doing so; and that
he is not liable to answer in the courts of California
on account of his part in that transaction.

" We therefore affirm the judgment of the Circuit
Court authorizing his discharge from the custody of
the sheriff of San Joaquin county."

CHAPTER XX.

Thus ends the history of a struggle between brutal violence and the judicial authority of the United States. Commencing in a mercenary raid upon a rich man's estate, relying wholly for success on forgery, perjury, and the personal fear of judges, and progressing through more than six years of litigation in both the Federal and the State courts, it eventuated in a vindication by the Supreme Court of the United States of the constitutional power of the Federal Government, through its Executive Department, to protect the judges of the United States courts from the revengeful and murderous assaults of defeated litigants, without subjecting its appointed agents to malicious prosecutions for their fidelity to duty, by petty State officials, in league with the assailants.

The dignity and the courage of Justice Field, who made the stand against brute force, and who, refusing either to avoid a great personal danger or to carry a weapon for his defense, trusted his life to that great power which the Constitution has placed behind the judicial department for its support, was above all praise.

The admirable conduct of the faithful deputy marshal, Neagle, in whose small frame the power of a nation dwelt at the moment when, like a modern David, he slew a new Goliath, illustrated what one frail mortal can do, who scorns danger when it crosses the path of duty.

The prompt action of the Executive Department, through its Attorney-General, in directing the marshal to afford all necessary protection against threatened danger, undoubtedly saved a justice of the Supreme Court from assassination, and the Government from the disgrace of having pusillanimously looked on while the deed was done.

The skill and learning of the lawyers who presented the case of Neagle in the lower and in the appellate courts reflected honor on the legal profession.

The exhaustive and convincing opinion of Circuit Judge Sawyer, when ordering the release of Neagle, seemed to have made further argument unnecessary.

The grand opinion of Justice Miller, in announcing the decision of the Supreme Court affirming the order of the Circuit Court, was the fitting climax of all. Its statement of the facts is the most graphic and vivid of the many that have been written. Its vindication of the constitutional right of the Federal Government to exist, and to preserve itself alive in all its powers, and on every foot of its territory, without leave of, or hindrance by, any other authority, makes it one of the most important of all the utterances of that great tribunal.

Its power is made the more apparent by the dissent, which rests rather upon the assertion that Congress had not legislated in exact terms for the case under consideration, than upon any denial of the power of the Federal Government to protect its courts from violence. The plausibility of this ground is dissipated by the citations in the majority opinion of the California statute concerning sheriffs, and of the federal statute concerning marshals, by which the latter are invested with all the powers of the sheriffs in the

States wherein they reside, thus showing clearly that marshals possess the authority to protect officers of the United States which sheriffs possess to protect officers of the State against criminal assaults of every kind and degree.

During the argument in the Neagle case, as well as in the public discussions of the subject, much stress was laid by the friends of Terry upon the power and duty of the State to afford full protection to all persons within its borders, including the judges of the courts of the United States. They could not see why it was necessary for the Attorney-General of the United States to extend the arm of the Federal Government. They held that the police powers of the State were sufficient for all purposes, and that they were the sole lawful refuge for all whose lives were in danger. But they did not explain why it was that the State never did afford protection to Judges Field and Sawyer, threatened as they notoriously were by two desperate persons.

The laws of the State made it the duty of every sheriff to preserve the peace of the State, but the Terrys were permitted, undisturbed and unchecked to proclaim their intention to break the peace. If they had announced their intention, for nearly a year, to assassinate the judges of the Supreme Court of the State, would they have been permitted to take their lives, before being made to feel the power of the State? Would an organized banditti be permitted to unseat State judges by violence, and only feel the strong halter of the law after they had accomplished their purpose? Can no preventive measures be taken under the police powers of the State, when ruffians give notice that they are about to obstruct the admin-

istration of justice by the murder of high judicial
officers? It was not so much to insure the punishment of Terry and his wife if they should murder
Justice Field, as to prevent the murder, that the
executive branch of the United States Government
surrounded him with the necessary safeguards. How
can justice be administered under the federal statutes
if the federal judges must fight their way, while going from district to district, to overcome armed and
vindictive litigants who differ with them concerning
the judgments they have rendered?

But it was said Judge Terry could have been held
to bail to keep the peace. The highest bail that can
be required in such cases under the law of the State
is five thousand dollars.

What restraint would that have been upon Terry,
who was so filled with malice and so reckless of consequences that he finally braved the gallows by attempting the murder of the object of his hate? But
even this weak protection never was afforded. Shall
it be said that Justice Field ought to have gone to
the nearest justice of the peace and obsequiously
begged to have Terry placed under bonds? But this
he could not have done until he reached the State,
and he was in peril from the moment that he reached
the State line. The dust had not been brushed from
his clothing before some of the papers which announced his arrival eagerly inquired what Terry would
do and when he would do it. Some of them seemed
most anxious for the sensation that a murder would
produce.

The State was active enough when Terry had been
prevented from doing his bloody work upon Justice
Field. The constable who had been telegraphed for

before the train reached Lathrop on the fatal day, but who could not be found, and was not at the station to aid in preserving the peace, was quick enough to *arrest Neagle, without a warrant, for an act not committed in his presence,* and therefore known only to him by hearsay. Against the remonstrances of a supreme justice of the United States, who had also been chief justice of California, and who might have been supposed to know the laws as well at least as a constable, the protection placed over him by the Executive branch of the Federal Government was unlawfully taken from him and the protector incarcerated in jail. The constable doubtless did only what he was told and what he believed to be his duty. Neagle declined to make any issue with him of a technical character and went with him uncomplainingly. If Neagle's pistol had missed fire, or his aim had been false, he might have been arrested on the spot for his attempt to protect Justice Field, while Terry would have been left free at the same time to finish his murderous work then, or to have pursued Justice Field into the car and, free from all interference by Neagle, have despatched him there. The State officials were all activity to protect the would-be murderer, but seemed never to have been ruffled in the least degree over the probable assassination of a justice of the Supreme Court of the United States. The Terrys were never thought to be in any danger. The general belief was that Judges Field and Sawyer were in great danger from them.

The death of Terry displeased three classes: first, all who were willing to see Justice Field murdered; second, all who naturally sympathize with the tiger in his hunt for prey, and who thought it a pity that so good a fighter as Terry should lose his life in seeking that of another ; and, third, all who preferred to see Sarah Althea enjoy the property of the Sharon estate in place of its lawful heirs.

It is plain from the foregoing review that the State authorities of California presented no obstruction to Terry and his wife as they moved towards the accomplishment of their deadly purpose against Justice Field. It was the Executive arm of the nation operating through the deputy United States marshal, under orders from the Department of Justice, that prevented the assassination of Justice Field by David S. Terry.

It only remains to state the result of the second trial of the case between Sarah Althea Hill, now Mrs. Terry, and the executor of William Sharon before the Superior Court of the city of San Francisco. It will be remembered that on the first trial in that court, presided over by Judge Sullivan, a judgment was entered declaring that Miss Hill and William Sharon had intermarried on the 25th of August, 1880, and had at the time executed a written contract of marriage under the laws of California, and had assumed marital relations and subsequently lived together as husband and wife. From the judgment rendered an appeal was taken to the Supreme Court of the State. A motion was also made for a new trial in that case, and from the order denying the new trial an appeal was also taken to the Supreme Court. The decision on the appeal from the judgment resulted in its affirmance. The result of the appeal from the order denying a new trial was its reversal, with a direction for a new trial. The effect of that reversal was to open the whole case. In the meantime William Sharon had died and Miss Hill had married David S. Terry. The executor of William Sharon, Frederick W. Sharon, appeared as his representative in the suit, and filed a supplemental answer. The case was tried in the Superior Court, before Judge Shafter, in July, 1890, and on the 4th of August following the Judge filed his findings and conclusions of law, which were, briefly, as follows:

That the plaintiff and William Sharon, deceased, did not, on the 25th of August, 1880, or at any other time, consent to intermarry or become, by mutual agreement or otherwise, husband and wife; nor did they, thereafter, or at any time, live or cohabit together as husband and wife, or mutually or otherwise assume marital duties, rights, or obligations ; that they did not, on that day or at any other time, in the city and county of San Francisco, or elsewhere, jointly or otherwise, make or sign a declaration of marriage in writing or otherwise; and that the declaration of marriage mentioned in the complaint was false, counterfeited, fabricated, forged, and fraudulent, and, therefore, null and void. The conclusion of the court was that the plaintiff and William Sharon were not, on August 25, 1880, and never had been husband and wife, and that the plaintiff had no right or claim, legal or equitable, to any property or share in any property, real or personal, of which William Sharon was the owner or in possession, or which was then or might thereafter be held by the executor of his last will and testament, the defendant, Frederick W. Sharon. Accordingly, judgment was entered for the defendant. An appeal was taken from that judgment to the Supreme Court of California, and on the 5th of August, 1892, Sarah Althea Terry having become insane pending the appeal, and P. P. Ashe, Esq., having been appointed and qualified as the general guardian of her person and estate, it was ordered that he be substituted in the case, and that she subsequently appear by him as her guardian. In October following, the appeal was dismissed.

Thus ended the legal controversy initiated by this adventuress to obtain a part of the estate of the deceased millionaire.